TEXT & PRESENTATIC

ALSO BY STRATOS E. CONSTANTINIDIS

Modern Greek Theatre: A Quest for Hellenism
(McFarland, 2001)

TEXT & PRESENTATION, 2004

Edited by Stratos E. Constantinidis

The Comparative Drama Conference Series, 1

McFarland & Company, Inc., Publishers
Jefferson, North Carolina, and London

ISSN 1054-724X / ISBN 0-7864-2205-X
(softcover : 50# alkaline paper) ∞

Cover photograph ©2005 Clipart.com

Manufactured in the United States of America

*McFarland & Company, Inc., Publishers
Box 611, Jefferson, North Carolina 28640
www.mcfarlandpub.com*

Acknowledgments

This issue of *Text & Presentation* and the 28th Comparative Drama Conference were funded, in part, by the Office of International Affairs Interdisciplinary Lectures, Seminars, and Conferences, the Department of Greek and Latin, the Middle East Studies Center, the Department of East Asian Languages and Literatures, the Department of Comparative Studies, the Department of English, the Department of Near Eastern Languages and Cultures, the Department of French and Italian, the Department of Spanish and Portuguese, the Department of African-American and African Studies, the Department of Germanic Languages and Literatures, the Department of Theatre, and the Department of Slavic and East European Languages and Literatures at the Ohio State University.

This publication would not have been possible without the commitment and expertise of our editorial board: Marvin Carlson (*City University of New York, Graduate Center*), William Gruber (*Emory University*), Harry Elam (*Stanford University*), William Elwood (*Southern Connecticut State University*), Les Essif (*University of Tennessee–Knoxville*), Jan-Lüder Hagens (*University of Notre Dame*), Karelisa Hartigan (*University of Florida*), Graley Herren (*Xavier University, Cincinnati*), William Hutchings (*University of Alabama–Birmingham*), David Krasner (*Yale University*), Jeffrey Loomis (*Northwest Missouri State University*), Helen Moritz (*Santa Clara University*), Jon Rossini (*University of California–Davis*), Elizabeth Scharffenberger (*Columbia University*), Tony Stafford (*University of Texas–El Paso*), Ron Vince (*McMaster University*), Kevin Wetmore (*California State University–Northridge*), Katerina Zacharia (*Loyola Marymount University, Los Angeles*). I am also grateful to a significant number of additional specialists who participated in the anonymous review of the many manuscripts submitted to me for publication consideration. I would like to thank our associate editor, Kiki Gounaridou (*Smith College*), who assisted with the proofreading of this volume, and our book review editor, Verna Foster (*Loyola University, Chicago*), who solicited, edited, and proofread the book reviews.

The past editors of *Text & Presentation* deserve recognition for their contribution in establishing the reputation and standards for this annual publication: Karelisa Hartigan (1980–1993), Bill Free (1993–1998), and Hanna Roisman (1998–1999).

Last but not least, I want to thank the Executive Board of the Comparative Drama Conference and the hundreds and hundreds of scholars who presented the results of their research — both creative and analytical — at the Comparative Drama Conference, an annual three-day event which is devoted to all aspects of theatre scholarship.

Contents

Preface

Text & Presentation is an annual publication devoted to all aspects of theatre scholarship and represents a selection of the best papers presented at the Comparative Drama Conference. For the past 28 years, participants at the Comparative Drama Conference have come from 35 countries: Australia, Austria, Belgium, Brazil, Bulgaria, Canada, China, Cyprus, Denmark, Egypt, England, Finland, France, Germany, Greece, Iceland, India, Iraq, Ireland, Israel, Italy, Japan, Jordan, Korea, Malaysia, New Zealand, the Philippines, Russia, Saudi Arabia, Scotland, Slovenia, South Africa, Taiwan, Tanzania, Turkey, and the United States of America.

This volume of *Text & Presentation* features sixteen research papers, one review essay, and five book reviews. The papers included here were among a total of 168 research papers which were presented and discussed at the 28th Comparative Drama Conference. The presentations, which were divided into 59 sessions of 75 minutes each, were discussed by 200 program participants at the Columbus Hotel (formerly Adam's Mark Hotel) in Columbus, Ohio, during a three-day period, April 29–May 1, 2004.

The four concurrent sessions per day were complemented by three plenary sessions and a show. The keynote address, "Fossilized Talking: Writing, Print, Drama," was given by Professor W. B. Worthen (University of California–Berkeley) on April 30. He pointed out that one of the theoretical challenges embodied by the history of stage performance arises at the interface between writing and enactment. While "the death of the print culture" and the displacement of print in the cultural imaginary by the spatial discourses of film, video, and digital media has become a cliché of cultural and performance criticism in the past decade, the relation between writing and performance — and more narrowly between print and performance — remains unstable and contested, as it has been at least since the rise of industries of professional theatre and professional publishing in the sixteenth century. In this context, Professor Worthen raised several questions and discussed the implications of the print form of plays from the controversies of contemporary Shakespearean editing — arguably the zone of scholarship most minutely involved in tracing performance into (or out of) the print record —

into the "*mise-en-page*" of modern plays. Professor Richard Dutton and Professor Hannibal Hamlin — both of the Ohio State University — responded to the keynote address.

The second plenary session, Author-Meets-Critic, on May 1, was devoted to the discussion of one of the books (*Rescripting Shakespeare: The Text, the Director, and Modern Production*) that was reviewed in the 24th volume of *Text & Presentation* (pp. 193–198). Its author, Alan C. Dessen (University of North Carolina–Chapel Hill), discussed his book with the following critics: Professor M. J. Kidnie (University of Western Ontario) and Luke Wilson (Ohio State University).

The third plenary session was a workshop — Anne Bogart's Viewpoint Training in the Rehearsal Process. It was conducted by Professors Jeanine Thompson and Maureen Ryan — both of the Ohio State University — on April 29 . They demonstrated how the essential elements of Anne Bogart's Viewpoint Training can be used in the rehearsal process.

The show, Leonard Bernstein's and Richard Wilbur's *Candide*, was produced jointly by the OSU School of Music and the Department of Theatre, and was performed at the Thurber Theatre on May 1.

Of special interest was Session no. 55: German Experiments. Chaired by Professor Jan-Lüder Hagens (University of Notre Dame), it featured presentations by William R. Elwood (Southern Connecticut State University), Hal H. Rennert (University of Florida–Gainesville) and Timothy Richard Wutrich (Université Catholique, Lyon, France).

In 2004 we published

Professor Timothy Richard Wutrich of Université Catholique (Lyon, France), presenting his paper, "Staging Act Five of Schiller's *Wilhelm Tell*" during Session No. 55 on *German Experiments* at the 28th Comparative Drama Conference in Columbus, Ohio on May 1, 2004.

Volume 24 and our last issue of *Text & Presentation: Journal of the Comparative Drama Conference* as a periodical. The new *Text & Presentation* is an annual publication in book form. The series title of this new annual is *The Comparative Drama Conference Series*. What would have been the 25th volume of *Text & Presentation: Journal of the Comparative Drama Conference* is now the 1st volume of *The Comparative Drama Conference Series* with the title *Text & Presentation, 2004*.

The Executive Board welcomes research papers presenting original investigations and critical analysis of research and developments in the field of drama and theatre. Papers may be comparative across disciplines, periods, or nationalities, may deal with any issue in dramatic theory and criticism, or any method of historiography, translation, or production. *Text & Presentation* is edited by scholars appointed by the Executive Board of the Comparative Drama Conference, of which it is the official publication.

Text & Presentation is indexed in the MLA International Bibliography.

Stratos E. Constantinidis
February 2005

1

Caught in Time
Creusa, Iphigenia, and Resolving the Past in Euripides' *Ion* and *Iphigenia in Tauris*

Angeline Chiu

Abstract

Euripides's tragedies the Ion *and the* Iphigenia in Tauris (IT) *may be read as companion plays of resolving the past, as the* Ion*'s protagonist Creusa and Iphigenia of the IT significantly echo each other. As a doublet, they demonstrate the power and problem of the past. From the beginning of their respective plays, they come to the stage already primed for disaster as the heiresses of violent family histories. Moreover, both as young girls suffer traumatic personal pasts which not only haunt them in the present, but actively propel present activities—to the point of nearly repeating those very traumas of kinslaying. Finally, Creusa and Iphigenia can only escape the vicious circularity of the past by a dramatic anagnorisis—a recognition—that brings a final resolution to divide troubled past from enlightened present.*

Euripides' *Ion* and *Iphigenia in Tauris* are both unusual tragedies which conclude with hopeful endings, "tragicomedies" in which the principal characters come to the brink of irreparable ruin, yet manage to avert it and achieve a happy resolution. As plays of "catastrophe survived," to use Burnett's phrase (1985), they have been compared as nontragic parallels to other tragedies or even aligned with comedies and satyr plays.[1] Nevertheless, it is also useful to compare these two plays more carefully with each other. In this paper, I suggest that the *Ion* and the *IT* may be read as companion plays exploring the power of the past and its need for resolution.[2]

For the *Ion*'s Creusa and the *IT*'s Iphigenia, family history is an essential and ever-present backdrop to the plot. Blood literally runs in these noble families in the form of familial violence and marks them from the onset as

5

heiresses to a history of bloodshed. In the *Ion*, the dark side of family history arises from the beginning of the Erechtheid house of Athens. The
founder of the ruling house, Erechthonius, was born from the earth, placed
in a golden box, and given by Athena to the daughters of Cecrops for safe-
keeping — with the injunction they must not open the golden box. They
opened it and paid for their transgression with their lives — they bloodied
the Athenian cliffs (272–4). The pattern of blood continues into the next
generations with Erechtheus and his daughter Creusa. The story of
Erechtheus sacrificing his children was part of the fame of the ruling house;
when Ion first meets Creusa at Delphi he eagerly asks her: "Did your father
sacrifice your sisters?" (277). Creusa answers that he did so for Athens, and
that she herself escaped the same fate because she was yet a baby:

> Ion: Did your father Erechtheus sacrifice your sisters?
> Creusa: He brought himself to kill the girls for the country's sake.
> Ion: How was it that you alone of the sisters survived?
> Creusa: I was a newborn child in my mother's arms [277–80].

This is no innocent exchange, though — Creusa does not forget that bloody
family pattern in part because she cannot: it is a matter of widespread public knowledge and fascination. Even Ion the sheltered temple acolyte has
heard of that history, and his question conjures up the immediacy of the past.

   For Creusa, moreover, there is also another facet to her heritage — its
mythical autochthony, being sprung from the earth.[3] It is a sign of the native
nobility of Athens, but it is also a mark of innate ambivalence, as Euripides
takes care to state that the earth also bore the monstrous Gorgon to battle
the gods (989–90).[4] Creusa's intimate connection with her double-sided heritage is typified in the golden bracelet she wears. Thorburn points out that
the playwright has a habit of "masking images and implements of violence
with a golden façade"(39)[5] and that Creusa's bracelet is nothing less than a
weapon hidden under a golden surface (44). It contains an inheritance from
her father — two drops of Gorgon blood, one which heals and one which kills.
As Segal reminds us, "The two drops of the Gorgon's blood are not just parts
of an inert mythical apparatus inherited from an archaic past, but signify
two different sides of Athens' autochthonous heritage" (98). Creusa later
declares bitterly that despite its nobility, her lineage doesn't help her—*to de
genos m' ouk ōphelei* (268). The statement is more fraught than first appears,
as her *genos* compasses past, present, and future, and their entanglement in
the play. More, that *genos* does not prevent her misfortunes but even spurs
them on.

   In the *Iphigenia in Tauris*, the story of the Tantalids, the house of Atreus,
is an inescapable backdrop.[6] Here also each successive generation has its share

of kindred bloodshed, beginning with Tantalus's banquet which served Pelops as a cannibalistic dish and began the "woe on woe" — *mochthos d'ek mochthōn* (191) for the family. The Chorus sings to Iphigenia:

> From the blessed kings in Argos
> <This disaster> took its beginning,
> And trouble from trouble came,
> <Ever since> with his whirling winged steeds
> Helios changed from its station
> The sun's holy radiant face,
> And now at one time, now at another there came to the house
> Woe from the golden lamb,
> Slaughter upon slaughter, grief upon grief.
> Hence from those long-dead sons
> Of Tantalus breaks out affliction
> Against the house, and not to be pushed forward are the designs
> against you that your <ill-starred> fate is hastening on [189–202].

The first word of the play itself is the name of Pelops, thus bringing immediately to the fore the history of the house.[7] Moreover, it is spoken by Iphigenia herself, tying her more closely to her background.[8] Sansone also points out the immediacy of this heritage in the setting of the action, for the plot enfolds at Tauris, location of the first crime in the familial series, Tantalus's sacrifice of Pelops (293). The violence has increased with the clan's most recent misfortunes — Agamemnon's attempted sacrifice of his daughter Iphigenia, his slaughter by his wife Clytemnestra, and her subsequent murder by their son, Orestes. In this last generation, the "woe on woe" of the family has dissolved into almost uncontrollable familial slaughter. The Chorus sings its lament of the family's misery, but it is also a commentary on Iphigenia herself: fate hastens on terrible designs.

Iphigenia is still more closely linked to this heritage by an ancestral spear of Pelops which was kept in her chambers at home in Argos (822–826). A spear may seem an odd item to place in a young girl's room, and Pelops' spear, besides signifying the Tantalid house, was also the weapon by which he killed his father-in-law Oenomaus. As Goff remarks, its presence specifically in Iphigenia's own room underlines "the intimacy of her relations with familial violence" (155).[9] It is the twin of Creusa's Gorgon-blood bracelet, a sign of a noble yet dubious identity. Furthermore, while Creusa's bracelet contains the potential for killing, Iphigenia's spear has actually shed blood before. For Iphigenia and Creusa, their noble heritage comes with the overt association of familial slaughter — a pattern and family curse which previous generations seemed to repeat inexorably over time. From the beginning, both have the potential of being caught in that pattern, of being forced into inexorable tragedy.

While that familial predisposition to violence sets the stage and tone for both the *Ion* and the *IT*, the past only becomes compelling in the form of deep personal injury for Creusa and Iphigenia. For each, a single shattering experience will define them thereafter; they will be caught up in remembering it. Each Greek princess suffers this as a *parthenos*— a young girl — who, instead of being married, is brutally traumatized in a perversion of marriage. Thus devastated at the threshold between childhood and womanhood, seemingly neither can truly recover nor move past it psychologically.[10]

In Athens, the young Creusa is raped instead of wed.[11] Apollo accosts her as she is wandering alone in a meadow, gathering golden flowers.[12] She later recalls this:

> You came to me with your hair
> Gold-gleaming as into the folds of my gown
> I was plucking flowers of saffron hue
> Reflecting the golden light.
> Seizing me by my pale white wrists
> As I cried out "Mother!"
> Into the cave that was your bed
> You took me, divine ravisher,
> Without pity,
> Doing what gladdens Cypris' heart [887–96].

She cries out to her mother in vain as Apollo seizes her by her "white wrists"— *leukois … karpoisin* (891), in what may be a violent caricature of a groom taking the bride by the wrist. There is no marriage for the young Creusa; though "unwilling"–*akousa* (941), she is taken "by force"–*biai* (11) in a sunless cave. For her, the trauma of sexual assault is further compounded by her secret pregnancy, lonely childbirth, and the despair of abandoning her child in the cave where Apollo raped her. In an ironic twist, Creusa who was saved from death as a babe in arms here does not take her own child in her arms, but abandons it. Now a grown woman, married to Xuthus but childless by him, she broods on the past. When Ion asks about her lack of children, she replies darkly that Phoebus knows how childless she is:

Ion: You have never been a mother, then? You are childless?
Creusa: Apollo knows my childlessness [305–6].

Her lack of a child as a married queen is a constant reminder of the infant she had conceived, borne, abandoned, and lost as a girl.

Iphigenia is not violated as Creusa was, but nearly slain as a human sacrifice. Believing that she was to marry Achilles, she traveled to Aulis at her father's summons. There he took her instead to be sacrificed to Artemis to secure fair winds for the Greek fleet to Troy, as she herself retells:

> There [at Aulis] the Greeks took me in their grasp like a calf
> and slit my throat, and the slayer was the father who begot me.
> Ah me (for I cannot forget the pain of that day),
> how many times did I reach out my hand to touch my father's chin
> [and, as I clung to them, his knees],
> uttering words such as these: 'O Father, I am given in marriage by you
> — a marriage of shame! Now, even as you are killing me, my mother
> and the Argive women are singing the wedding song for me,
> and the whole house resounds with piping!
> And yet it is death I receive at your hands!
> The husband you promised me in the chariot
> as you ferried me deceitfully to my blood-stained marriage
> was Hades, not the son of Peleus! [359–71].

There is no marriage for Iphigenia, no happy normative end for her girlhood innocence, as there is for Creusa. Iphigenia herself says that there was death instead of marriage: Achilles was Hades, not the son of Peleus (369). We may recall Creusa, seized while gathering flowers, as Persephone was seized by Hades, when death and marriage appear one and the same. Furthermore, Iphigenia seems to conflate the sacrifice and the deceitful promise of marriage, calling her ordeal a "bloody wedding"–*haimatêron gamon* (371).[13]

For Iphigenia, the aftermath of the near-sacrifice is likewise troubling. Though Artemis snatches her from the altar, the goddess takes her to the barbaric land of the Taurians, where she serves as priestess of the Tauric Artemis's cult. As in the case of Creusa, the one saved from death now engages in inflicting it, albeit indirectly: Iphigenia the maiden nearly sacrificed to Artemis at Aulis has become a priestess preparing human sacrifices for Artemis in the land of the Taurians. But she also relives her own near-sacrifice every time she performs the Taurian blood rites, and a Taurian herdsman in the play even says this explicitly (336–9).[14]

Neither Creusa nor Iphigenia can forget their personal traumatic pasts or resolve them and move past those experiences — in this sense, they are "caught in time," ever reliving the past and suffering its psychological repercussions. Because of this, their past will drive the present — with near-disastrous results. The opening speeches of both plays refer immediately to the personal histories of Creusa and Iphigenia, marking the urgency with which the past may impinge on the present. Hermes in the opening of the *Ion* candidly relates the story of Creusa's violation (8–27), while Iphigenia herself retells her near-murder in the opening of the *IT* (1–34). The past and its personal trauma will not only inform but almost dictate the plot. For both women, long-pent-up emotions will explode once a breaking point is reached; as the dam bursts, a surge of unrestrained impulses to violence is the result.

And the bitter memories of the past and emotions linked with them have been pent-up for a very long time indeed. Both Creusa and Iphigenia tell and retell their stories throughout the plays, cycling repeatedly through the same horrific memories.[15] Symptomatic of their psychological imprisonment is Creusa's first appearance at Apollo's shrine, where she weeps over her memories; they are clearly never far away from her thoughts, and she seems to forget she is in Delphi, not Athens the scene of her trauma.[16] Later in her encounter with Ion, his innocent questions bring her past rushing back once more:

> Stranger, your attitude
> — your wondering at my tears — is well bred.
> Looking at Apollo's temple, I remembered
> something that happened long ago [247–50].

Creusa refers specifically to "retreading an old memory"—technically in the Greek, re-measuring it like a road (250)— she has literally been down this road before, and often. Iphigenia, mulling over her near-murder, interrupts her retelling of Aulis with a stark cry, *oimoi–kakôn gar tôn tot' ouk amnêmonô*—Alas! I cannot forget those evils" (361). For both of them, the pain of the past is still fresh though years have elapsed, and the plays resonate with it.

Caught in their violent family histories and their own past, both Creusa and Iphigenia are trapped. For both of them, however, a breaking point is required to transform them from passive sufferers into active agents capable of repeating their history and willingly inflicting suffering on others. But it is true despair — the sting of a faint but long-held hope now extinguished — that goads them both onward into open violence. For both Creusa and Iphigenia, that breaking point is the (perceived) confirmation that their secret and desperate hope is gone. Creusa has come to Delphi with her husband Xuthus to inquire about their childlessness, but she yet hopes her own secret child lives (384–91). Iphigenia, on the other hand, hopes that her brother Orestes — whom she last saw as a baby — is yet alive; she has long kept a letter addressed to him, waiting for a messenger to deliver it for her (578–96).

Both these hopes are seemingly dashed in the course of the plots. When Creusa's chorus of maidservants tells her that she will never bear a child, she despairs, leaping to the conclusion that her child is dead (916–918). Iphigenia faces a similar despair with a dream which she interprets to confirm Orestes's death (50–8). Their loss of hope translates almost immediately into an acceleration of violent intent, as if now Creusa and Iphigenia willingly embrace the darker side of their heritage. Both women jump to the worst possible conclusion, the thing they have dreaded the most: the death of their longed-for kinsmen. The logic for both is flawed — the Delphic oracle makes no mention of the death of Creusa's abandoned child, and Iphigenia's dream does not specifically state Orestes' death, but Creusa and Iphigenia leap to their conclusions based not on logic, but on long-held fear and dread.[17] Moreover, both these perceived deaths signify the end of their respective family lines and seemingly this end will come, as did the beginning of the line, with a surge of blood — now driven by Creusa and Iphigenia, as nobler impulses seem submerged in visceral despair.

In Creusa's case, the change from the passive mourner to active avenger is decisive. It is even a change which apparently the gods of the play had not calculated upon.[18] She declares that she will no longer strive for virtue — *aretē*—as she flings away self-restraint and the moderating effect of shame:

> My heart, how shall I keep silent?
> But how shall I reveal the secret
> Union and lose my sense of shame?
> What stands in my way to halt me?
> With whom am I contending for the prize of goodness? [859–63].

She continues: "I am being robbed of my house, robbed of children, my hopes are gone" (865–6). She then plans to poison Ion, whom she does not recognize as her own son, but thinks is her husband's illegitimate child and a threat to the Athenian throne.[19] Creusa, having in effect "killed" Ion once before as a baby, now moves toward killing him again as a youth. Moreover, she would be doing so for the sake of preserving Athens — the reason for the sacrifice of her sisters. And the poison she would use is none other than the deadly drop of Gorgon's blood on her wrist — and the image of Athenian heritage's dark side come to the fore.

Iphigenia for her part declares that she has become embittered in her despair over Orestes' supposed death. She has become savage — *ēgriōmetha*:

> O my woe-laden heart! Till now you were mild
> and full of pity toward foreigners
> and gave your meed of tears to your fellow
> Greeks whenever you took any as your prisoners.
> But now because of the dreams that have made me savage,

> thinking that Orestes no longer looks upon the sun,
> you who have arrived here will find me unkind [344–50].

She says that she wishes she could sacrifice Menelaus and Helen, whom she sees as enemies, but even as she does so, she draws closer to sacrificing Orestes, whom she does not recognize as her brother. Even in her conversation with him, she is determined to fulfill her deadly, priestly role (617–20). She evidently no longer feels hesitation or regret about shedding blood.

Caldwell notes that she echoes Clytemnestra, as "an innocent man is about to suffer, at the hands of his mistaken sister, the same fate that their guilty father suffered at the hands of their fully cognizant mother" (25). Blind violence seems to be the motive now instead of calculating purpose, as the tragic family pattern asserts itself. But Iphigenia also becomes a direct parallel to her father Agamemnon, the priest at her own near-sacrifice. She is, in effect, set to reenact Aulis by the shores of the Black Sea and so repeat the crimes of her family — including the sacrifice she so deplored.[20] At this point, both tragedies seem to march relentlessly toward hopeless error and bloodshed repeated, all further driven onward by the troubled family histories and personal pasts of Creusa and Iphigenia. Tragedy would seem to beget more tragedy.

Yet the past does not reassert itself. The *Ion* and the *Iphigenia in Tauris* emphatically do not conclude with tragic error and death. Instead, in both cases a remarkable *anagnorisis*— a recognition — takes place on the cusp of catastrophe which dramatically alters everything, including perhaps even the genre of the play. For both Creusa and Iphigenia, their long entrenchment in the troubled past have led to a belief that their respective houses are doomed to extinction — a belief which culminates in near-disaster: Iphigenia is on the verge of sacrificing Orestes, and Creusa attempts to kill Ion — who in turn attempts to kill her.[21] But recognition comes suddenly to intervene.

In the *Ion*, a murderous impasse has arisen, as Creusa, her plot revealed, takes refuge in Apollo's sanctuary, where Ion comes in his attempt to kill her (1261ff). Familial bloodshed seems inevitable; in this case, this is not the gods' plan, and the actions of Creusa and Ion in a very real sense force the gods' hand — and intervention. The Delphic priestess, like a *dea ex machina* and in great degree as Apollo's agent, interrupts the scene. She enters to stop the conflict and prevent bloodshed within the sacred precinct and to redirect the action by bringing forth Ion's cradle and the tokens within which lead Creusa and Ion to recognize each other as mother and son (1320ff).[22]

In the *Iphigenia in Tauris*, Iphigenia's own waiting letter lead her and Orestes to recognize each other as sister and brother (788ff). Significantly, this recognition comes in a scene in which Orestes refuses to let Pylades die with him as the required Greek victim (687ff) and in which Pylades, in agreeing to convey Iphigenia's letter to Orestes, insists on oath-keeping to an extraordinary degree (744ff).[23] Together these two details present a new idea that seems key to breaking the Atreid blood cycle: the combination of desires to both prevent innocent bloodshed (Pylades') and to avert treachery (oath-keeping). Both stand as the first real articulation by a cognizant individual wishing to act contrary to previous instances (and patterns) of slaughter and perfidy. Pylades then touches off the *anagnorisis* by handing Orestes the letter in Iphigenia's presence.

In both plays, the apparently self-driven cycles of bloodshed in the immediate family are also broken in no small part by the insertion of external figures of the Pythia and Pylades into the action.[24] Their introduction helps to prise open Creusa's and Iphigenia's entrenched, private worlds of pain, and the effect in both cases is electric: they, and their patterns of violence, are interrupted. For the pairs of Creusa-Ion and Iphigenia-Orestes, the recognition of personal identities is also a recognition of the powerful and violent past in which all have been enmeshed up to this point — a recognition which enables the characters to attempt a new set of independent actions. This conclusion as a happy set of interruptions is also a striking echo of the stories' beginning, an unhappy set of interruptions — Apollo's assault on Creusa and the would-be sacrifice of Iphigenia that interrupted their previously "normal" lives. More, recognition not only arrests impending violence, but brings about a much greater change. Caldwell thinks it brings about a change of genre entirely in the *IT*: "Recognition is a means of escape... *from tragedy itself*" (30). The same is true for the *Ion*. The tragic past is confounded as violence is arrested in mid-motion. Bloody expectations give way to the extraordinary realization that new possibilities have arisen.

As Creusa in despair thought Ion was dead, so had Iphigenia thought Orestes. In a sense, the recognition scenes are also scenes of resurrection — the "dead" live again.[25] Ion himself famously says that he is both one who died and is not dead:

> Creusa: O my child, dearer than sunlight to your mother
> (the god will forgive my saying this), I have you in my arms,
> a finding I had not looked for, a child I thought
> dwelt below with the shades and with Persephone!
> Ion: Well, dear mother, now I have come to your arms,
> I who died and am now alive! [1439–1444].

For Iphigenia, the unrecognized Orestes' declaration that her brother is alive, but exiled, breaks through her self-proclaimed hostility and hints at the *anagnorisis* to come:

Orestes: He lives, unhappy man, both nowhere and everywhere.
Iphigenia: Farewell, false dreams! I see now you were worthless! [568–569].

Soon after, the tokens of recognition cement the mutual discovery between brother and sister, and Iphigenia sings of her new joy:

Iphigenia: At that time still a babe
            I left you in the arms of your nurse,
            Newborn in the palace.
Orestes: O how great is my good fortune, greater than words can
            tell!
Iphigenia: O my soul, what am I to say? These events surpass wonder and
            beggar speech!
Orestes: From now on may we enjoy good fortune together! [834–840].

There is immediate release from Creusa's and Iphigenia's lingering personal pasts and resultant self-proclaimed savagery. Moreover, the recognitions connote the end of the cycles of family violence as well. As Orestes and Ion are respectively the heirs to the Atreid and Erechtheid families, their restoration is also the restoration of their houses, freed from the patterns of generational violence. Ion may even be seen as Erechtheus reborn, re-founding the family.[26] Light, as Creusa and Iphigenia both declare, has returned to the house:

Creusa: No longer am I childless, barren!
           The house has its hearth, the land its king!
           Erechtheus is young once more!
           The house of the earthborn race no longer looks upon night
           But recovers its sight in the rays of the sun! [*Ion*, 1463–1467].

Iphigenia: How strange is the pleasure I have received, my friends!
           I am afraid that out of my hands to heaven
           It may take wing and flee!
           O hearth built by the Cyclopes, O homeland,
           Dear Mycenae,
           I feel gratitude for his life, for his nurture,
           That you raised to manhood this brother of mine
           To be a beacon to the house! [*IT*, 842–849].

Finally, aetiologies — new establishments — cap these stories of catastrophe survived. Dunn notes that aetiologies mark the distance between past and present (48). Here we see the vivid contrast between past misery and present restoration. Athena appears, *dea ex machina* in both plays, to decree that both reunited pairs will return to Athens, and proceed from there to a future free from inevitable bloodshed.[27] Moreover, Athens is the final destination for the reunited families. Notably, while Creusa and Ion are Erechtheids and would naturally return to Athens, the Argive Orestes and Iphigenia will not return to Argos, but start life afresh in Athens instead. Ion will found the Ionians (1573–88), and Creusa's future children with Xuthus several Greek tribes (1589–94).[28] Orestes will establish the sacred rites at Halae (1446–61), and Iphigenia the new cult of Taurian Artemis at Brauron (1462–7), eventually to receive cult of her own — the clothing of women dying in childbirth (1464–7). These future events are a sort of recompense and a conclusion to the resolution of tragic pasts both familial and personal. The past cannot be recovered or relived, but its power no longer hangs over the present as a sword of Damocles. The focus is now firmly on the future.

The twinned figures of Creusa and Iphigenia finally find release from the relentless memory of their traumatic pasts. Further vicissitudes of life will confront them — Iphigenia and Orestes, for instance, yet must escape from the land of the Taurians, and Creusa and Ion must keep his true Apolline identity a secret from Xuthus — but now the power of the past is broken. The companion stories of the *Ion* and the *Iphigenia in Tauris* thus conclude, ending the circles of violence and beginning the possibilities for prosperity with two impending murders resolved into two radiant restorations.

PRINCETON UNIVERSITY

Notes

Acknowledgment. My thanks to Mark Buchan, John Thorburn, Froma Zeitlin, and the anonymous readers of *Text & Presentation* for their feedback and kind suggestions during this paper's various drafts. Any remaining errors are my own. All translations come from the most recent Loeb edition of David Kovacs (1999).

1. Such as *Hippolytus*, the three plays of the *Oresteia*, and *Oedipus Tyrannus*. Rabinowitz 1993 compares Ion to Hippolytus (190) and considers the play *Ion* as a mini–*Oresteia* (210). Segal 1999 compares the *Ion* to the *Choephoroi* (95) and to the *Oedipus Tyrannus* (101). Caldwell 1964 considers the *IT* with the *Oresteia*. Burnett 1985: 72 n. 23 sees the *IT* in terms of the *Eumenides* and the *Proteus*, the *Oresteia*'s satyr play; she also compares it to the *Cyclops*. Note also Sutton 1972 on satyric elements in the *Iphigenia at Tauris* and the *Helen*. Burian 1996: 4 points out similarities between the *Ion* and Menander's fragmentary 4th century BC comedy *Arbitration*, or *Epitrepontes*.

2. Note to Neumann's useful 1995 study. Also in terms of resolving the past and its violence, it is worth noting that both these plays date to approximately the same time period — the 410s BC, when, incidentally, the Peace of Nicias was failing to prevent further bloodshed in the Peloponnesian War.

3. See also Loraux 1990 for a detailed treatment of the theme of Athenian autochthony.

4. It is also interesting that when Creusa's handmaids come on stage as tourists to Delphi in the opening scenes, they note the shrine's artwork, part of which depicts a battle between Olympian deities and chthonic monsters (191–218). Note to Rosivach 1977.

5. Recall also in the *IT*, Iphigenia mentions the ancient quarrel over the golden lamb as part of her family's violent heritage (813).

6. Note especially in the aftermath of Aeschylus's landmark treatment of the Atreid house in the Oresteia trilogy of 458 BC.

7. Hartigan 1986:120 points to this as the alignment of Iphigenia specifically to Pelops as her model for later behavior in first tricking and then fleeing Thoas.

8. O'Brien 1988 specifically focuses on the Pelopid, not Tantalid, part of Iphigenia's background.

9. For an opposing view of the spear as a harmless object, see Burnett 1985: 64, which regards the spear as "thoroughly tamed, for it turns up like some beribboned Heracles among the princess' gowns in the Argive gynaeceum."

10. Note also Electra in the Euripidean tragedy of the same name, who declares that her marriage is like death: *egêmamesth', ô xeine, thanasimon gamon.*—"I have made a marriage, stranger, a marriage that is like death" (247). She is likewise unable to escape her past, mulling constantly over her misfortunes: Agamemnon's murder, the treachery and subsequent rule of Clytemnestra and Aegisthus, and her mistreatment at their hands — being forced into marriage to a poor peasant. For Electra, as for Creusa and Iphigenia, the past is inescapable and serves only to bring ever-present pain in the here and now. I owe this observation to Tracy Jamison in conversation.

11. See Segal 1999: 72 on how this incident becomes the "interruption" of a *parthenos*'s normal life cycle.

12. Thorburn 2000: 41–42 suggests the influence of the Homeric Hymn to Demeter in Creusa's golden flowers and the crocus-like narcissus Persephone is about to pick (*HH* 2.428). For more on Creusa as a Persephone (and also Demeter) figure, see Loraux 1990: 199–203. Segal 1999: 86 notes that the sunless cave of Creusa's trauma, suggests Hades and death. Note also Rehm 1994.

13. Wolff 1992: 321.

14. See also Hartigan 1991: 91.

15. For Creusa especially, these repetitions are also important for the development of the plot in terms of when, how, and in what context the recollection occurs. See also Wolff 1963: 170–171.

16. See also Lee 1996: 89, noting "so powerful is the evocation of the past that she seems to lose consciousness of where she is."

17. Compared this too with a significant passage in another of Euripides' "tragicomedies"— the *Helen*, where Helen, on hearing a news report, leaps to the conclusion that Menelaus is dead. When the Chorus admonishes her that she is indeed leaping to an unconfirmed conclusion *es xumphora gar anti tagathou fere*—"You say this because you rush toward woe, not blessing" (311), she replies plainly that this is true: *phobos gar es to deigma peribalôn m'agei*—"Yes, anxiety surrounds me, drives my thoughts toward fear" (312).

18. See too Burian 1996:14. Hermes' original plan was set out in the opening scene of the play at 61–3.

19. For further discussions of Ion and issues of identity, see Zeitlin 1996.

20. Several critics have asserted, as in Goward 1999: 139 that Iphigenia is "psychologically incapable" of vengeful murder. Even so, her harsh statements, at least in the scene in which they are spoken, depict her, however temporarily but effectively, as a potential killer. Iphigenia's conflicted nature may be, according to Vellacott 1975: 239, "the fullest picture in Euripides of a heart struggling to free itself from anger which demands revenge."

21. Ion's sudden transformation from innocent unworldly acolyte into vengeful youth on the verge of disregarding the sanctity of a suppliant (even if the suppliant on the altar is Creusa) mirrors Creusa's own transformation from sympathetic Athenian queen to would-be murderess of a temple servant. Note also that Ion as much as Creusa is part of the Erechtheid family in both its benign and malign manifestations.

22. Also in this scene, the past comes surging back, as the basket-cradle is not unlike a time capsule, preserving within it the weavings done by the young Creusa to be the infant Ion's swaddling clothes. In a real sense, the older Creusa is able to confront her past and see the tokens in Ion's basket both as a memory of her abandoned baby and as a confirmation of his identity (and recovery into her life) as he stands beside her.

23. Note particularly 755–8, in which Pylades focuses on what amounts to very specific conditions in a binding verbal contract.

24. Admittedly, Pylades is a kinsman to both Orestes and Iphigenia. Nevertheless, he is not a member of the immediate, nuclear family where the bloodshed has been repeatedly spilled.

25. Note this is also a significant theme in Euripides' *Helen*, particularly in the escape from Egypt (1517ff).

26. See also Loraux 1990.

27. See Hartigan 1991:104 on Athena as a final and critical element of resolution in both plays: "The final recognition of the *Iphigeneia in Tauris*, as of the *Ion*, lies in the role of Athena and her polis." The gods lurking in the backdrop of the plays — Apollo in the *Ion* and Artemis in the *IT* (and to an extent, Apollo in Orestes's case) — do not appear; Athena as a new divine figure is also in a sense a sign that the plots have turned a corner and will veer into new possibilities unfettered by the past which those previous deities had created.

28. Dunn 2000: 22–23 discusses the founding of the Ionians and the other tribes as "mystification with a vengeance" with respect to the status of the founders.

References Cited

Burian, Peter. "Introduction," In *Euripides, Ion*. Translated by Peter Burian and W.S. Di Piero, 3–19. New York: Oxford University Press, 1996.

Burnett, Anne Pippin. *Catastrophe Survived: Euripides' Plays of Mixed Reversal*. Oxford: Oxford University Press, 1985.

Caldwell, R. "Tragedy Romanticized: The *Iphigenia Taurica.*" *Classical Journal* 70.2 (1974): 23–40.

Dunn, Francis. *Tragedy's End: Closure and Innovation in Euripidean Drama.* Oxford: Oxford University Press, 1996.

Goff, Barbara. "The Violence of Community: Ritual in the Iphigeneia in Tauris." In *Rites of Passage in Ancient Greece: Literature, Religion, Society.* Edited by Mark W. Padilla, 109–125. Lewisburg and London: Bucknell University Press, 1999.

Goward, Barbara. *Telling Tragedy: Narrative Technique in Aeschylus, Sophocles and Euripides.* London: Duckworth Press, 1999.

Hartigan, Karelisa. "Salvation via Deceit: A New Look at the *Iphigeneia at Tauris.*" *Eranos* 84 (1986): 119–125.

_____. *Ambiguity and Self-Deception: The Apollo and Artemis Plays of Euripides.* Studien zur klassischen Philologie 50. New York and Frankfurt am Main: P. Lang Press, 1991.

Hoffer, Stanley. "Violence, Culture, and the Workings of Ideology in Euripides' *Ion.*" *Classical Antiquity* 15 (1996): 289–318.

Lee, Kevin. "Shifts of Mood and Concepts of Time in Euripides' *Ion.*" In M.S. Silk, *Tragedy and the Tragic.* Edited by M.S. Silk, 85–109. Oxford: Oxford University Press, 1996.

Loraux, Nicole. "Kreousa the Autochthon: A Study of Euripides' *Ion.*" In *Nothing to Do with Dionysus?* Edited by John J. Winkler and Froma Zeitlin, 168–206. Princeton: Princeton University Press, 1990.

Mastronarde, Donald. "Iconography and Imagery in Euripides' *Ion.*" *California Studies in Classical Antiquity* 8 (1975): 163–76.

Neumann, Uwe. *Gegenwart und Mythische Vergangenheit bei Euripides.* Stuttgart: Franz Steiner Verlag, 1995.

O'Brien, Michael. "Pelopid History and the Plot of *Iphigenia in Tauris.*" *Classical Quarterly* 38 (1988): 98–115.

O'Bryhim, Shawn. "The Ritual of Human Sacrifice in Euripides." *Classical Bulletin* 76.1 (2000): 29–37.

Rabinowitz, Nancy Sorkin. *Anxiety Veiled: Euripides and the Traffic in Women.* Ithaca and London: Cornell University Press, 1993.

Rehm, Rush. *Marriage to Death: The Conflation of Wedding and Funeral Rituals in Greek Tragedy.* Princeton: Princeton University Press, 1994.

Rosivach, Vincent. "Earthborns and Olympians: The Parados of the *Ion.*" *Classical Quarterly* 27 (1977): 284–94.

Sansone, David. "The Sacrifice-Motif in Euripides' *IT.*" *Transactions of the American Philological Association* 105 (1975): 283–295.

Segal, Charles. "Euripides' *Ion*: Generational Passage and Civic Myth." In *Rites of Passage in Ancient Greece: Literature, Religion, Society.* Edited by Mark W. Padilla, 67–108. Lewisburg and London: Bucknell University Press, 1999.

Thorburn, John E. Jr. "Euripides' *Ion*: The Gold and the Darkness." *Classical Bulletin* 76.1 (2000): 39–49.

Vellacott, Philip. *Ironic Drama: A Study of Euripides' Method and Meaning.* Cambridge: Cambridge University Press, 1975.

Wolff, Christian. "The Design and Myth in Euripides' *Ion.*" *Harvard Studies in Classical Philology* 69 (1963): 169–194.

_____. "Euripides' *Iphigenia Among the Taurians*: Aetiology, Ritual, and Myth." *Classical Antiquity* 11.2 (1992): 308–334.

Zeitlin, Froma. "Mysteries of Identity and Designs of the Self in Euripides' *Ion*." In *Playing the Other: Gender and Society in Classical Greek Literature*. Edited by Froma Zeitlin, 285–338. Chicago and London: University of Chicago Press, 1996.

2

"Because you spoke abuse against the king"
Parresia and Tyrannicide in Euripides' *Medea*

Mary Frances Williams

Abstract

Three important political themes in Euripides' Medea *are free speech, tyranny and how tyranny punishes speech that is opposed to it, and resistance to tyranny. Since both opposition to tyranny and freedom of political speech (parresia) are defining characteristics of Athenian democracy, these were important ideas for Euripides' Athenian audience. The Corinthian king Creon exiles Medea because of her abusive speech about him, thus depriving her of democratic rights, and Medea is depicted as a tyrannicide who murders Creon because he has exiled her. But Medea is also portrayed as a tyrant herself, and since Medea kills on the basis of self-interest and without regard for law, she is an example of the sophistic ideal tyrant who is motivated by self-interested political action and ignores the law.*

Three important political themes in Euripides' *Medea*[1] are free speech, tyranny and how tyranny punishes speech that is opposed to its rule, and tyrannicide. Since both opposition to tyranny and freedom of political speech (parresia) are defining characteristics of an Athenian democracy that had only recently driven out its own tyrants and had been created to guard against tyranny, these were significant ideas for Euripides' Athenian audience, who would have immediately noticed these themes in the *Medea*. Creon's punishment of Medea through a decree of exile for "speaking against the king" (*basileôn* 453; *su d' ouk anieis môrias, legous' aei/ kakôs turannous* 457–58) and Medea's antagonism towards the tyrant Creon (453, 457–58, 607) and her murder of him would have won Medea sympathy from an audience that considered arbitrary exile to be an action of a tyrant. Medea would have appeared not only politically acceptable to Athenians but also similar to the heroic tyrannicides of the Athenian democracy. But Euripides adds political complexity to the play by also depicting Medea herself as a new and dangerous kind of tyrant.

Parresia

The ancient Greeks defined democracy as a type of government in which there exists equality before the law and freedom of speech, *isonomia* and *parresia*. A number of ancient authors specifically cite *isonomia* (e.g., Hdt. 3.80, 142; 5.37; Thuc. 3.82.8; 4.78.3; Pl. *Rep.* 563b),[2] *parresia* (Ar. *Th.* 541; Isoc. 2.3, 8.14; Pl. *Rep.* 557b; Aes. *Pers.* 591–3),[3] and *isonomia* together with *parresia* (e.g., Polyb. 6.9.4–5; 6.47.7; 4.31; cf. Polyb. 6.8.4; 27.4.7) as the bases of democracy. The Athenians especially claimed freedom of speech as their privilege, and Euripides includes the word *parresia* in his dramas (e.g., Eur. *Hipp.* 422; *Ba.* 668; *Ph.* 391; *El.* 1049, 1056; *Ion* 475).[4] Ion, for example, prays that his mother may be Athenian so that he may enjoy freedom of speech, something that he thinks is particularly Athenian (Eur. *Ion* 672, 675).

In Euripides' *Medea*, Jason rebukes Medea and explains that she caused her own exile, because she did not submit to political authority but instead was always speaking ill about Creon. He declares that she has been exiled for her speech against the "tyrant:"

> I have noticed many times, this not the first,
> how willfulness runs on to self-destruction.
> You could have kept this country as your home
> by obeying the decisions of your betters,
> but futile protests send you into exile.
> They do not worry me. You can go on forever saying
> Jason is a scoundrel;
> but when it comes to slandering [tyrants],
> count yourself lucky you were only banished.
> I wanted you to stay — tried all the time
> to pacify the anger of the [tyrant];
> but you persevered in folly, and continually spoke
> ill of him, and so you must be banished.
> [Arnott 446–59].

Jason's words emphasize Creon's "tyranny" and Medea's continual speech in opposition to "tyranny" (*es turannous esti soi lelegmena* 453; *legous' aei/ kakôs turannous: toigar ekpesêi chthonos* 457–58), a choice of words that an Athenian audience would have noticed. Jason's insistence on Medea's abusive speech which he calls "foolish" (*logôn mataiôn* 450; *môrias* 457), rather than on Creon's fear of Medea, reveals a political motive for her exile rather than a personal one. He declares that Medea could have remained in Corinth if she had submitted to the decrees of those in power (*soi gar paron gân tênde kai domous echein/ kouphôs pherousêi kreissonôn bouleumata* 448–49). Jason repeatedly insists that because of Medea's insulting speech, which is the indication of her non-submission to the power of the king, she must be exiled (450, 454, 458).[5]

Jason's claim is supported by other evidence. Creon himself declares that he "controls discourse" (*brabeus logou* 274).[6] Through this boast, Creon reveals that he is in charge of *parrasia* and in effect controls the power of speech of his citizens. Creon is concerned about hostile political speech and he punishes those who speak against him. Creon is a tyrant in a bad sense and inimical to everything dear to Athenian democracy since he is opposed to freedom of speech, one of the basic foundations of democracy, and is willing to exile or kill to enforce his power over the speech of his subjects. Tyrants generally opposed freedom of speech and used violence to deprive citizens of it (e.g., Plut. *Dion* 5.4, 34.3)—just as tyrants characteristically retain power by destroying those "of independent spirit" (Arist. *Pol.* 5.11, 1313a34; 1314a5).

Jason cites Medea's words in opposition to Creon (*ha d' es turannous esti soi lelegmena* 453, 457–58) as one reason for her exile. But Jason also points to Medea's curses against the royal family as another reason (605, *agas turannois anosious arômenê* 607). Medea does curse Jason, his new bride, and their house in her very first words (160–65). The Nurse says that Medea has frequently rebuked Jason for his betrayal (20–23), and the Chorus has heard her curses (205–09). Medea's curses are indications of dangerous rebellion against the king and her hostility towards Jason is considered to be hostility towards the ruling house of Corinth, of which Jason is now a member. Furthermore, Medea's threats are one more reason that her speech is deemed dangerous, and Creon consequently fears that Medea will harm his family (282–3, 287–9).

Although Medea announces that she has no praise for a fellow citizen who causes pain by his "lack of sense" and says that a foreigner must be compliant (223–224)—a suggestion that she herself does not condone causing disruption by criticism of government — Medea is dissembling and her meekness is not sincere, but it does indicate that she is aware that public dissent will cause problems. Nevertheless, Medea easily and frequently speaks ill of her enemies, even if they are kings. Medea is exiled because of her abusive words, curses, and threats against Jason and Creon's family. Creon must control Medea's speech in order to control Medea herself.

Tyranny in the Medea

Creon clearly is an absolute ruler; the democratic Athenian audience, which despised both kingship and tyranny equally, would have considered him to be a negative figure, both a king and a tyrant,[7] and the words for tyranny and kingship are utilized indistinguishably in the play.[8] Euripides' language emphasizes Creon's non-democratic authority: various old-fashioned words refer to Creon's position as sole ruler (e.g., *aisimnai* 19; *koiranos* 71; *kreissonôn* 449; *turannous* 453, 458; *basileôn* 455; *turannois* 607, 934; *archei* 702; *turannikos* 740; *basileôs* 783; *koiranois* 875; *turannôn* 1298; Luschnig 2–4). Aristotle calls Creon's office of *aisimnêtês* (19) an "elected tyranny" (Arist. *Pol*.3.9, 1285b14; 1295a12–14).[9] Other language stresses Jason's association with Corinthian royalty ("royal," *basilikois* 18; "tyrant," *turannon* 42; "king," *basileôn* 455, 594) and reiterates the theme of kingship and tyranny. It suggests that Jason hopes for political power and tyranny for himself through alliance with the Corinthian king (Luschnig 3). Jason announces that he never opposes the desires of kings (455–6) and seeks a royal marriage (18, 554); Medea informs Aegeus that Jason "loves tyranny" (698, 700);[10] and Jason hopes that his sons will become rulers of Corinth someday (916–17). Medea repeatedly calls Jason's new bride a "tyrant" (*gamous turannôn* 778, 877; *têi turannôi makariai numphêi* 957, *numphê turannos* 1066; *hê turannos* 1356; Luschnig 3, 6), and Creusa, the daughter of a king (554, 783), delights in her robe and crown, insignia of royalty (1159–66). Creon, Creusa, and Jason are continually linked with royalty and tyranny, while Medea is in opposition to them. Medea, indeed, contrasts herself with royalty and tyranny, declaring that she is weak and powerless but her enemies are royal, wealthy, powerful, and "tyrannical" (*turannikos* 739–40).

Furthermore, Creon's exile of Medea is arbitrary and in a democratic context is beyond the law since he answers to no one for his deeds. Tyrants generally rule according to self-interest and answer only to themselves (Hdt. 3.80; Arist. *Pol*. 4.8, 1295a17–22; 4.8, 1311a2–5). There is no public discussion about Medea, only rumor that Creon, "lord of the land" (*têsde koiranos chthonos* 71), intends to banish her from Corinth (67–71). Before Medea speaks, Creon abruptly declares in his very first words that Medea is exiled because she is "dark-faced and scowling with rage against [her] husband" (*se tên skuthrôpon kai posei thumoumenên* 271–76). Medea must be punished not for what she has done but because she is not sufficiently submissive to her husband, and to Creon (449–50), in regard to the new marriage.

Creon eventually grants Medea one extra day to remain in Corinth, believing that this is compassionate. Since Creon declares that his "spirit least of all is tyrannous" (*hêkista toumon lêm' ephu turannikon* 348), it is clear that Creon himself considers tyranny to be harsh and unjust, although he does not consider his actions to be "tyrannical."[11] Nevertheless, Creon insists that if Medea delays more than one day, she will die (351–54). A ruler's decree of death on the basis of whim or personal fear rather than violation of law is one of the characteristics of despots, such as Xerxes, who possessed absolute power over their subjects;[12] and the Greeks associated tyranny with hubris and violence from an early date (e.g., Hdt. 3.80).[13] The harshness of Creon's decree would have shocked an Athenian audience, where even homicide was punished with exile rather than death and where ostracism had been instituted as a protection against arbitrary exile.[14] Athenians would have noticed Creon's reference to tyranny and his wielding of absolute authority.

The play's robe and crown imagery underscores the importance of the themes of royalty, tyranny, and tyrannicide. Medea's gift of rich robes and golden crown, attributes of royalty, are her means of murdering Creon and Creusa. The poet repeatedly emphasizes how the robes and crown bring death (784–88, 803–09, 976–95, 1159–62, 1167–94). Jason even wonders why Medea feels the need to give such gifts, since a royal house contains many golden robes and crowns (960–61). But the gifts provide an appropriate allusion to royal rule and symbolically indicate how a tyrant can never have sufficient power. It is the crown that kills Creusa (1186–87, 1191–92); it grips her tight and burns her, and gore mixed with fire drips from her head and the crown (1199).[15] The robe also kills Creon when he attempts to help his child (1213–14), which is what Medea says she intended (787–89)[16] (and Medea had previously declared her intention to kill Creon (374–75)). Since the Greeks had long associated tyranny with wealth and luxury,[17] Medea's tools for carrying out murder, the crown and robes, both represent the riches that tyrants possess and symbolize Creon's royal power and absolute rule. Medea exploits Creusa's desire for royal power and for wealth (1159–66) in order to lure her to her death. At the same time, Medea punishes Jason's aspirations for tyranny and for royal connections by killing his royal bride and she appropriately uses a crown and robes, symbols of royalty, both to harm Jason and to signify her opposition to Creon's authority. Medea's choice of the means of murder indicates that Medea envisions herself as a tyrannicide who acts from political motivations since she uses symbols of royal and autocratic power to strike a blow against tyranny.

Tyrannicide

The Athenians prided themselves on their history of opposition to tyranny (*Ath.Pol.* 22.3), and the radical Athenian democracy was created in order to guard against tyranny (McGlew 149). The Athenians had violently killed their tyrants (Thuc. 1.20.2, 6.53.3–59; Hdt. 6.123.2; Arist. *Rh*.1401b; *Pol.* 5.8, 1311a37–39; Pl. *Sym*.182c), and the tyrant-killers were honored at Athens (e.g., Athen.15.695a) with a state cult and a statue commissioned by the city.[18] The tyrannicides were "symbols of civic identity" and were regarded as heroes.[19] In the fifth century, the threat of tyranny still exerted a strong influence on democratic life at Athens (McGlew 1), and Athenians considered attacks on democracy to be a form of tyranny (McGlew 12). Democratic Greek opinion generally condoned tyrannicide (e.g., Hdt. 6.123; Arist. *Pol.* 2.4, 1267a.14–16; Polyb. 2.58.15; 2.60.2). Tyrannical acts were punished in Athenian law, which held tyranny to be beyond the law and decreed that whoever killed a tyrant "shall be holy and blameless."[20]

Medea's opposition to Creon's tyranny on personal grounds is consistent with Greek history and is not incompatible with tyrannicide: Aristotle points out that many rose against tyrants for revenge because of the tyrants' insolence and abuse of individuals (Arist. *Pol.* 5.8, 1311a31–1131b37) and the Athenian tyrannicides sought revenge, not liberation (Thuc. 6.56–57). Medea's emotionalism also evokes the motivation for the overthrow of tyrants: Aristotle describes opposition to tyranny in the same terms that Medea debates murdering her children (1057), contrasting "emotion" (*thumos*) and reason (Arist. *Pol.* 5.8, 1312b28–32; McDonald 302–303). Medea's act of murdering Creon and his daughter, carried out through her feigned submission to authority and by weapons disguised as gifts, contains overtones of tyrannicide since tyrant killing at Athens had involved deception and hidden weapons (e.g., Harmodius and Aristogeiton hid their daggers in myrtle-branches (Athen. 15.694b) and tyrants were often assassinated "by stealth" (Pl. *Rep.* 566b)). Moreover, Medea certainly thinks of herself as acting not just personally but also politically, not only because of family but also for her fellow women (214–66). It is true that Medea cites Jason's new marriage, the marriage-alliance, and her banishment as her reasons for killing (400). But tyrants, such as Peisistratus, often gained power through marriage (Hdt. 1.60; Cawkwell 74), and since Medea connects Jason's new marriage with his love of tyranny and desire for power (700), her opposition to his marriage may be interpreted as political opposition to tyranny. Medea evokes political oppression when she declares, "the tyrant of the land has decreed my exile" (*epei turannois gês m' aposteilai dokei* 934), ironically using the language of democratic civic resolutions but with *dokei* not referring to the council or people but rather to Creon as sole ruler. Medea also obliquely raises the concept of democracy when she objects to Creon's actions since Medea casts herself in the role of advocate for democracy and freedom from tyranny, and she uses this public role to excuse her actions, whatever her personal motivations, such as when she laments the plight of all women.

Moreover, the Chorus pities both Medea's loss of husband and her dishonorable exile (435–38), the personal and the political, since *atimos* (438) means "loss of citizen rights."[21] *Atimia* is the punishment in Athenian pre–Solonian law for aiming at tyranny or conspiring in setting up a tyranny (*Ath.Pol.* 16.10; Ostwald 106). The word emphasizes the importance of tyranny and opposition to it in the play, and Euripides' language not only indicates the Chorus' political sympathy for Medea but also suggests a relationship between Creon's actions and tyranny.

McGlew notes that both early tyrants and their enemies were pervaded by "notions of hubris, divine necessity, and most importantly and conspicuously, justice."[22] Creon claims that he acts to punish Medea's arrogance and out of necessity, and he does not believe himself to be unjust. Medea, likewise, is outraged at the arbitrary decree of the king and insists both that she is compelled to kill (1238–45) and that she has justice on her side (1391). The Chorus declares that Jason's misfortune is just (1231–32), and sees the murders as the vengeance of a divine Fury (1258–60; Kovacs 1260 n.b). Thus, the Creon-tyrant/Medea-tyrannicide antithesis in the *Medea* employs the conventional images of tyrant, autocrat, tyrannicide, and liberator (McGlew 6) while evoking the traditional ideas of justice, fate, and punishment for hubris.

When Jason blames Medea for her exile, she reminds Jason of how she helped him gain the Golden Fleece, abandoned her father (the king of Colchis), and slew Pelias (the king of Iolcos) (476–87). Medea has a history of opposition to kings, although her resistance is always motivated by personal considerations. Medea, the daughter of a king, who disobeyed his orders (483, 502–03, 798–801) and who killed another king, Pelias (9–10, 486–87, 504–05), is exiled by yet another king, Creon. It is true that Medea is assisted by Aegeus, the king of Athens, but Aegeus is only used and duped by Medea, bringing murderous pollution upon his city (824–55).[23] Medea consistently opposes kingship and recognizes no authority other than her own.

Finally, the Athenian regard for tyrannicide and protection of it in law provides an interpretation for the end of the *Medea*, since Medea herself, like many tyrannicides, escapes punishment for her murders and takes refuge in Athens (771, 1384–85).[24]

Medea tyrannos

But Medea is not simply portrayed as a tyrannicide; her political character is much more complex. Euripides also associates Medea herself with royalty and tyranny. Medea is the daughter of a king, and the Nurse refers to her as both royal (119–30) and a "tyrant" (*turannôn* 119)[25] whose mind she fears since tyrants "often command and seldom obey, and suffer violent changes of mood." Medea herself mentions her "noble father" and descent from Helios (406). When the Chorus refers to Creusa as "another princess (*basileia*), superior to [Medea's] marriage" (443–45), it reminds the audience that Medea, too, is royalty.[26] Medea's possession of the crown and robes that she gives to Creusa connects Medea herself with the wealth and luxury that the Greeks associated with tyranny,[27] and Medea, like many aristocratic tyrants (Cawkwell), is aided by aristocratic connections.

Other similarities include: Medea, like Creon, acts because of personal whim — one of Aristotle's definitions of a tyrant (Arist. *Pol.* 4.8, 1295a17–22; *NE* 8.10.2, 1160b; Hdt. 3.80; McGlew 27). Medea is consumed by passion, and Plato characterizes the tyrant as one driven by passion (Pl. *Rep.* 573–575) and tyranny as an example of unrestrained political desire (Pl. *Rep.*616d). Medea disregards the law and is a killer; and the tyrant turns the laws upside down and puts people to death (Hdt. 3.80). Moreover, Aristotle claimed that opposition to tyrants arose because they were feared (Arist. *Pol.* 5.8, 1311b37–38; cf. Thuc. 6.55.3). Medea generates fear in many, such as the Nurse (119) and Creon (280–291).

Medea is a barbarian (536, 591), and since barbarians are frequently connected with despotism in Greek tragedy,[28] and the Greeks associated tyrants "with alien and barbaric ways" (O'Neal 22), and they believed that barbarians were more servile and tolerant of tyranny by nature (Arist. *Pol.* 3.9, 1285a17–25), the barbarian Medea is automatically associated with tyranny. Medea's willingness to kill her own children suggests barbarian and authoritarian practice: the Persians, for example, considered their sons slaves and Aristotle considers this tyrannical (Arist. *NE* 8.10.4, 1160b; cf. Hdt. 3.30–31). Moreover, Medea's murder of her children is the ultimate act of a tyrant since despots in the ancient world often turned their power and violence against their own family.[29]

Euripides' language enhances Medea complex character; she is not only the opponent of a tyrant, eventually a tyrannicide, but is also both royal and a tyrant herself. Even Medea's exile contains overtones of punishment for tyranny, since the Chorus calls her "without rights" (*atimos*), which was the penalty in Athenian law for aiming at tyranny or conspiring at tyranny (*Ath.Pol.* 16.10; Ostwald 106). This word would have reminded the Athenian audience that Medea not only opposes tyranny but also acts like a tyrant herself.

But it must be remembered that the ancient world had many kinds of tyrants. One was the absolute ruler who could become corrupt and despotic (Hdt. 3.80;[30] Arist. *Pol.* 3.5, 1279b5–7). But for Plato, too much equality between men and women and too much freedom in a democracy lead to the degeneration of democracy (Pl. *Rep*. 563–564).[31] A corrupt form of democracy eventually dissolves into mob rule, which gives rise to a new form of tyrant who uses the claim of acting on behalf of the people in order to gain power (Hdt. 3.82.4; Pl. *Rep*. 565c) and who disregards the law (Arist. *Pol*. 4.4, 1292a).[32] Political sympathy for Medea becomes intertwined with suspicion of clever-speaking demagogues, who claim to speak and act for the people but who themselves have despotic tendencies (e.g., Cleon (Thuc. 3.36.6–3.37)). Medea herself is articulate, commanding, and controlling; like a demagogue, she is highly persuasive and rhetorical. Medea persuades the chorus of Corinthian women and Aegeus to support her; and the masculine Medea, who claims to act on behalf of the suffering of all women, gains her greatest power by disregarding all law.

In the fifth century, the sophists postulated and admired a new kind of tyrant, who aimed at obtaining absolute power and who acted purely in his own self-interest without regard for conventional law. McGlew remarks:

> When tyrants had disappeared from most of the Greek world, tyranny nevertheless remained an object of general fascination and horror. The fifth century invested the tyrant with considerable ideological force. The advocates and enemies of democracy made various uses of him as a negative image of citizenship, while the more radical sophists embraced him, for yet other purposes, as a positive image of deliberately self-interested political action [McGlew 1].

Medea embodies the radical sophistic image of deliberately self-interested political action[33] since her opposition to Creon's tyranny is purely self-motivated and because she acts without regard for her children or conventional law and solely in her own interest. Like Callicles in Plato's *Gorgias*, she believes that it is better to do wrong than to suffer it (Pl. *Grg*. 482d). Through her murders, Medea becomes an example of the fifth-century sophistic and philosophical "ideal" tyrant. Medea appears to be aware of this since she even holds herself up as an example for others to admire when she reveals she will kill her children and then declares, "Most glorious is the life of such as I" (Way 810; *tôn gar toioutôn eukleestatos bios* 810).

Conclusion

Euripides portrays Medea as a tyrannicide who undertakes the murder of the royal house of Corinth because of her opposition to arbitrary and tyrannical rule, and because the tyrant Creon deprives her of basic democratic rights, including the freedom to speak publicly about political and personal matters. This portrayal would have generated sympathy for Medea among a democratic Athenian audience, in addition to empathy for her personal problems.

But Euripides also explores problems raised and discussed by the sophists: moral virtue's connection with political theory, the relationship between power and justice, and the "disruption to civic life caused by the reckless pursuit of self-interest."[34] Medea is a tyrant herself, who bases her exercise of power on claims of justice and who disrupts the civic life of Corinth. She is an example of the sophistic tyrant who acts purely from self-interest (e.g., Pl. *Rep.* 344; Arist. *Pol.* 4.8, 1295a17–22; Thuc. 3.37.2; 3.40.4; 5.107) and exemplifies fifth-century political theory. Medea is the epitome of the persuasive tyrant who rises up out of an aberrant democracy,[35] claiming to speak and act on behalf of all women (e.g., 230–51), winning the support and sympathy of the women of Corinth, and bending the law (including the murder of her children) to suit herself. Medea acknowledges this and describes herself when she presciently remarks, "To my mind, the plausible speaker who is a scoundrel incurs the greatest punishment. For since he is confident that he can cleverly cloak injustice with his words, his boldness stops at no knavery (trans. Kovacs 581–83)."[36] Medea herself eloquently argues that Jason deserves the murders of Creon, Creusa, and his children and that these brutal killings, although of an innocent woman and of children, are just. The character of Medea through her words and actions provides a warning to the democratic Athenian audience about the dangers of excessive freedom. She demonstrates how an articulate and self-interested demagogue can disregard the law while claiming to act justly on behalf of democracy and can become a new, more terrible kind of tyrant who is motivated only by self-interest, is consciously "most impious" (796), and is unrestrained and unpunished by any conventional or natural law or by the norms of society. Medea's pursuit of self-interest and individually defined justice leads to the "disruption of civic life," but it exemplifies fifth-century sophistic political theory.

In a political context, just as in a personal one, the character of Medea generates both sympathy and confusion. As Murray noted, Medea's character is bewildering.[37] An Athenian audience would have found the political complexity of the *Medea* and the depictions of Medea and Creon disturbingly challenging because of their sympathy for Medea. As Lawrence remarks, "The spectators (and especially the men) are compelled thereby to view, however reluctantly, Medea's psychology as relevant to their own" (Lawrence 49). An Athenian audience would expect that the barbarian and female Medea would support tyranny since barbarians were believed to be more tolerant of tyranny (Arist. *Pol.* 3.9, 1285a17–25) and women were thought to be sympathetic towards it (Arist. *Pol.* 5.9, 1313b31–41), but Medea instead adopts the Athenian male attitude of opposition to tyranny. Moreover, although Medea, as a barbarian and a woman, had no true political rights, her masculine and heroic behavior would have caused her male audience to identify with her and sympathize with her plight of exile: this is another example of the complexity of Medea's character. Should not opposition to tyrants and tyrannicide be praised as just? Why should the arrogant decrees of a despotic ruler be tolerated and accepted? It is the tyrant, after all, who "turns the laws upside down," and outrages women, and puts people to death (Hdt. 3.80).

Yet Medea's portrayal as a sophistic tyrant who murders her own children would also have been upsetting to Euripides' audience, who would have been equally shocked by her new and dangerous form of despotism. The audience, forced to ponder a choice between sympathy for a traditional tyrant or for a tyrannicide who was also a new kind of tyrant herself, must have felt confusion. Which "tyrant" has upset the laws, which tyrant is preferable, the old or the new, Creon, the arbitrary despot, or Medea, who has abandoned the character of the submissive female and adopted not only the male heroic guise[38] of tyrannicide but also sophistic self-interested tyranny and even infanticide? In an Athenian's eyes, which of Euripides' two kinds of tyrant would have been worse for the *demos*, the king who opposed critical speech and therefore democracy itself or the sophistic hero, the cleverly persuasive, self-motivated woman who would not submit to the rules of law and society, something essential to democracy? And which of the two tyrants would a democratic audience prefer, the repressive and autocratic Creon who tried to exile a killer, or the murderous Medea who ignores all law to suit herself?

INDEPENDENT SCHOLAR

Notes

1. The text is that of Diggle but I retain lines 1056–80.

2. Podlecki 140. Page *PMG* 896. Cf. Thuc. 2.37.1 where Pericles in his Funeral Oration stresses that all Athenian citizens are equal before the law.

3. Cf. Thuc. 2.40.2 where Pericles praises public discussion.

4. Liddell and Scott. Although the word *parresia* also has a bad sense, meaning "license of tongue" (e.g., Isoc. 11.40; Plato *Phaed.* 240e), which how Creon uses it with respect to Medea, this was not a common meaning at Athens, where speech of all types was prized.

5. Jason also complains about Medea's "wearisome prattling" (*glôssalgian* 525). Green *ad* 453 says, "Jason hints that even death might have been the penalty for treasonable words."

6. Luschnig 8. von Arnim and Weil say the word means an athletic referee. But Kovacs and Mastronarde *ad* 274–75 translate it as "enforcer of this order."

7. McDermott 98–99. Authors as early as Herodotus used the word "tyrant" with both a good and bad meaning (Ferril 386–88; W.W. How and J. Wells, eds. *Commentary on Herodotus*. Vol. 2. Oxford, 1928. 338; White; O'Neal; Andrewes 20–30). Although Aristotle (Arist. *NE* 1160b) and others distinguished between kingship and tyranny, with tyranny being a degenerate form of kingship, the Athenians despised both equally (White 3). Mastronarde *ad* 119 says both tyrant and king were odious to the Athenians. Heath 76: "The 'one-man' theory of the state is never acceptable in Greek (or more precisely and more revealingly, in democratic Athenian) tragedy."

8. O'Neal 35; Mastronarde *ad* 119.

9. Weil *ad loc.* says that the word is used of elected officials and tyrants. Luschnig 4.

10. Hdt. 1.96: Deioces "loved tyranny" (*erastheis turannidos*).

11. Page *Medea ad loc*: the word tyrant did not have a bad meaning in the fifth century at Athens where pride in democracy and hatred of tyrants was common (e.g., Soph. *Ant.*1056; *O.T.* 873; Eur. *Med.* 119 *deina turannôn lêmata*). Luschnig 9: an Athenian audience would have considered Creon a tyrant in the bad sense. McDermott 100 believes Creon is no longer tyrannical when he yields to Medea. However, McGlew 28–29 notes that tyrants were frequently benevolent: this was a sign of their absolute power.

12. Cf. Lateiner 172–79; Gray 364.

13. O'Neal 29, 35; e.g., Solon fr.32, 34 West; Soph. *O.T.* 873.

14. Kinzl 209. But ostracism was used against all outstanding men (Arist. *Pol.* 3.8, 1284a 2–23).

15. Page xxvi believes that the crown is unimportant in the play since it is the robe that causes the deaths and suggests that the crown came from tradition while the robe was invented. But this misses the symbolic significance of both.

16. *kakôs oleitai pas th' hos an thigêi korês:/ toioisde chrisô pharmakois dôrêmata* (788–89).

17. O'Neal 27–28; Isoc. 2.4–5; Heraclitus 643–44; Xenophanes fr.3 West; Solon fr.33 West.

18. McGlew 150–56. Podlecki 129. Raaflaub 261; Paus.1.29.3, 15; *SEG* 10 320; *IG* I³ 520.

19. McGlew 153. Podlecki 129.

20. McGlew 185; Andocides (*de myst.*) 1.96–98. Athenian laws against tyranny date back to the time of Draco (Ostwald).

21. Mastronarde *ad* 438 who also remarks that Medea as a woman would not have had citizen rights.

22. McGlew 5. O'Neal 29: tyranny was associated with hubris and violence. Hdt. 3.80.

23. McDermott 98–99, 101–04. Page *Medea* xiii; Grube 152.

24. Medea is glad to hear that Creon and Creusa are dead; the messenger wonders if she is mad since she has "outraged the royal house" but is not afraid (1128–31).

25. Mastronarde *ad* 119: Euripides may be "exploiting the resonance" of the term "tyrant." McDonald 302: Medea becomes a tyrant and uses power. Cf. Sourvinou-Inwood 256.

26. Grube 156–57 says that the Aegeus scene reminds the audience that Medea is a princess and can hold her own with kings.

27. O'Neal 27–28; Heraclitus 643–4; Xenophanes fr.3 West; Solon fr.33 West.

28. Cf. Hall 154–56, 192–95.

29. McGlew 33 & n.40; Hdt.1.92, 3.30, 3.39; *FGH* 90 F 61. Plato calls the tyrant a parricide (Pl. *Rep.* 569b, 574c).

30. Cf. Ferril 392–93; O'Neal.

31. Cf. Arist. *Pol.* 1.1, 1252b5–9: among barbarians, females and slaves are the same as men; and Arist. *Pol.* 5.9, 1313b31–41: the dominance of women in the home gives rise to tyranny.

32. Guthrie 533–34: the tyrant who rises up out of a democracy ignores law and convention, and driven by lust and immorality is a violent criminal (Pl. *Rep.* 572–75). The demagogue is mentioned at Ar. *Ra.* 419; And. 4.27; Polyb. 3.80.3.

33. McGlew 1. Pl. *Rep.* 344. It is difficult to accept Medea's words as trustworthy. Tyrants are similar: their language is often "chosen for maximum political benefit" and is "utterly self-serving" (McGlew 3–4).

34. Allan 148–50. The sophists were also interested in the relativity of virtue and the power and abuses of rhetoric, two themes that are prominent in the *Medea*. Cf. Conacher on the sophists and Euripides.

35. Sourvinou-Inwood 256 believes that when the Nurse characterizes Medea as a tyrant, this distances her from "the normality of the democratic *polis*." However, this ignores the relationship between democracy and demagogues.

36. Cf. Vellacott 106: Medea is a "heroic figure championing the whole female world."

37. "Euripides' treatment of his subject was calculated to irritate the plain man in two ways. First it was enigmatic. He did not label half his characters bad and half good; he let both sides state their case and seemed to enjoy leaving the hearer bewildered. And further, he made a point of studying closely and sympathetically many regions of thought and character which the plain man preferred not to think of at all" (Murray 83).

38. Barlow 161; Knox 197, 201–02.

References Cited

Allan, W. "Euripides and the Sophists: Society and the Theater in War." *Euripides and Tragic Theater in the Late Fifth Century.* Ed. Martin K. Cropp and D. Sansone. Illinois Classical Studies 24–25. Champaign, IL: Illinois University Press, 1999–2000. 145–156.

Andrewes, A. *The Greek Tyrants.* London: Hutchinson University Library, 1956.

Arnott, Peter D., trans. *Three Greek Plays for the Theatre.* Bloomington, IN: Indiana University Press, 1961.

Barlow, S.A. "Stereotype and Reversal in Euripides' *Medea*." *Greece & Rome* 36 (1989): 158–171.

Cawkwell, G. "Early Greek Tyranny and the People." *Classical Quarterly* 45.1 (1995): 73–86.

Conacher, Desmond. *Euripides and the Sophists: Some Dramatic Treatments of Philosophical Ideas.* London: Duckworth, 1998.

Diggle, James, ed. *Euripides.* Vol. 1. Oxford: Oxford University Press, 1984.

Ferril, A. "Herodotus on Tyranny." *Historia* 27 (1978): 385–398.

Gray, Vivienne J. "Herodotus and Images of Tyranny: The Tyrants of Corinth." *American Journal of Philology* 117.3 (1996): 361.

Green, W.C., ed. *Euripides Medea.* Cambridge, 1872.

Grube, G.M.A. *The Drama of Euripides.* London: Methuen, 1941.

Guthrie, W.K.C. *A History of Greek Philosophy.* Vol. 4. Cambridge: Cambridge University Press, 1975.

Hall, Edith. *Inventing the Barbarian. Greek Self-Definition Through Tragedy.* Oxford: Clarendon Press, 1989.

Heath, Malcolm. *The Poetics of Greek Tragedy.* London: Duckworth, 1987.

Kinzl, K.H. "Athens: Between Tyranny and Democracy." *Greece and the Eastern Mediterranean in Ancient History and Prehistory. Studies Presented to Fritz Schachermeyr on the Occasion of His Eightieth Birthday.* Ed. K.H. Kinzl. Berlin & New York: W. de Gruyter, 1977. 199–223.

Knox, Bernard. "The *Medea* of Euripides." *Yale Classical Studies* 25 (1997): 193–225. Rpt. in *Word and Action. Essays on the Ancient Greek Theater.* Ed. Bernard Knox. Baltimore: Johns Hopkins University Press, 1979, 295–322.

Kovacs, David, ed. & trans. *Euripides. Medea.* Cambridge, MA: Harvard UP, 1994.

Lateiner, D. *The Historical Method of Herodotus.* Toronto and London: University of Toronto Press, 1989.

Lawrence, Stuart. "Audience Uncertainty and Euripides' Medea." *Hermes* 125.1 (1997): 49–55.

Liddell, Henry George, and Robert Scott. *A Greek-English Lexicon.* Oxford: Clarendon Press, 1996.

Luschnig, Cecilia A.E. "Medea in Corinth: Political Aspects of Euripides' Medea." *Digressus. The Internet Journal for the Classical World* 1 (2001): 8–28 <http://www.digressus.org>.

McDermott, Emily A. *Euripides' Medea: The Incarnation of Disorder.* University Park, PA: Penn State University Press, 1989.

McDonald, Marianne. "Medea as Politician and Diva. Riding the Dragon Into the Future." *Medea. Essays on Medea in Myth, Literature, Philosophy, and Art.* Ed. James J. Clauss and Sarah Iles Johnston. Princeton, N.J: Princeton University Press, 1997. 297–323.

McGlew, James F. *Tyranny and Political Culture in Ancient Greece.* Ithaca, NY: Cornell University Press, 1993.

Mastronarde, Donald, ed. *Euripides Medea.* Cambridge: Cambridge University Press, 2002.

Murray, Gilbert. *Euripides and His Age.* NY and London: H. Holt, 1913.

O'Neal, J.L. "The Semantic Use of *turannos* and Related Words." *Antichthon* 20 (1986): 26–40.

Ostwald, Martin, "The Athenian Legislation Against Tyranny and Subversion." *Transactions of the American Philological Association* 86 (1955): 103–128.

Page, Denys L., ed. *Euripides Medea.* Oxford: Oxford University Press, 1955.

_____, ed. *Poetae Melici Graeci.* Oxford: Oxford University Press, 1962.

Podlecki, A.J. "The Political Significance of the Athenian Tyrannicide-Cult." *Historia* 15 (1966): 129–141.

Raaflaub, Kurt A. "Zeus Eleutherios, Dionysos the Liberator, and the Athenian Tyrannicides. Anachronistic Uses of Fifth-Century Political Concepts." *Polis and Politics: Studies in Ancient Greek History. Presented to Mogens Herman Hansen on His Sixtieth Birthday, August 20, 2000.* Ed. Pernille Flenstead-Jensen, Thomas Heine Nielsen and Lene Rubinstein. Copenhagen: Museum Tusculanum, 2000. 249–276.

Sourvinou-Inwood, Christiane. "Medea at a shifting distance: images and Euripidean tragedy." *Medea. Essays on Medea in Myth, Literature, Philosophy, and Art.* Ed. James J. Clauss and Sarah Iles Johnston. Princeton, N.J: Princeton University Press, 1997. 253–296.

Vellacott, Philip. *Ironic Drama.* Cambridge: Cambridge University Press, 1975.

Von Arnim, Hans, ed. *Medea.* Berlin, 1886.

Way, Arthur S., trans. *Euripides.* Vol. 4. Cambridge, MA: Harvard UP, 1912.

West, Martin L., ed. *Delectus ex Iambis et Elegis Graecis.* Oxford: Clarendon Press, 1980.

Weil, Henri, ed. *Euripides Médée.* Paris, 1899.

White, M. "Greek Tyranny." *Phoenix* 9 (1955): 1–18.

"When I am laid in the earth"
Dido and Aeneas, Nahum Tate and Anglo-Irish Consciousness
Michael P. Jaros

Abstract

Dido and Aeneas, *Henry Purcell's 1689 opera, with libretto written by Nahum Tate, offers a powerful condemnation of the seventeenth century English imperial project. With Purcell's music and Tate's libretto, the warrior queen becomes the hero over the vacillating Aeneas, who cannot choose between love and destiny. Additionally, the curse Virgil gives to Dido at the end of Book IV of* The Aeneid, *vowing eternal enmity between Rome and Carthage, is absent from the opera. The last lines of the newly forged heroine are a paean to memory and reconciliation. Scholars have proffered several possibilities for why such a Dido should emerge in an age well on its way toward empire. What has not been taken into account, however, is the Irish authorship of the work. This paper discusses that Irish dimension, positioning Tate's libretto as an early example of the invention of an Anglo-Irish idea of "Ireland" which would reach its zenith in the next century with Farquhar, Swift, and Sheridan.*

But rise up from my bones, avenging spirit!
Harry with fire and sword the Dardan countrymen
Now, or hereafter, at whatever time
The strength will be afforded. Coast with coast
In conflict, I implore, and sea with sea
And arms with arms: may they contend in war,
Themselves and all the children of their children.
Virgil, The Aeneid¹

When I am laid in the earth may my wrongs create
No trouble in thy breast
Remember me, but ah! Forget my fate.
Purcell and Tate, Dido and Aeneas²

As she ascends her own funeral pyre, Virgil's Dido announces a legacy of violence that will last for countless generations and consume the lives of thousands, "necessitating" three Punic wars between Carthage and Rome. Cato's famous command, "Carthage must be destroyed," is reified in *The Aeneid*, which dually functions as both a Roman foundational epic and as an "historical" justification for imperial pacification of the warlike Other: Augustus' "Pax Romana" must be bought in the blood of the barbarian state, here feminized as a passionate, vengeful woman.

Virgil's exhortation to violence is absent from the conclusion of Henry Purcell's 1689 opera *Dido and Aeneas*, in which Dido announces an alternate legacy: one of faithful remembrance *without* bloodshed. Superficially, the vogue for "happy" endings so common in the theatre of the time explains this: Nahum Tate, the opera's librettist, is perhaps most infamous to theatre historians for penning the happy ending to Shakespeare's *King Lear*. Digging deeper, however, one unearths a much more critical departure from the source text. In Purcell and Tate's adaptation of the Virgilian epic, Dido becomes the hero, not Aeneas. Tate moulds her into a sympathetic, tragic character led astray not by her own "barbarous" emotions, but by a coven of deceitful witches — like happy endings, another vogue of the late seventeenth century English stage — who replace Dido as the barbarians of the new story. Purcell supports this refashioning by giving his heroine some of the most powerful and memorable music of the early modern period. The heroic and forgiving Dido, embodied so, stands in stark contrast to the vacillating, unsympathetic Aeneas, who cannot seem to choose between his present love and his future empire.

This refashioning of the barbarian Carthaginian queen appears antithetical to the ideology of a nascent British Empire eager to equate itself with the grandeur of Imperial Rome. The Dido of King William's Glorious Revolution is hardly a justification for European imperialism, especially when she is compared to later models.[3] This apparent incongruity has been addressed in various ways: Deborah Fisk and Jessica Munns posit that it reflects imperial "anxiety" on the part of both Purcell and Tate concerning the recent loss of the colony of Tangiers (25). Andrew Walkling, arguing that the opera was written earlier (1687 as opposed to 1689), maintains that the work is in actuality an allegory for the political fate of the soon-to-be-deposed King James II (Aeneas) at the hands of evil Catholic councilors (the witches), who force him to abandon a distraught Dido (England).[4] Ellen Harris argues that the opera is absent of any political subtext, merely serving as a morality play that was originally performed at a school for young women (McDonald 48–9).

What these accounts fail to take into consideration is the anxiety many felt regarding events then transpiring in the most immediate colony, Ireland, especially Nahum Tate's reaction to those events as a member of the nascent Anglo-Irish Ascendancy, the Protestant class that would rule Ireland for the next two centuries.[5] At the very moment that *Dido and Aeneas* was being performed, the fate of Protestant England was being decided in Ireland, where William of Orange, proclaimed king of England, was fighting the deposed James II and his Catholic army. The reverberations within British and Irish history of the Stuart-led Catholic insurrection in Ireland, which ended with James II's decisive defeat at the Boyne, are incalculable: it cemented the position of British colonial interests in Ireland, assured the Catholic majority there colonized status for the next several centuries, and provided the justification of an imperial policy of subjugation which would legitimate the "Pax Britannia" of the next two centuries, the British empire. It is highly unlikely that Tate himself was not aware of the unfolding events: he himself was a third generation Anglo-Irishman who had been raised in Dublin, and had attended Trinity College.

To address this "apparent incongruity" between Tate and Purcell's Dido and later versions, one must first place the opera within the context of developing ideas of both empire and colony in British and Irish colonial discourse, specifically the creation of cultural histories on both sides that emulated classical civilizations. On the British side, this led to the promulgation of a foundational myth that established a direct hereditary link with Rome. As Elizabeth Cullingford notes, this Romano-British myth maintained that Brutus, the grandson of Aeneas, first settled in Albion, which would become England (223). From here the idea was expanded upon in numerous ways. Most interesting for the purposes if this study was the practice of equating the English king with either Aeneas or the Caesar that Virgil's hero had stood in for: Catholic James II was cast as Caesar in 1687 and then the Protestant William of Orange in 1691 in an eerily seamless transition between two vastly disparate regimes. Nahum Tate himself was responsible for this: In 1687 he had written a poem to James comparing him to both Caesar and Aeneas, and only four years later William took his place (Fisk and Munns 37, Walkling 554). It is easy to see how Tate could have had either monarch in mind for the role of Aeneas in Purcell's opera.

The Irish were cast as the Other in this classical analogy, especially the Celtic Catholics that lived beyond the Pale of Tate's Dublin. English poet Edmund Spenser, writing in 1596, grafted a fictive Scythian ancestry onto the Celts to explain their "barbarity." Cullingford notes that various Celtic "hairstyles, battle cries and keens are identified — and deplored — as Scythian" (224). Spenser's codification of the barbarism of the Celtic Catholic Irish left Anglo-Irish settlers worried over where their identity fit between these two disparate codes of empire and barbarian. A century later, Englishmen born in Ireland began to see themselves as something between Irish and English, and began to speak to what that meant.

Within such a framework, Tate can be seen as one of the first examples of the type of colonial criticism that would reach its zenith in the next century with the writings of George Farquhar, George Berkeley, and Jonathan Swift. It is just this group of people, Declan Kiberd maintains, that set about inventing their own Ireland. The Anglo-Irish playwrights Farquhar and R.B. Sheridan, Declan Kiberd notes, often took up the role of "Anglo-Irish gentlemen returned in disheveled desperation to remind the London smart-set of the cultural price being paid for empire by its sponsors on the periphery, a place often repressed from the official consciousness" (Kiberd 16). Suddenly, Tate's abandoned Dido makes a lot more sense crying for us to remember her from the imperial periphery.

These "disheveled" Anglo-Irish writers attempted to place themselves somewhere between the Roman civilian and the Scythian barbarian. In the 18th century, Anglo-Irish linguists appropriated Edmund Spenser's Scythian connection for their own uses, claiming that the Irish language, although originating in Scythia, had made its way to Ireland via the more civilized peoples of Phoenicia and Carthage (Cullingford 225). They were thus able to subvert Spencer's trope by establishing a "civilized" Other in the place of his barbarian one. Importantly, this civilizing move remained an identity figuration *in opposition* to the native Irish living outside the pale. George Farquhar's 1698 play *Love and a Bottle* asserts this newfound anti-imperial "civility." When Roebuck, the Anglo-Irish protagonist of the play, reveals his Irish nationality, Lucinda, an Englishwoman, inquires after the strange tales she has heard:

Lucinda: Tell us some news of your country; I have heard the strangest stories — that the people wear horns and hoofs!

Roebuck: Yes, faith, a great many wear horns: but we had that, among other laudable fashions, from London...

Lucinda: Then you have ladies among you?

Roebuck: Yes, yes, we have ladies, and whores, colleges and playhouses, churches and taverns, fine houses and bawdy-houses, in short, everything you can boast of, but fops, poets, toads and adders [qtd. in Leerssen 103–4].

Through wit rather than barbarity, Farquhar's protagonist effectively feminizes the English: Irish "cuckoldry" (the pun of wearing horns) is solely an import from England and Ireland, unlike England, is without the emasculated "venom" of fops and would-be poets.

The Ascendancy's practice of distancing themselves from the Catholic Irish was employed not only to resist negative Anglo-Irish characterization in English letters: it also had direct political implications, specifically to mollify English paranoia about Irish loyalty, a paranoia stemming from various

Catholic uprisings in Ireland. In 1641, Catholics in Ulster had driven Protestant settlers from their homes, killing and injuring a significant number. When pamphlets broadcasting the news were printed in England, the event was already couched in highly stilted "barbarian" rhetoric. As late as 1678 — more than a quarter century after the uprising — "unbiased" historical accounts ran with preambles such as:

> An account of the bloody massacre in Ireland, acted by the instigation of Jesuits, priests and friars, who were the promoters of horrible murthers, prodigious cruelties, barbarous villainies, and inhumane practices executed by the Irish papists upon the English Protestants in the Year 1642.[6]

Importantly, it was the *Catholicism* of the native Irish that the English pamphleteers feared most: Catholics had been blamed for the great fire of London in 1666, as well as for plots to assassinate King Charles II and replace him with his openly Catholic brother, James. These tales set about casting Catholics — especially Irish Catholics — as an anarchic, evil, and very un–English specimen of humanity.

This anti–Catholic paranoia was in no way aided by King Charles' sudden death in 1685. James ascended to the throne, and his open Catholicism brought Protestant English paranoia to a boiling point. Many were convinced that the "triumph of Popery" was at hand (Walkling 545). Simultaneously, anti–Irish paranoia was augmented when James began placing Catholic officers in the Irish army, which until that point had been a stalwart, Protestant-controlled force that ensured English colonial interests in the country. James' importation of these Irish regiments into England, along with the birth of a Catholic heir in 1688, pushed the majority of his subjects too far, and in that year Parliament asked William of Orange and his wife Mary to take the throne by force (Foster 140–41). James fled the country to France. When the deposed king landed in Ireland and amassed a loyal army, William met him at the Boyne, where James' attempt to reclaim power ended in decisive defeat. Although victory belonged to William, the new king's triumph did little to sway English public opinion from regarding "Irish," "Catholic," and "rebellious barbarians" as interchangeable terms.

This was the political environment within which Nahum Tate wrote his libretto. Tate had already compared both James and William to Caesar in poetic odes, and if one accepts the later date for the opera,[7] it is plausible to visualize William as Aeneas. This certainly appears to be Tate's intent in the prologue, which features the lines "The greatest blessing Fate can give/ Our Carthage to secure, and Troy revive. When Monarchs unite, how happy their state/They triumph at once over their foes and fate" (32). If this opera is only a celebration of the Glorious Revolution and the joint monarchy with

Mary, as some scholars have maintained, then why is Aeneas effectively feminized and Dido made the hero? Why do witches conspire towards the ruin of both?

Tate's placement within the Anglo-Irish context elucidated above explains these moves. On one side, Tate was adamant in proclaiming his loyalty to William. In 1694 he collaborated with Purcell again on an ode sung to mark the centenary anniversary of his alma mater in Dublin, Trinity College. Tate equated the future of his college with that of his class, which had been "delivered" from James II, a king he had ironically praised only several years before:

> Great Parent, hail! All hail to Thee,
> Who hast from last Distress surviv'd
> To see this joyful Year arriv'd
> Thy Muses second Jubilee
> Another Century commending
> No decay can in thee trace
> After War's Alarms repeated
> And a circling Age compleated,
> Vig'rous Off-spring thou dost raise [qtd. in Spencer 22].

Delivered from distress by William, the college of the Ascendancy could now launch into its golden age with the "off-spring" it would raise. Tate's paeans of loyalty to William had not gone unnoticed, for when Thomas Shadwell died in 1691 Tate became Poet Laureate of England. From this position, however, Tate offered not only praise but also veiled criticism. As Fisk and Munns note, the year Tate become Poet laureate, even in the poem in which he compared William to Caesar were buried criticisms of imperial maneuverings, comparing the inhabitants of "distant nations" to "ghosts" slain by William (38).

Seeing *Dido and Aeneas* in an Irish context should now be easy: Dido's newfound prominence in the story, along with her lack of barbarity, clearly reflected the Ascendancy's need to assert a place for themselves somewhere between the British Romans and the Irish barbarians. This strange and often unstable balance of loyalty with criticism of the emerging Empire would dominate Anglo-Irish writing in the coming decades. Remember Ireland, but forget its fate: a conciliatory gesture of forgiveness (for the various rebellions) and an admonition to the King to remember Ireland and his "loyal" Anglo-Irishmen. For this complicated move to work, Dido would have to be deprived of her barbaric incitement to violence in *The Aeneid*. Unable to find a convenient scapegoat in the Latin original, Tate invented one. Dido's tragic demise could be conveniently blamed on the witches in a deft move that distanced Dido from the culpability given to her in Virgil. Tate had a ready-made model for this anomalous addition. Above all, they were an allegory to the Catholic paranoia elucidated above, and were a mainstay of the English theatre, perhaps for this very reason. Also, the practice of witchcraft fit very nicely into the barbarian trope applied to the Catholic Irish. In 1682, his predecessor as laureate, Thomas Shadwell, had written a play called *The Lancashire Witches*, which Tate was doubtless aware off. As Joep Leerssen notes, Shadwell's play spoke directly to the paranoia of the time, directly equating witchcraft with Catholicism and Irishness in the person of the priest Tegue O'Devilly. O'Devilly's extravagant behavior lead one character to remark:

> I do not know what to think of his Popish way, his words, his Charms, and Holy Water, and Relicks, methinks he is guilty of Witchcraft too, and you should send him to Gaol for it [qtd. in Leerssen 94].

Shadwell, as Leerssen notes, took great pains to bury any trace of Irishness in his own past (his father was from Galway), and took great pains to defend his Englishness when the playwright John Dryden later lampooned his closeted Irish roots.

Tate, as has been shown, was much more open about his Irishness. Considering the Trinity College address, however, this was an Anglo-Irishness defined in opposition to the "barbarous" Catholics Shadwell had lampooned in *The Lancashire Witches*. Tate was doubtless aware of the associations the audience would readily make with the witches, yet he still found them to be a very effective tool to distance the Carthaginian queen from direct responsibility for her actions. Inhabiting the borderlands of queen Dido's kingdom, they live only for anarchic destruction. At the opening of the Opera's second act, the sorceress enters and summons her sisters to a "mischief that shall make all Carthage flame":

> Enchantress: Say beldame what's thy will?
> Sorceress: Harm our delight and mischief all our skill.
> The Queen of Carthage, whom we hate,
> As we do all in prosperous state.
> Ere sun-set shall most wretched prove,
> Deprived of fame, of life and love.
> Chorus of Witches: Ho ho ho ho ho ho! [Tate 38].

Unlike Virgil's original, it is a witch, not the actual God, which appears to Aeneas in the shape of Mercury, giving the hero a command to abandon Dido and sail on to his Roman destiny. The "tragedy" that befalls the two lovers is therefore solely the responsibility of the sorceress and her coven.

Furthermore, such a move calls into question the very concept of Aeneas' destiny to found the Roman Empire. Here, it is his very belief in his own destiny that the witches exploit to their own malicious ends. Dido is as a result the more sympathetic character of the pair: she is the victim of both the witches' conspiracy to destroy her kingdom and her lover's magic-inspired hallucination of imperial destiny.

The story becomes Dido's story, and her fate becomes truly tragic. Dido's actual passing is marked by the most beautiful and memorable piece of music in the opera. Although directed onstage towards Belinda, her sister and confidante, it is also a metatheatrical message to the audience, encouraging Christian forgiveness in place of Virgilian vengeance: "Remember me, but ah! Forget my fate." With all forgiven, Dido no longer so barbaric, and Aeneas' own motivations called into question, the Carthaginian queen becomes a likely heroine of an Anglo-Irish class eager to both heal divisions with the mother country and at the same time assert a certain amount of independence from the imperial center. This idea of Ireland, sadly, reified existing divisions within the country, for barbaric stereotypes were not so much subverted by this formation of Irish consciousness as they were passed on to the other Irish the witches stood in for, specifically the disenfranchised Catholic majority of the Island who now lived outside the walls of Dublin in the south and Derry in the north. "Beyond the Pale" became just as much a synonym for barbarism as it was as a physical location outside the gate, called the Pale, of Tate's Dublin.

Three centuries later, Irish playwright Frank McGuinness (who claims that he writes from a "Catholic" perspective) returned to this very set of ideas to forge a much more inclusive idea of what it meant to be an Irish Carthaginian.[8] His 1988 play *Carthaginians* both opens and closes with Dido's famous lament from Purcell and Tate's 1689 opera. This seems an apt choice for a play concerning the 1972 Bloody Sunday murders in Derry, a city under siege by the forces of James II the very year the opera was first performed.[9] Nor does McGuinness seem ignorant of the place both Dido and Carthage play in constructions of Irishness: Cullingford notes that he included sections of Spenser's 1596 *A View of the Present State of Ireland* in the original program for his play (223). Whereas Tate's Dido, however, seemed founded on a reconciliation that was exclusionary, McGuinness' Dido is anything but: an openly gay cross-dressing Catholic. The new Dido keeps Tate and Purcell's aura of Christian forgiveness, but sheds the exclusionary idea of Irish identity attached to the original. (S)he becomes a force of both survival and healing in the face of the continued sectarian divisions of Irish society today. The play ends not only with the repetition of the Operatic Lament, "When I am laid in the earth, remember me, but Ah! Forget my

fate!" but also with Dido's own proclamation, which seems a fitting place to
end this examination of the Carthaginian queen's strange voyage through
the formation of Irish identities: "How's Dido? Surviving. How's Derry?
Surviving. Carthage has not been destroyed" (McGuinness 379).

UNIVERSITY OF CALIFORNIA, SAN DIEGO

Notes

1. Trans. Robert Fitzgerald (New York: Vintage, 1990) 119.
2. Nahum Tate, Libretto, *Dido and Aeneas,* 56.
3. See, for instance, Deborah Fisk and Jessica Munns' description of Prince
Hoare's 1792 opera, *Dido, Queen of Carthage.* See also the libretto of Berlioz' *Les
Troyens,* in which Dido herself validates empire in her final, prophetic vision: 'Ah!
Carthage will perish.... Rome.... Rome.... Eternal!' trans. David Cairns, 1971: 320.
4. Walkling covers this theory extensively in his article, "Political Allegory in
Dido and Aeneas."
5. The phrases "Anglo-Irish" and "Ascendancy," used interchangeably throughout this paper, refer to the Protestant ruling class in Ireland who were primarily the
descendents of English settlers placed there from the reign of Elizabeth I onward.
6. Quoted in Leerssen 59. The rebellion actually began in 1641.
7. As was noted above, there is a large debate over when the libretto was actually written. Walkling argues for an earlier date (1685–7), whereas others, such as
Fisk and Munns, argue for a later one (1689–90) after James had fled. This paper's
analysis, as may be now be clear, assumes a later date, and that the work is directed
at King William.
8. Besides McGuinness, described below, Dido also appears in Irish letters in
various 18th century Aisling poems, and indirectly in the last lines of Brian Friel's
1984 *Translations,* where the character Hugh quotes from Book I of the Aeneid in a
comparison between the erasure of Gaelic culture and the fall of Carthage. Friel,
Translations, Modern Irish Drama (New York: Norton, 1991) 374. The term "Irish
Carthaginian" is taken from Elizabeth Cullingford's article title, cited below.
9. Derry, it should be noted, is the Catholic (or Republican) name for this city.
It is also called Londonderry by the Protestant Unionists in Northern Ireland today,
who hold "Orange" marches each year to celebrate the victory of King William of
Orange over James II at the Boyne. These marches have often been the flashpoint
of paramilitary violence between the Protestant Ulster Volunteer Force (UVF) and
the Catholic Irish Republican Army (IRA).

References Cited

Cullingford, Elizabeth Butler. "British Romans and Irish Carthaginians: Anticolo-
nial Metaphor in Heaney, Friel and McGuinness." *PMLA* 111.2 (1996): 222–39.

Fisk, Deborah, and Jessica Munns. "Clamorous with War and Teeming with Empire: Purcell and Tate's *Dido and Aeneas.*" *Eighteenth Century Life* 26.2 (2002): 23–44.

Foster, Roy F. *Modern Ireland: 1600–1972.* London: Penguin, 1988.

Kiberd, Declan. *Inventing Ireland: The Literature of the Modern Nation.* London: Vintage, 1996.

Leerssen, Joep. *Mere Irish and Fior Ghael.* 2nd ed. Cork: Cork University Press and Field Day, 1996.

McDonald, Marianne. *Sing Sorrow: Classics, History and Heroines in Opera.* London: Greenwood, 2001.

McGuinness, Frank. *Carthaginians. Plays 1.* London: Faber & Faber, 1996.

Spencer, Christopher. *Nahum Tate.* New York: Twayne, 1972.

Tate, Nahum. Libretto. *Dido and Aeneas.* Music by Henry Purcell. Orch. The Academy of Ancient Music. Cond. Christopher Hogwood. Decca, 1992.

Walkling, Andrew. "Political Allegory in Dido and Aeneas." *Music and Letters* 76.4 (1995): 540–71.

Oskar Blumenthal and the Lessing Theater in Berlin, 1888–1904

William Grange

Abstract

Oskar Blumenthal (1852–1917) was Berlin's most feared theatre critic in the early years of the new German Reich. He had the audacity of referring to Goethe as "an egghead" who had no understanding of what made plays effective for audiences, and in other critiques he ridiculed Kleist, Hebbel, and other "important" playwrights — prompting an adversary publicly to call him a "one-man lynch mob." In the 1880s Blumenthal himself began writing plays, and he was so successful that many self-appointed cultural guardians accused him of damaging the German theatre beyond repair. His became the most frequently performed plays on any German stage well into the new twentieth century, and when he built the Lessing Theater in 1888 he became a theatrical entrepreneur whose triumphs were unsurpassed. Then he leased the Lessing to the man who had criticized him most vociferously and general rejoicing followed "Bloody Oscar" into retirement. Extremely few since Oskar Blumenthal have matched his record as influential critic, successful playwright, and prosperous theatrical entrepreneur. Even fewer have any idea who he was, when he lived, or what he accomplished.

Oskar Blumenthal was the most successful, the most frequently performed, the most envied, and probably the most hated theatre man of the Wilhelmine Era. He was born in Berlin on March 13, 1852, and twenty years later he earned a doctorate in German literature at the University of Leipzig. Within two years he became Feuilleton (an "arts and leisure" section) editor of the Berliner Tageblatt. At that newspaper he became the most widely read theatre critic in Berlin, where he presided as the city's most feared critic, known within many theatre circles as "Bloody Oscar." A good example of Blumenthal's merciless appraisals is the night he and a companion attended the premiere of what both men considered a new play. The companion said he was "surprised the audience didn't hiss the actors off the stage." "Well," Blumenthal said, "it's difficult to yawn and hiss at the same time" (Hoffmeister 28). Blumenthal directed many of his most severe reviews at a Norwegian playwright who by the late 1870s was beginning to develop a reputation in Berlin, namely Henrik Ibsen. Blumenthal dismissed Ibsen's innovative use of dramatic structure as "ornamental illustrations of the playwright's perspicacity;" Ibsen's interest in the inner tensions of character Blumenthal termed "psychological steeple chasing" (Blumenthal 112). Blumenthal liked "accessibility" in plot construction and character development. Anything inchoate or recondite he usually condemned in his reviews.

That opinion placed Blumenthal at the opposite end of a cultural spectrum stretching all the way to a remote space occupied by the newspaper critic Otto Brahm (1856–1912) and his Freie Bühne organization. Brahm and his organization worked to subvert police censorship and present controversial plays that treated social problems. Brahm and his backers objected to Blumenthal's plays, and most other contemporary German plays like them, because they offered "absolutely no way out of the problems of our contemporary world. The primary concern of the German theatre-goer has been is to amuse himself as much as possible." Brahm indeed dismissed most popular German plays as "freshly baked goods that go stale almost as soon as they hit the shelves" (Brahm, *Theater* 257). Blumenthal, in contrast, felt that popular plays were the theatre's life-blood.

Blumenthal admired playwrights like Adolph L'Arronge, Gustav von Moser, Paul Lindau, or Franz von Schönthan. He likewise esteemed the theatre managers who presented their plays, men like Theodor Lebrun, August Wolff, Adolf Ernst, or Sigmund Lautenburg, who had become highly adept at discovering entertainment based on a "reproduction of success formulae" (Harden vii) that would pack their houses night after night for months. Many Berlin playwrights and managers who used those formulae became extremely wealthy, for the Wilhelmine years were ones in which live theatre performance faced little competition for the disposable income of growing numbers of middle-class audiences.[1]

Brahm and his sympathizers lamented such developments. "No bourgeois audience," said Siegfried Jacobsohn, "can have a theatre [of its own] because it is bourgeois first of all and an audience thereafter. Audiences like those in ancient Athens or in Elizabethan London had a different temperament, a different epidermis, different needs and different longings," he pontificated. "People who have just put in a full workday, or read news reports about brutish events taking place in all the major cities of the western world come to the theatre with an altogether different set of aesthetic principles from those held by the citizens of Athens, the artisans of the Middle Ages, or the cavaliers of Shakespeare's day." Berlin's theatres in the later Wilhelmine era had almost without exception, Jacobsohn concluded, "bowed at the feet of social classes who comprised their clientele, creating theatres which were simply meeting production demands in what had been an intellectual activity. [Such theatres] had now gained a complete foothold" (Jacobsohn 14; Sollmann 145).

Blumenthal began his playwriting career in the early 1880s under the pen name "Otto Guhl," and by 1883 he enjoyed impressive success with *Der Probepfeil* (The Trial Balloon), which premiered at L'Arronge's Deutsches Theater. Blumenthal's playwriting bespoke the dramatic qualities he had advocated as a critic. *The Trial Balloon*, however, earned him the enmity of colleagues, and that enmity grew proportionally with his continued achievements. No other playwright in the 1880s and 1890s could match Blumenthal's total of hit plays. When he became a manager in 1888 by building his own superbly equipped and tastefully appointed theatre near the new Reichstag building in Berlin, he had few peers in the knack of making enormous sums of money from the enterprise of theatre. *The Trial Balloon* became the second most-frequently performed comedy throughout Germany during the 1883-1884 season.

It was a likable satire on decadent aristocrats, brazen coquettes, and society pianists, all of whom were gaining social prominence during the 1880s in the Second Reich. Blumenthal subsequently wrote or co-wrote a dozen hit comedies. Some of them were so successful that they often competed with each other in several theatres in the same German city. His most successful season came in 1897-1898, when three of his plays were among the top five most frequently produced on German stages. One of them, *Im weiss'n Rößl* (*The White Horse Inn*) remained one of the most frequently performed comedies for years after it initially premiered. Another of his comedies, adapted by David Belasco in 1900 as *Is Marriage a Failure?*, ran for 366 performances during the 1909-1910 season on Broadway.

What was perhaps most significant in his multifaceted, successful career was his characteristic refusal to voice any regrets or apologies for his success — a tendency that gained him additional hostility in the press. Blumenthal's playwriting success was based, his critics noted and as he himself admitted, on supremely well-crafted superficiality, consisting of formulaic plots and a whole-hearted embrace of aphorism and badinage. Critic Julius Bab said Blumenthal's plays were always characterized by "a paucity of any real interest in human motivation" (Bab 62). Another critic said his characters "lacked gravity" and were little more than "husks full of effective witticisms" (*Schaubühne* 14). Jokes "came out of the character's mouth and did not emanate from the character's inner dramatic being, while the characters themselves had only a loose connection to the plot," complained Rudolph Lothar (282). One could have anticipated such playwriting, however, by having read Blumenthal's theatre reviews. As a critic, he had always prized facile exchanges over internal development. He realized that most audience members did not understand internal development in characters, and if they did understand it they did not care about the niceties of a character's "inner dramatic being," "human motivation," or "gravity" in general.

Blumenthal's success as a playwright enabled him to construct the Lessing Theater, a facility with suitable pretentiousness, observers noted, for the ostentatiousness of the audience Blumenthal wanted to accommodate. Its architects, Hermann von der Hude and Julius Hennicke, had built several hotels in the area and numerous apartment buildings in the fashionable Tiergarten district, using a similar mock Italian Renaissance building style. They provided façades for Blumenthal that were likewise imposing. The auditorium retained box-pit-gallery arrangements to some extent, though there were several doorways into the auditorium — one door for every two rows of seats — of which at the time no other Berlin theatre could boast. The galleries likewise had easily accessible exits, while the lobbies and other gathering places were large enough to allow patrons to show off their finery. Audiences at many of Berlin's boulevard theatres consisted of "the aristocracy ... mixing with hustlers, coquettes, sophomoric dandies, middle-aged playboys, and elderly peacocks" (Turszinky 48). At the Lessing, "jobbers, sportsmen, and do-nothings" along with "the banking and stock market speculators found everything to their taste" (Zabel 102). The objections of such viewpoints notwithstanding, such individuals were the financial basis of Oskar Blumenthal's operation.

Oskar Blumenthal personified what Max Martersteig claimed was a collusion among the Berlin press, its commercial interests, and its middlebrow literary circles. Blumenthal's beginnings as a newspaper theatre critic led him to write the "new German *Gesellschaftsstück*," a middlebrow society play he felt was an antidote to the "social play" of Ibsen. In the process Blumenthal attracted substantial attention from theatre professionals in Berlin, who like most theatre professionals were afraid to confess the fact that literary plays dealing with social problems rarely attract audiences for an entire season. Blumenthal had no such fear, agreeing with fellow critic and successful playwright Paul Lindau that "in modern [theatre] art, reality seems to begin where soap leaves off."

Martersteig esteemed Blumenthal for writing plays that captured the ethical consciousness of his day (Martersteig 641). Blumenthal's *Das zweite Gesicht* (Two-Faced) *Die grosse Glocke* (The Big Bell), *Der schwarze Schleier* (The Black Veil), and *Ein Tropfen Gift* (A Drop of Poison) were far more genuine and less affected than the flimsy comedies of his predecessors Hugo Lubliner, Gustav von Moser, or Carl Lauffs. Like them, Blumenthal was convinced that most people went to the theatre "to be entertained, to laugh and not to cry, to avoid thinking about the sad world outside the theatre" (Booth 169). Unlike them, he wanted theatre to provide not just an evening's entertainment but rather an entire experience based on accessibility and what he later called a "theatre of the living."

He constructed the Lessing Theater for those purposes. By "living," he claimed a desire to present contemporary playwrights like Ibsen, Maurice Maeterlinck, and Hermann Sudermann — though in most cases the "living playwright" was Blumenthal himself. He offered his audiences an experience within a splendid building that accommodated them comfortably and afforded them a feeling of improved self-esteem. He wanted his patrons to feel as good about themselves as he did about himself. When construction on his Lessing Theater began in 1887, it marked the first time since Karl Friedrich Schinkel (1781–1841) in the 1820s that architects had been specifically commissioned to design and build a new free-standing theatre structure in Berlin.[2]

Blumenthal opened his new theatre on September 11, 1888, with Lessing's *Nathan der Weise* (Nathan the Wise). Few critics were impressed — though Blumenthal surprised everybody on October 10, 1888, by staging the first fully unabridged version of Ibsen's *A Doll's House*, in which Nora for the first time on a German stage actually deserted her husband and children. Blumenthal's audiences found Ibsen intolerably preachy and morally smug, so *A Doll's House* ran for only seventeen performances. Yet Blumenthal wanted to show Berlin that he, alone among producers in Berlin, had the financial fortitude, the attorneys, and the influence with police censors to present Ibsen uncut. Perhaps his secret desire was to demonstrate to everybody that no matter how one presented Ibsen, few audiences were interested. What audiences really wanted was a *Serienerfolg*, a play that could run an entire season in a repertoire of other less popular offerings. Such a play needed to feature comic situations, witty dialogue, and erotic sensationalism. Blumenthal's audiences also expected showy effects of every kind, especially jewelry, fancy hairdos, and lavish make-up on the female star performers, a combination often referred to in German theatre reviews as *eine blendene Toilette*, or a "blinding toilette."

On January 5, 1889, Blumenthal opened the kind of play his new theatre needed, namely Sardou's *Let's Get a Divorce*—in Blumenthal's translation as *Cyprienne*. The translation was perhaps the only novelty Blumenthal could offer, as the play had been done several times in Berlin during the 1880s. Blumenthal also presented Dumas *fils'* *The Clemenceau Case* that season, and it was the only production of the play anywhere in Germany, since

Blumenthal secured exclusive German-language rights to it from Dumas *fils* himself. *The Clemenceau Case* created a sensation in Berlin by featuring barely concealed nudity at the play's beginning. Louisa Brion, a beautiful young actress Blumenthal had hired to play the love interest of the sculptor Clemenceau, assumed the pose of a classic Greek goddess covered only by diaphanous material. Otto Brahm cast a fairly predictable skepticism over the success of both the production and on Louisa Brion herself by stating the play "would have a long run on the legs of a gorgeous actress" Brahm *Freie Bühne* 523). Brahm concluded his review by quoting a popular ditty of the day that approximated Blumenthal's premiere season:

> So sad he had to sit there,
> Hoping at last he had a hit there.
> There then unfolded quite a story
> When lo, a girl appeared in all her glory,
> Trading off a tat for tit there [Wilcke 30].

Police censorship of the nudity question never presented a problem in *The Clemenceau Case* because the character Luisa Brion so skillfully portrayed was a woman of dubious repute to begin with. That she appeared to be nude on stage seemed a natural consequence of her actions both as the sculptor's model and as his mistress. But Blumenthal, along with his attorney Richard Grelling, had developed skillful techniques to deal with the Berlin police by the 1890s, often convincing them that controversy in comedy was not nearly so dangerous as controversy in straight drama.

Hermann Sudermann's first play *Ehre* (Honor) followed *The Clemenceau Case*, and its unanticipated success surprised just about everybody — including critic Albert Soergel, who claimed the play bespoke a "modernist façade, allowing audiences to 'feel' modern but providing them an exit before any genuine socio-critical moments were allowed to disturb anyone's consciousness" (Soergel 86). Blumenthal staged *Honor* for the very reasons Soergel described: it was make-believe modernism, something his audiences would actually come to see and afterwards feel good about actually liking something that seemed up-to-date. He then presented the German-language premiere of Ibsen's *Hedda Gabler*, but like *A Doll's House*, it failed to attract attention. In the spring of 1891 Blumenthal premiered a play he and actor Gustav Kadelburg had written, titled *Die Grossstadtluft* (Big City Airs). It became the colossal success that solved all of Blumenthal's financial concerns as a producer. "A wind that sits in the sails of the good ship Blumenthal-Kadelburg and Co.," wrote Maximilian Harden, "allows it to sail wide of the shoals besetting many a premiere. The authors have cleverly created a play that meets all their audience's expectations.

Blumenthal for his part has forsaken any literary ambitions dogging his heels, while Kadelburg brings an unusual freshness to the work, borne of his wide experience as an actor. Kadelburg knows how gladly old acquaintances greet each other in the theatre, and that applies to audiences who are delighted to see time-honored gimmicks on full display" (Harden *Köpfe* 80). Blumenthal wrote the badinage, word plays, *bon mots*, and jokes, while Kadelburg developed the situations, though they were distinctly secondary in importance for the comedy's success. Actors played their roles "well below the demands of their talents" (Vossische Zeitung, 24 October 1891). Blumenthal's next effort with Kadelburg, *Gräfin Fritzi* (Countess Fritzi) was even more popular, though in it Blumenthal tried to restrain Kadelburg's enthusiasm for creating chance meetings, convenient happenstance, withheld information, and startling reversals. That was a shame, said Paul Lindau, because "There isn't a joke too old or too often heard before in *Countess Fritzi*. They're all there" (Lindau, Berliner Börsen Courier). The success of *Big City Airs* and *Countess Fritzi* set the stage for more plays like it at the Lessing, such as the Milland and Najac variation on the *Cyprienne* divorce-theme titled *Paragraph 330*. In this play a divorcing couple find themselves falling in love with each other during the trial hearings. Ludwig Fulda's *Das Recht der Frau* (A Woman's Rights) parodied feminist aspirations, Paul Heyse's *Wahrheit?* (Reality?) lampooned Naturalism by making fun of Zola, Hauptmann, and other proponents of the so-called "new" theatre.

The most curious success of 1893 was the world premiere of Hermann Sudermann's straight play *Heimat*. This play, in its English version titled *Magda*, was one of the few originally in German to attract an English-language audience in the 1890s. It featured a preternatural conflict between Magda and her father and evinced Sudermann's aptitude for coupling a fashionable dilemma (female emancipation vs. patriarchal control) with effective stage performance. The play did not, of course, disclose much in the way of intellectual content; Magda and her father remained two-dimensional, and Maximilian Harden condemned *Heimat* as "a masterpiece of theatrical falsehood. Every tone is screamingly spurious, and the tricks [Sudermann] uses to prolong the play's tension in the final act have absolutely nothing to do with anything remotely artistic" (Wilcke 39). Harden was referring to the father's convenient collapse from a cerebral hemorrhage just as the play's climax was reaching its conclusion. It was an ideal play for the Lessing Theater.

The Lessing was a bastion of anti-modernist theatrical taste, and Oskar Blumenthal's exertions there formed a bulwark against encroaching modernist sentiments, many of them emanating from the aforementioned Otto Brahm. Brahm had been Blumenthal's most articulate competitor when both men were newspaper critics. When Brahm likewise became a theatre manager and director, their competition intensified. Indeed the Oskar Blumenthal-Otto Brahm relationship reveals a great deal about the dynamics of the Wilhelmine theatre as a whole. Blumenthal and Brahm were approximately the same age, both extremely well educated, both from bourgeois Jewish families, both had begun their careers in journalism, and both became extraordinarily successful in subsequent theatrical pursuits. Yet an enormous gulf in aesthetic taste and political conviction separated them. Brahm as the director of the Freie Bühne organization had advocated the cause of Naturalism and a wholesale reform of the German theatre for the sake of what he termed "modern life." When in 1894 he took over the reins of the Deutsches Theater in Berlin, he turned the Deutsches into a literary showplace, presenting one Gerhart Hauptmann premiere after another and continuing the Freie Bühne tradition of "theatre for modern life." He maintained the position that a stage director's two most important abilities as "the art of staging and the art of literary discovery" (*Vossische Zeitung* 29 September 1883). Brahm's vision ultimately conquered Blumenthal's, and the conquest ironically took place in the very building Blumenthal had constructed as a monument to his own vision of what the German theatre should accomplish.

How could that happen? How could Oskar Blumenthal, one of the most successful personalities the Berlin theatre had ever known, simply disappear into the mists and allow modernism to reign triumphant in his theatre? Throughout the 1890s and well into the new century, the Lessing had continued to provide Berlin audiences with popular, middle-brow theatrical entertainment, for which Blumenthal had been such a staunch advocate and of which he became a most prolific and successful creator. By the end of the nineteenth century, however, Blumenthal had become restless. "They say a year in war is two years in peacetime, and a year in the theatre is like two years of war," Blumenthal said, "so in effect, I'm leaving after a thirty-year career" (*Neuer Theater-Almanac* X 1899, 151). The ironic conclusion to Blumenthal's career in Berlin was his unadmitted defeat at the hands of modernism, for the man to whom Blumenthal leased his theatre in 1904 was none other than Otto Brahm.

Brahm proceeded to do not just Ibsen's plays, but cycles of Ibsen's plays. By the time of his death in 1912, Brahm had produced and staged at the Lessing nearly every play Ibsen ever wrote, along with more Hauptmann premieres, and even premieres of Arthur Schnitzler's gloomy depictions of melancholy in turn-of-the-century Vienna. The Lessing Theater in Berlin thus became a kind of microcosm of the way Berlin's theatre began to change during the later Wilhelmine years. What had begun as the center of a thriving "boulevard culture" ultimately died an unmourned death and was buried in an unmarked grave. Who, for example, in the dawning years of the twenty-first century has even heard of Oskar Blumenthal? Who remembers the titles of his stupendously popular plays? Is it rhetorical to ask further, who would dare nowadays to produce one of them ? Some students of the German theatre, admittedly very few of them, have speculated on those questions, along with the question of why Blumenthal turned the Lessing over to Brahm. One answer may be that Blumenthal wanted to give Otto Brahm enough rope to hang himself with, knowing that Brahm would serve up as much Ibsen, Hauptmann, and Schnitzler as possible and thereby give final proof that most audiences simply rejected the modern "social problem play." Another reason may have been financial, since the lease on the Lessing was extremely expensive. Perhaps Blumenthal hoped Brahm would have to break the lease and finally convince everybody that Ibsen and the others were essentially box office poison.

As it turned out, Brahm did not break the lease, but Ibsen did in most instances prove to be a box-office failure. Of all the plays Brahm staged in Blumenthal's theatre, the sentimental nationalistic melodrama *Glaube und Heimat* (Faith and Homeland) by Karl Schönherr was the most popular, followed by Hermann Bahr's domestic comedy *Das Konzert* (The Concert). Along with Bahr's comedy and Schönherr's melodrama, Brahm featured the preposterous farce *Der Raub der Sabinerinnen* (The Rape of the Sabine Women), the very same farce that Blumenthal had run since 1888. Thus both Blumenthal and Brahm could claim a victory of sorts: Blumenthal proved, through Brahm, that a producer could not concentrate solely on literary plays. He had to combine them with popular fare like *The Concert*, *Faith and Homeland*, and *The Rape of the Sabine Women* if his theatre were to survive. Yet Brahm proved that Ibsen could indeed attract audiences, if those audiences had been sufficiently exposed to the "socially conscious" play to develop a taste for it. Both men were losers to economic forces beyond their control, of course: the motion picture had by 1905 established a foothold in Berlin, and the result was a rapid loss of theatre's near-monopoly on the mass audience. It is altogether likely that both men could see that kind of handwriting on the walls of the Lessing Theatre; fortunately neither of them lived long enough to witness the German theatre's wholesale collapse as an entertainment medium and its ultimate capitulation to modernism, with its attendant insistence upon and its embrace of an elitism that drove away what was left of the middlebrow audience.

UNIVERSITY OF NEBRASKA, LINCOLN

Notes

1. In a survey of the German theatre's "social economics," Gustav Rickelt listed Blumenthal, August Wolff of the Belle-Alliance Theatre, Adolf L'Arronge at the Deutsches Theater, Ludwig Barnay of the Berliner Theater, Sigmund Lautenburg of the Residenz Theater, and Adolf Ernst of the Adolf-Ernst Theater as men who had become millionaires as theatre managers in Berlin (91).

2. The Lessing Theater was destroyed in a 1943 Allied bombing raid over Berlin.

3. The first Berlin production of *A Doll's House* opened in October of 1880 at the Residenz Theater in the "reconciliation" version in which Nora looks in on her sleeping children and remains with her husband. It was based on the first German production staged Munich of March 1880 (Frenzel 23).

4. Brahm presented Hauptmann performances a total of 1169 times between 1894 and 1904, or one third of his total of 3,000 performances (Goldmann 13). One reason he did so was Hauptmann's grant to Brahm of exclusive performance rights to his plays in Berlin.

5. All of these questions are doubtlessly rhetorical, although a Berlin production of *Im weiss'n Rössl* (The White Horse Inn) took place in 1997. It was not the Blumenthal original, however. It was the Ralph Benatsky musical based on the play, starring Max Raabe and Otto Sander.

References Cited

Bab, Julius. *Der Mensch auf der Bühne*, Berlin: Oesterheld, 1910.

Blumenthal, Oskar. *Theatralische Eindrücke*. Berlin: Hofmann, 1885.

Booth, Michael. *Theatre in the Victorian Age*. New York: Cambridge University Press, 1991.

Brahm, Otto. *Freie Bühne für modernes Leben*. Vols. I and II. Berlin: Fischer, 1891.

_____. *Theater, Dramatiker, Schauspieler*, Ed. Hugo Fetting. Berlin: Henschel, 1961.

_____. "Literarische Entdeckung ... " *Vossische Zeitung*, 29 September 1883.

Frenzel, Herbert. "Ibsens *Puppenheim* in Deutschland." Diss. University Berlin, 1942.

Gesnossenschaft Deutscher Bühnen-Angehöriger, *Neuer Theater-Almanac* X (1899).

Goldmann, Paul . *Aus dem dramatischen Irrgarten*, Frankfurt: Rütten und Löning, 1905.

Harden, Maximilian. "Zukunft" in his *Köpfe* Vol. 1. Berlin: Reiss, 1910.

Harden, Maximilian, Foreword to Paul Linsemann, *Die Theaterstadt Berlin*. Berlin: Tändler, 1897, iv–xi.

Hoffmeister, Heribert. *Anekdotenschatz*. Berlin: Verlag Praktisches Wissen, 1957.

"Hülsen wirkungsvoller Bonmots." *Schaubühne* 13 (1917) 14–17.

Jacobsohn, Siegfried. *Das Theater der Reichshauptstadt*. Munich: Langen, 1904.

Lindau, Paul. Rev. of *Gräfin Fritzi*, *Berliner Börsen Courier* 30 September 1895.

Linsemann, Paul. *Die Theaterstadt Berlin*. Berlin: Tändler, 1897.

Lothar, Rudolph. *Das deutsche Drama der Gegenwart*. Munich: Müller, 1905.

Martersteig, Max. *Das deutsche Theater im neunzehnten Jahrhundert*. Leipzig: Breitkopf und Härtel, 1924.

Rev. of *Die Großstadtluft*, *Vossische Zeitung*, 24 October 1891.

Rickelt, Gustav. *Schauspieler und Direktoren*. Berlin: Langendscheidt, 1910.

Sollmann, Kurt. "Zur Sozialgeschichte des Kaiserreichs" in Viktor Zmegac (ed.) *Deutsche Literatur der Jahrhundertwende*. Königstein: Athenäum, 1981, 140–152.

Soergel, Albert. *Dichtung und Dichter der Zeit*, Leipzig: Voigtländer, 1928.

Turszinky, Walter. *Berliner Theater*. Berlin: Seemann, 1908.

Wilcke, Joachim. "Das Lessingtheater unter Oskar Blumenthal." Diss. Freie University Berlin, 1958.

Zabel, Eugen. *Zur modernen Dramaturgie*. Oldenburg und Leipzig: Schulze, 1905.

Comedian of the Seventeenth Century

Ostrovskii's Dialogue with Russian Theatre History

John W. Hill

Abstract

In 1872, A.N. Ostrovskii wrote the play Komik XVII-ogo stoletiia (Comedian of the 17th Century) to mark the "bicentennial" of the Russian theatre. The historical event celebrated was the performance for Tsar Alexei Mikhailovich of the play Esther on October 17th, 1672. Ostrovskii's play, which takes as its subject preparations for the performance of Esther, draws on medieval popular performance (skomorokhi) and folk theatre traditions. The principal character, Yakov, is identified as a skomorokh, or minstrel: his natural comic ability leads to his being drafted into the theatre company. In the traditional view, represented by his strict father, acting was an unwholesome pastime. The way Yakov and the producers of Esther overcome this prejudice is one aspect of the play. Another is Ostrovskii's use of dramatic elements of the traditional wedding ritual and the folk theatre. Thus Ostrovskii engages the past and challenges received wisdom in his tribute to Russia's theatrical roots.

In 1872 Aleksander Ostrovskii wrote the play *Komik XVII-ogo stoletiia* (*Comedian of the 17th Century*) to mark the "bicentennial" of the Russian theatre. On October 17th, 1672, Tsar Alexei Mikhailovich was present at a performance of *Esfir* (*Esther*), otherwise known as *Artaksersovo deistvo* (*The Artexerxes Play*). *Comedian* concerns preparations being made in the summer of that year for the production. Ostrovskii had explored the life of performers in his play *Les* (*The Forest*); and he had also set several plays in the sixteenth and seventeenth centuries. In *Comedian of the 17th Century*, however, he combined the genre of historical drama with reflections on the actor's place in Russian society and the nature of performance.

Esther, based on the eponymous Old Testament book, established a strong tradition of social and political commentary from the Russian stage, in this case through an allegory of the contemporary Muscovite court.[1] Although referred to as a *Komediia*, *Esther* was serious and didactic. Ostrovskii's treatment of the 17th century performance of *Esther*, however, was comic, a genre that had been widely used in Russia at least since Denis Fonvizin's *The Minor* (1782). This "corrective" notion of comedy highlighted various characters' flaws, delusions and virtues to critique society and government policy.

The year 1672, the setting of *Comedian*, is both an appropriate date for the birth of Russian theatre and a misleading designation. Ostrovskii demonstrates in his play that he was well aware of both sides of this paradox. The year 1672 is arbitrary because of other instances of Western style theatrical performances in Russian lands that were contemporaneous and even predate the premier of *Esther* such as scholastic dramas and presentations of plays in the private homes of the high-ranking nobility.[2] Still, *Esther* does mark the beginning of a discrete performance tradition. The type of theatrical performance seen in the fall of 1672 in the newly constructed *komediinaia khoromina* (comic chambers) in the settlement of *Preobrazhenskoe*, the Tsar's favorite summer retreat, closely followed its European model. It featured painted sets, sewn costumes, and props, all specifically prepared for the performance. There was a written, rehearsed text acted by specially prepared performers; there were even what today we would call producers and directors. The performance took place in a specially designated space with actors on one side of the room and audience on the other. Most importantly, however, this was a performance called into being by the ruler and executed for his entertainment and for the prestige of the state.

Russia in the second half of the seventeenth century was at a crucial turning point in its history. Perhaps no other period displays so many vivid ambiguities and contradictions. Tsar Alexei Mikhailovich began, and his son Peter the Great would continue, to make extensive changes to Russia's religious, military, administrative and cultural institutions. The ruling classes looked to the West for examples and inspiration. The rest of the population did not always share this enthusiasm for things European. Often western ideas and customs came into violent conflict with time-honored native beliefs and habits. Eventually, though, most western ideas were subsumed into Russian culture after being transmuted to varying degrees — Russified.

This is what happened to the performance traditions imported during the reign of Alexei Mikhailovich. The court theatre emerged in a land that could already claim a long and rich history of performance. Ostrovskii states unequivocally in his play that these native performance traditions not only influenced the development of Russian drama, they constitute an integral part of Russian theatre as a whole.

In his play, Ostrovskii both marked the anniversary of Russia's first theatrical production and indicated the complexity of the emergence of the Russian theatrical tradition. In addition to his treatment of the historical events of 1672, Ostrovskii included material that clearly derives from three folk-based performance traditions in Russia: folklore *per se* in the form of the wedding ritual, the *skomorokh* tradition of popular entertainers in early Russia, and the popular theatre. Ostrovskii's celebration of these forms conveyed through their inclusion into the dramatic fabric of his play shows that he believed they were as important to the development of Russian drama as was the fact of transplanting the European stage play tradition.

Ostrovskii labeled his play a comedy in verse in three acts with epilogue. Act one is concerned with the impending marriage of Yakov and Natal'ia. Only in passing do we learn of Yakov's involvement with the production of *Esther*: he has been drafted as one of the actors. Dramatic tension is created and maintained throughout the majority of this act by the conflict between Yakov's and Natal'ia's parents, who are negotiating the terms of their marriage. Weddings in Russia traditionally consist of a highly complex set of rituals. Folklorists and theatre scholars have found many dramatic elements in the traditional marriage rite.[3] These discussions invariably begin with the Russian expression for nuptials: *igrat' svad'bu*, to "play" a wedding (same verb as the Russian for "to act"). The first "act" in the wedding "play" is the matchmaking process. According to custom, this involves people other than the future bride and groom exploring the possibility of a union and negotiating the material arrangements of the ceremony and life of the new family. In this part of the marriage ritual, preparations and planning for the wedding itself take place. Thus matchmaking is a rehearsal for the wedding day in the same way that rehearsals for *Esther* are underway in *Comedian*. By juxtaposing the two, Ostrovskii seems to be saying that the life of the Russian people has inherently theatrical qualities.

While the steps in matchmaking certainly demonstrate dramatic features, ritual conflicts by themselves do not constitute drama. This idea was put forward by Larisa Ivleva in *Doteatral'no-igrovoi iazyk russkogo fol'klora* (*The Pre-Theatrical, Play-Based Language of Russian Folklore*). She writes that traditional theories about the birth of theatre in Russia, which fit into two categories — the idea that 1) ritual by its very nature is theatrical, or, 2) that theatre grew up naturally from proto-theatrical ritual forms, — "are nothing more than attempts to retroactively rehabilitate the history of professional theatre in [Russia] by presenting the fact of its borrowing as an insignificant graft onto the already existing tree of so-called theatre (pre-theatre) proper"

(Ivleva 32). She describes as flawed the conclusion that since folklore and theatre contain many analogous elements and that since the latter developed after the former, then theatre evolved organically from folk ritual. Instead of the "genetic" approach to the origins of theatre in Russia, she proposes a structural and typological method that would allow these two phenomena to be compared in ways more significant than a purely mechanical or a cause and effect relationship (Ivleva 35). Ostrovskii's views, as will be seen by the end of this analysis, are quite similar to Ivleva's. For both scholar and playwright, ritual forms were highly dramatic but did not constitute drama *per se.*

Thus in Act 1 Yakov's father, Kirill Kochetov, and Natal'ia's mother, Tatiana, repeatedly spar over the dowry. In the Russian village, these ritualized confrontations were based on economic necessity. While negotiating the dowry and other issues involving property, each party — bride's and groom's families — would strive to get as much and give as little to the other side as possible. For Ostrovskii, the custom of haggling during matchmaking negotiations, i.e., ritual, does not inherently contain enough tension to make a scene dramatic. His solution is to add sympathetic characters and real human feelings to provide a foil for these collisions over money. In the very first scene of the play, before the parents are introduced, we meet Natal'ia and Yakov. She has been preparing for the visit of his parents but expects him to be working at his job as clerk in the Ambassadorial Office. He has run away. We discover why only later. While this scene does foreshadow Yakov's troubles at work, an important element in the plot, it also shows a moment of affectionate banter between the two young people (Ostrovskii I–i, 296–297), thus establishing the warmth of the characters and the sincerity of their relationship.

Only by establishing this relationship at the beginning will the conflict that follows between the parents seem like something is at stake. The audience must believe that the threat Tatiana makes to call things off is real. She admits, later, at the end of the act after the Kochetov family has gone home, that she always intended to go through with the wedding, "We'll disagree a few more times, then make arrangements proper [...] I won't back down, it's just not in my nature (Ostrovskii I–vii, 317–318).[4] Since financial considerations did frequently make or break marriage negotiations, since Tatiana's confession comes after the confrontations, and since we know none of the characters particularly well at this early stage, the viewer would have no reason to be sure the adults were not sincerely expressing an antagonism that could potentially wreck the future happiness of Yakov and Natal'ia.

Ostrovskii does not restrict his treatment of the folk ritual involving marriage to just the financial negotiations. He also has fun with other features of the traditional scenario. A key element of the marriage rite, or indeed any folk rite, was the songs. In the marriage ritual there were a great number of occasions for many different kinds of songs sung by various "actors" in the wedding drama: bride's laments, wedding feast songs, songs for dressing the bride, and so on. Ostrovskii takes the genre of mothers' song. Here the bride's mother mourns the loss of her daughter while other adult women commiserate. While it is likely that Ostrovskii wrote an original dialogue based on folk models rather than copy an existing folk song, the following exchange contains both folk form and imagery:

Anisia:	(*Yakov's mother*). Fathers have it easy...
Tatiana:	(*Tatiana's mother*). But what about us?
Anisia:	We gave them birth...
Tatiana:	And didn't we see pain?
Anisia:	We raised them...
Tatiana:	And kept them like our eyes.
Kochetov:	(*Yakov's father*). Oh, that's enough!
Tatiana:	We cleaned their little faces.
Anisia:	And fed them...
Tatiana:	Didn't we finish off their table scraps?
Anisia:	And they grew up...
Tatiana:	Like juicy little apples.
Kochetov:	(*stamping his foot*). Oh, that's enough!
Anisia:	Our hearts aren't made of stone.
	[Ostrovskii I–iii, 304].

Stock phrases like "kak oko sobliudali" ("and kept them like our eyes") and comparing young girls to ripe apples are common tropes in folk poetry and wedding songs. Furthermore, it was the "role" of the bride's mother to lament the loss of her daughter, whether she would really miss the girl or not.[5]

Since the matchmaking negotiations are conducted either by parents or designated matchmakers, the young people can seem to become almost like puppets. In another scene, the adults are disputing whether Tatiana should give up her chest of loose pearls to decorate Natal'ia's wedding headdress.

Anisia:	Give them up!
Tatiana:	I won't!
Kochetov:	She's mighty stubborn.
Tatiana:	That's how I am. The older I get
	The less I change. Natal'ia! Get away
	From Yakov!
	(*Natal'ia walks to the other side*)

Anisia: (*to Tatiana*). What's wrong with you! Children,
          Don't listen to her, go off in the corner!
          (*Natal'ia goes towards Yakov*)
          [Ostrovskii I–iii, 307–308]

and later

Anisia: (*to Yakov & Natal'ia*). You've separated again? Come together,
          Talk, God's will is that
          Things work out for the best.
Tatiana: Then we'll shake on it?
Kochetov: We will. God's blessing on it. And, oh,
          I ought to get a hat of belly fur from you.
Anisia: A hat? Whatever for?
Kochetov: I just
          Thought it would be good.
Tatiana: Aha! You've greedy eyes, I see!
          Natal'ia, get away from Yakov!
          (*Natalia walks away from Yakov*)
          [Ostrovskii I–v, 313]

It is apparent, then, that Ostrovskii, in his tribute to the founding of the western stage play tradition in Russia, did not forget the contribution and influence of the native tradition of folk ritual. In his own way, through the fabric of his dramatic text, Ostrovskii seems to foreshadow by a hundred years Larisa Ivleva's position that while ritual was not the direct progenitor of Russian drama, through the color and vividness of its language, the playful, theatrical character of its dialogues and other exchanges, and the variety it demonstrated in meter and genre in its songs, it did provide a source of much rich artistic material and inspiration.

Ostrovskii is not content with just including folk ritual. He also addresses folk theatre proper by exploring the legacy of this tradition in Act 2 of *Comedian*. Set in "a chamber of the state palace" (Ostrovskii II–i, 318), this space is apparently a rehearsal room, as the platforms indicate. Participants in the scene include Yakov, who has been fetched back to rehearsal at the end of Act 1 by his supervisor, other "comedians" and real historical figures like German pastor Johann Gottfried Gregory, playwright and director of *Esther*, and producer Artemon Sergeevich Matveev. It is apparent that Ostrovskii will now present some aspect of preparations for the performance. At the time he wrote *Comedian of the 17th Century*, the text of *Esther* was believed lost. Only in 1954 did several copies of the play almost simultaneously come to light in France and Russia. There is little doubt that Ostrovskii could have invented a convincing recreation of a portion of the play based on knowledge of the Old Testament and the surviving literature of the time. He did not do so, but instead chose to engage in the speculative recreation of one of the *intermediia* or comic interludes between the acts of the serious, didactic story of Esther, which, unlike *Esther*, remain lost to this day.[6]

Ostrovskii gives us the following "interlude." Yakov, as a gypsy, is alone on stage and complains of extreme hunger. At the end of a sixteen line monologue lamenting his situation he decides to go to sleep with the hope that he will dream of food and at least get some satisfaction from that. He does indeed see a piece of pork fat in his sleep, which he tries to grab, only to wake up empty handed. Enter a doctor and his servant carrying a box of medicines. The doctor, a foreigner, speaks only Latin. The misunderstanding that follows due to the servant's mistranslation results in the gypsy having a tooth pulled instead of getting something to eat. The gypsy runs out. The doctor then switches to Russian and upbraids the servant for not collecting a fee.

> Doctor: Where's the money? He must pay!
> Servant: Go ask that gypsy, 'fore he gets away!
> Doctor: (*beating the servant*) Take that! You think it's funny,
>   To let a patient go without collecting money?

The servant then turns the tables on the doctor, throwing him to the ground, beating him with a stick and advising this "un-baptized forehead," this "mangy little wig" ("*Nekreshchenyi lob, parshivyi parichishko*") that this is the way Russians fight back ("*Nechego delat', davat' tebe sdachi. Po-russki vot kak!*") (Ostrovskii II–v, 328–333).

While this scene clearly derives from the traditions of folk theatre, it is not easy to determine exactly which one. Some scholars speculate that comic exchanges like this first appeared in the *vertep* tradition. The *vertep* was a Christmastime puppet theatre that developed in the western part of the Russian Empire — the Ukraine, Belarus and Western Russia, where Orthodoxy and Catholicism had intermingled during Polish domination, resulting in a fertile mixture of eastern and western traditions (Davidova; Kelly 34). Primarily concerned with representing serious scenes from the Christmas story — the gift of the Magi, the murder of the innocents, the death of Herod, and so on (Davidova) — there were also comic episodes "of a low, farcical kind"(Kelly 34) in which "healing" has been identified as "potential thematic material for the second half of the drama" (Davidova).

Although some scholars trace the beginnings of the *vertep* as far back as the sixteenth century, practically all irrefutable documentation of it date to the late eighteenth, early nineteenth centuries (Davidova). And there is no solid agreement among scholars as to the nature of the *vertep*'s relationship to another similar genre of folk theatre, the marketplace drama or *balagan*. Since the *balagan* featured only comic scenes, one might conclude that it developed from the *vertep*. However, since both genres were first recorded sometime in the eighteenth century, it would be pointless to try to determine which tradition spawned the other, especially since both seem to also be related in some way to the *intermedia* of the seventeenth century scholastic drama of the eastern Slavic lands (Aseev 141–148). Furthermore, all three genres were heavily influenced by western theatrical traditions —*commedia dell' arte*, Punch and Judy shows, and peep shows (Kelly 34–35). It is perhaps wise not speculate too much about which specific tradition Ostrovskii was citing but instead see his creation of an *intermedium* for *Esther* as a tribute to the popular theatre in general.

The ethnic stereotyping present in the interlude must certainly trouble many readers today.[7] Two things can be said, however. Firstly, Ostrovskii realized that the tradition of folk theatre, be it fairground or puppet theatre, which could incidentally be performed by live actors (Kelly 34), was too important an element in Russian theatrical culture to be left out of his tribute to Russian performance traditions. Secondly, Ostrovskii chose ethnic humor instead of the other evergreen motif in the folk theatre, satirical treatments of the clergy (Aseev 146–148). Had Ostrovskii decided to write an interlude about priests and monks, he would have guaranteed that *Comedian of the 17th Century* would never have been published or performed on an imperial stage due to censorship restrictions. Furthermore, it is highly unlikely that satire of the clergy would have been included in a play based on Biblical history and performed for such a devout monarch as Alexei Mikhailovich.

The final aspect of the native tradition of Russian theatrical performance that Ostrovskii explores in *Comedian* is the *skomorokh* tradition. *Skomorokhi* were professional entertainers in Old Russia. Whether permanently settled or itinerant, their repertoire could include singing, dancing, playing instruments, story-telling, stand-up comedy, animal acts, tumbling and leading the population in those folk rituals of pagan origin that had survived in some form into the Christian era.[8] Indeed, the *skomorokhi* seem to have originated in Russia's murky pagan past based on their close relationship with remnants of pre–Christian ritual. They were always bitterly opposed by the church for this reason. Throughout the medieval period, the secular authorities would alternatively persecute and patronize them, sometimes both at the same time.[9] The common people loved them. In the middle of the 17th century, the central government began taking unprecedented measures to wipe out *skomoroshestvo* (*skomorokh* performance) completely. As a living performance tradition, the era of the *skomorokhi* ends at this time.[10] It is ironic that this took place under the same ruler who organized the first European-style theatrical performance, Alexei Mikhailovich Romanov.

Ostrovskii explores stereotypes and prejudices about actors and the acting profession, the nature of theatrical performance and the place of theatre and actors in society through the *skomorokh* theme. It is important to remember that while the western-influenced ruling elite would have drawn a clear line separating the native tradition of popular entertainment represented by the *skomorokhi* from the imported, western stage play, other elements of society, such as peasants, artisans and low level government functionaries would surely have identified any secular performance activity as *skomoroshestvo*. Thus in *Comedian*, Yakov is motivated to run away from rehearsal, courting the displeasure of his director, leading noblemen and, ultimately the Tsar himself, for fear of what his father's reaction will be when he learns that his son has become a *skomorokh*.

Kirill Kochetov, Yakov's father, bases his conduct and world view on a sixteenth century text, *Domostroi* (*The Home-builder*), a list of rules for social, religious and family life that includes instructions on how to brew beer as well as what size stick to use to beat one's wife. Kochetov even sits down to read *Domostroi* in Act 3 to relish the, "verbal honey and food for the soul" (Ostrovskii III–ii, 341), to be found in its pages. The book serves to associate Kochetov with the strict ideology of Russian medieval church culture. Thus Kochetov takes an uncompromising view of the *skomorokhi*, absolutely the worst thing in heaven or hell that his son could become. He responds to another character who accuses Yakov of being a *skomorokh*:

> Vasily,
> Don't speak in vain! Call him what you will,
> Label him a thief, a robber of church goods,
> A murderer, if you've no fear of God,
> If you're possessed by devils, but don't
> You call him skomorokh!
> [Ostrovskii III–v, 349]

This is a fairly accurate picture of the vehemence of the anti-theatrical prejudice in mid–17th century Russia in a section of the population that extended from the semi-literate to lower level government functionaries.

Much of the higher nobility, of course, supported the Tsar in his attempt to charter an official theatre. Some noblemen, like the Tsar's father-in-law, I.D. Miloslavsky, had sponsored theatrical productions even before the celebrated premier of *Esther* (Vsevolodskii-Gerngross 65). The problem was how to overcome the resistance of the social layer immediately beneath the upper aristocracy, the resistance of which would doom any reform or innovation.

Ostrovskii highlights this problem by committing a slight anachronism. The actors who performed the premier of *Esther* were Pastor Johann Gregory's countrymen: German students living in Moscow. Ostrovskii would have known this.[11] For his play he chose to make the actors in the first performance of *Esther* Russian.

The nature of Yakov's inner struggle, even more than the external conflict with his father, demonstrates how Ostrovskii imagined that the inertia of the anti-theatrical prejudice was overcome in the seventeenth century. On the one hand, Yakov has a gift for comic performance. His director recognizes this when Yakov once again runs away after the rehearsal of the interlude.

Matveev:	I see you are upset,
	Find a replacement for him!
Gregory:	Is talent
	Like a shoe that you can throw away
	And go put on another?

[Ostrovskii II–vi, 336]

His colleagues acknowledge Yakov's gift.

3rd Comedian:	You made us bust a gut with laughter
	The time you told that story called
	"Father's sitting and you are standing."

[Ostrovskii II–i, 321]

Even Yakov admits to the pleasure he gets from performing in a confidential talk with Natal'ia.

Yakov:	It's even sometimes fun,
	And were it not a dreadful sin,
	And did I not so fear my dad…
	I'm drawn to it somehow,
	I dream of it at night.

[Ostrovskii I–v, 312]

On the other hand, Yakov must first overcome his own deep-seated cultural stereotypes about acting.

Yakov:	And should I entertain,
	Transform myself and take up foreign guises,
	–Gypsy, Jew, Estonian, pulling them onto
	An Orthodox Russian countenance,
	Being merry and making others merry,

> When the gates of hell beckon wide,
> And my father's curse awaits!
>
> [Ostrovskii II–vi, 334]

It is very telling that the example Ostrovskii gives of Yakov's comic talent aside from his performance in the interlude is the imitation of his father he does for his colleagues in Act 2.

> Yakov: … He takes his glasses off.
> "What's that stupid grin for? Or have you stolen something?
> Don't you know we're born in sin,
> That we must repent and not laugh?
> If you don't know, then let me teach you.
> Give me that belt that's hanging from the nail!
> Despair is what becomes a youth
> Despair and not a foolish grin,
> Despair, despair.." And he whacks
> Me up and down, from heel to shoulder…
>
> [Ostrovskii II–I, 321]

Ostrovskii seems to be saying that this ability to laugh at one's misfortunes, to find humor in misery, is the trait that has allowed Russians to survive: it is a part of the Russian character that goes deeper than the ideology *du jour*.

Indeed, the comic is central to Ostrovskii's fundamental ideas about Russian theatre. The material of the Book of Esther has much potential moral significance: obey the king; for he knows best; and willful, disobedient nobles will be punished. This is clearly the reason the subject was chosen for the first stage play to be done in Russia. During the reign of Alexei Mikhailovich, autocracy in Russia was entering a new phase — not only would the Tsar control the state, the state would directly control as never before more and more aspects of people's lives by absorbing different institutions into the state apparatus. The moralistic potential of a play based on the Book of Esther, though, did not suit Ostrovskii's purpose. Ostrovskii chose to concentrate on Yakov and his interlude, believing that comedy was the conscience and moral mirror of the nation. It should come as no surprise that Ostrovskii has this message spoken at the end of the play by Pastor Gregory.

> Gregory: And everyone will see
> Their own lives and their acts,
> And what each thinks alone at night
> And who neglects his conscience, and doesn't know
> Its judgement — that person will find judgement there

Volynskii: (*a nobleman*) And who will be my judge?
Gregory: The comedian.
Volynskii: In foreign lands that's true, I guess,
        But not with us.
Gregory: It will be so
        In Russia too. And you will not
        Be able to escape the comic. For in our souls
        There is one gift among God's bounty
        That's salutary: it makes things base and wicked
        Seem humorous, and gives them up to ridicule.
        To praise the greatness of the heroes
        Of one's country is right and good;
        But there's more honor, worth and glory
        In teaching folks by demonstrating morals.
            [Ostrovskii Epilogue–ii, 362–363]

The person to do this teaching, Ostrovskii makes clear, is the comedian. And let the patriots and chauvinists not worry, for the foreigner, Johann Gregory, Lutheran pastor, is only stating what Russians themselves have always had the ability to do. The proof is in the person of Yakov Kochetov, comedian.

The subject matter and the date of the first performance of *Comedian of the 17th Century* (October 26th, 1872) seem to indicate that Ostrovskii sincerely considered Russian theatre to have begun with the premiere of the first production for the Tsar's official court theatre. In many ways this view is correct: theatrical performance was a government monopoly in Russia until 1882, and even after Tsar Alexander III abrogated the government's exclusive right to determine what was seen on the stages of the Empire, theatre continued to follow the trajectory set for it 200 years earlier. This was the tradition of Moscow's Maly and Petersburg's Alexandriiskii, the theatres that most closely collaborated with Ostrovskii. A closer look at *Comedian*, however, indicates that Ostrovskii did not believe that the performance traditions of the Russian theatre were started from scratch in the 1670s. Popular genres and performance traditions of folk culture were present at the "birth" of Russian theatre and continued to influence its development and character. In addition to providing a kind of genealogy for Russian performance, Ostrovskii explores how attitudes about performance in society began to change from the perception of actors as suspect, immoral individuals to important bearers of culture and even a kind of morality. This change in attitudes was more than a historical reference: it resonated in Ostrovskii's day because even then the transition was far from complete.

THE UNIVERSITY OF MICHIGAN, ANN ARBOR

Notes

1. Esther would have stood for Alexei Mikhailovich's new, second wife, the young Natal'ia Kirillovna Naryshkina. The contemporary Mordecai was nobleman, Tsar's advisor and former guardian of Natal'ia Naryshkina, Artemon Sergeevich Matveev. The Muscovite Haman could have been disgraced counselors Afanasii Lavrent'evich Ordin-Nashchokin or Bogdan Matveevich Khitrovo (Kudriavtsev 40).

2. This is the view of Soviet theatre historian V.N. Vsevolodskii-Gerngross (Vsevolodskii-Gerngross 64).

3. The connection of folk ritual with drama became practically axiomatic in studies of the origins of Russian theatre through most of the twentieth century.

4. All translations in the present article done by John W. Hill. *Comedian* has apparently never been translated into English.

5. The mother and father of the bride were "theatrical figures" in the way that they played "the traditional role of the loving parents who must give up their daughter into a strange family regardless of their true feelings about their daughter and her wedding" (Pomerantseva 176).

6. None of the existing copies of *Esther* contains any comic interludes, although there is reference to them elsewhere, such as the list of actors which mentions five participants in the *interstseniia*, the "inter-scenes" (Vsevolodskii-Gerngross 67). Ostrovskii's interlude for *Comedian*, "Tsygan i lekar'" ("Gypsy and Doctor"), though, is based quite closely on an actual text: the *Proludium secundum* cited by N. Tikhonravov 1859: 40–42 (Kashin 130–131).

7. The portrayal of gypsies is negative, "I don't feel much like working, Just wander all day long, There's nothing even around to steal…" (Ostrovskii II–v, 329) The foreign doctor is ridiculed, abused and even slurred as a Jew, "…thin-legged *Zhid* (derogatory word for Jew in Russian)," and "un-baptized forehead" (Ostrovskii 332, 333).

8. These include non–Christian elements in marriage and funeral rituals. See Vlasova.

9. During the sack of Novgorod in the 1570s, for instance, Ivan the Terrible destroyed this center of *skomorokh* culture, scattering performers throughout Russia. The very best *skomorokhi*, though, were taken back to Moscow to entertain the Tsar, who was by all accounts quite a connoisseur of this type of entertainment.

10. But not, of course, as a cultural tradition.

11. Ostrovskii consulted extensively with historians Ivan Zabelin and Nikolai Tikhonravov when working on *Comedian* (Ostrovskii 581). Tikhonravov cites Yuri Mikhailov's commission to collect "foreign children of various ranks from civil servant and merchant families, 64 in all" (Tikhonravov 1874: xi). Soon after this, a Russian troupe was formed (Vsevolodskii-Gerngross 65).

References Cited

Aseev, Boris Nikolaevich. *Russkii dramaticheskii teatr: ot ego istokov do kontsa XVIII veka.* Moscow: Iskusstvo, 1977.

Davidova, Mariia Georgievna. "Vertepny teatr v russkoi traditsionnoi kul'ture." *Traditsionnaia kul'tura*. Moscow, 2002. No. 1, pp. 20–37. 15 December 2003. <http://booth.ru/vertep/vert_hist/david_istor_vert.doc>.

Ivleva, Larisa Mikhailovna. *Doteatral'no-igrovoi iazyk russkogo fol'klora*. St. Petersburg: Izdatel'stvo "Dmitrii Bulanin," 1998.

Kashin, Nikolai Pavlovich. "Komik XVII stoletiia." *Trudy Vsesoiuznoi biblioteki im. V.I.Lenina. Sb. 4*. Moscow, 1939. 121–153.

Kelly, Catriona. "The Origins of the Russian Theatre." *A History of Russian Theatre*. Eds. Robert Leach and Victor Borovsky. Cambridge: University Press, 1999. 18–40.

Kudriavtsev, Il'ia Mikhailovich, ed. *Artakserksovo deistvo: pervaia p'esa russkogo teatra XVII v*. Moscow, Izdatel'stvo akademii nauk SSSR, 1957.

Ostrovskii, Aleksandr Nikolaevich. *Polnoe sobranie sochinenii v 12-i tomax, tom 7: piesy (1866–1873)*. Moscow: Iskusstvo, 1977.

Pomerantseva, Erna Vasilievna. "Semeinaia obriadovaia poeziia." *Russkoe narodnoe poeticheskoe tvorchestvo*. Moscow: Uchpedgiz, 1954. 171–188.

Tikhonravov, Nikolai Savvich. *Letopisi russkoi literatury i drevnosti*. St. Petersburg: Tipografiia Gracheva, 1859.

Tikhonravov, Nikolai Savvich. *Russkiia dramaticheskiia proizvedeniia: 1672–1725 godov*. St. Petersburg: Izdanie D.E. Kozhanchikova, 1874.

Vlasova, Zoia Ivanovna. *Skomorokhi i fol'klor*. St. Petersburg: Aleteia, 2001.

Vsevolodskii-Gerngross, Vsevolod Nikolaevich. *Istoriia russkogo dramaticheskogo teatra v semi tomakh, tom 1: Ot istokov do kontsa XVIII veka*. Moscow: Iskusstvo, 1977.

Critical Mimesis
Investigating Gender Roles with Ellen Terry

Lauren Love

Abstract

Victorian actress Ellen Terry left correspondence, rehearsal notes and memoirs that offer insight on her acting methods and on conventional gender roles. In her reflections, Terry reveals a process in which her conceptions of her own Self are profoundly challenged as she prepares to play the role of Lady Macbeth. This negotiation also reveals the historical conditions that allow Terry to imagine and publicly present herself as a Victorian and a Woman. By taking acting techniques themselves as productive modes of critical inquiry, I suggest that self-conscious imitation followed by critical scrutiny can be useful to historians, actors and feminists interested in challenging constricting gender identities. I use mimetic writing to inform this historical investigation. Critical mimesis is meant as a practical application of research techniques through embodied practices, such as imitative writing and acting. It offers the historian a new proximity to the object of inquiry and to the performing subject an experiential awareness of constructed social roles.

Near the end of her published *Memoirs*, the nineteenth-century British[1] actress, Ellen Terry, reflects on the self and her life's work:

> If I have not revealed myself, (Myself? Why even I, I often think, know little of myself!) I hope I have given a true picture of my life as an actress, and shown what years of labour and practice are needed for the attainment of a permanent position on the stage. To quote Mrs. Nance Oldfield: "Art needs all that we can bring to her, I assure you!" [Terry et al. 367].

Is it possible that Ellen Terry is admitting in these closing comments to her written *Memoirs*, that the self is an expression of or adherent to Art? It might be said that Victorian British women were expected to attain a "permanent position on the stage" of everyday life by expertly performing their identities within clearly defined and rather narrow parameters. Terry's approaches to her performances as a social subject, public persona and actress suggest a complex negotiation with gendered discourses and practices. As a professional actress playing the roles of various women, Terry was able to manipulate boundaries, mix and match predefined "feminine characteristics" and question the absoluteness of human attributes categorized according to gender. Perhaps it is precisely the professional performer who can teach us that we continuously recreate our own selves artfully. Investing in a space of art, Ellen Terry practiced acts of self-transformation that may be instructive to twenty-first century feminists.

By focusing on Terry's long acting career and then on some of her comments, reflections and working notes relating to her 1888 performance of Lady Macbeth, I hope to display some of the Victorian views of Womanhood with which Terry negotiated. Those ideologies circulating around gender and propriety in this period necessarily constructed Terry's understanding and performance of her self and her characters as variations of the Victorian Woman. Analyzing historical actresses' professional processes can help us to understand gender as a performance — a performance that can be reworked, refined and relished, even if limited by social expectations. An actor's performance is limited by the text, but also made possible by it. An actor's imagination and physicalization of that same text in turn, stretches and transforms the text's potential meanings. Just as Ellen Terry, for instance, relied on text and learned to read its nuances to suggest actions, thoughts and emotions which she could imagine and then imitate, a contemporary actor (in everyday life or on the stage), might practice self-transformation through a kind of "critical mimesis."

Can techniques learned for acting on a conventional western stage inspire techniques for living? Can actively imitating an imagined subject enliven our understanding and uses of history? Even as I write, after all, I can decide to begin re-constructing the object of my inquiry (Ellen Terry) through *mimesis*: expressing my impressions of her "character" following a period of close textual scrutiny (research). *Self-consciously*, purposefully, I am transcribing fragments of her (writing) style while knowing *full well* that my representation is *impure*, clouded by the sediment of my *own* experiences, leading me to make my particular choices which I can *never* guarantee are (even) similar to those Ellen Terry may have made at *any particular time*. It is my very self-consciousness, my understanding that I have not 1) become Ellen Terry (am not): 2) channeling Ellen Terry; and 3) (do not) stand in for Ellen Terry, which betrays my training as an actor. This is what I believe is informed by my training to act on the stage *and* my desire to think things through from a "gendered" perspective.

In the preceding paragraph I have briefly demonstrated my interpreted imitation of the printed facsimiles I have seen that *themselves* translate the *hand* of the letter-writing, memoir-writing, note-scribbling, *emphatically-voiced* Ellen Terry. I will tell you now that I cannot sustain the emotional *intensity* I have imaginatively felt emanating from these translations of Ellen Terry's "writing of her self." She, too, doubted her *own endurance*— told herself that she had fallen short *as an actress* because she could not sustain emotion — even though she did recognize sustained pathos in the characters she encountered. She too believed she *could not match* the object she strove to re-present through Art.

What I am thus far suggesting is that art, specifically an actor's art, offers us opportunities to imagine and practice living otherwise. What I am about to suggest is that treating historical texts as potential performance texts can enliven the present. We can imagine and imitate historical figures, working their very different approaches to living into our own performative creations. But I am also arguing that every performance text must be scrutinized critically, placed in its social context, measured against our own assumptions, and used to create something unique and new, thereby upsetting assumptions historical *and* contemporary.

As for history as I read it, by 1888, the year Ellen Terry would take on Lady Macbeth, she and Henry Irving had come to stand for an expression of Legitimate theatre to themselves and to many of their Victorian contemporaries. Skilled in commercial practices, Irving instructed his team to spin out his affirmations of the moral value of theatre arts through the dissemination of pamphlets, programs and press releases. His choice to hire Terry to join him at London's Lyceum Theatre in 1878 was a brilliant business maneuver. Terry was already admired for her ability to seemingly "melt into" theatrical *mise en scenes*, striking a balance that seemed at once to conform to stringent middle-class morality *and* to resonate with secret, erotic Victorian fantasies.

Terry was a lauded pictorial actress, a perfect counterweight for Irving's virtuosic *tours de force*. Where Irving might pierce through the proscenium arch, Terry traipsed about within the frame, delightfully bringing a painterly depiction to life. The pictorial stage acting for which Terry was renowned was a mode of enlivening the static painterly arts through live performing bodies. It was not only Terry's resemblance to idealized Shakespearean female figures that enthralled audiences — it was more so those elusive qualities generated by a body, mind and voice in motion. As Stokes, Booth and Basnett observe in their study of Victorian actresses,

> [T]he contribution that theatre could make to prevailing sexual ideologies, was intricate and long-lasting. Pictorialism could make a spectacle of the

human body; it could not, even in *tableaux vivants*, turn the body into an inorganic object though the temptation was often there [8].

Although pictorialism could reinforce wider cultural notions about the legitimate place of men and women in Victorian society, it could not contain and stabilize pure models or the dynamics generated between performing bodies and the perceptions of audiences. By reworking received ideas and practices from myriad discourses circulating in her environment, Ellen Terry, like other actors of her time and ours, created a Lady Macbeth uniquely wrought and presented. Terry's process — a series of thoughtful encounters with numerous ideas and their embodied rehearsal — allowed her to experience new modes of self-perception and expression. The historical record of her approach to Lady Macbeth includes Terry's own written record and reveals some surfaces of the movement of her thought. We can see that she drew on pictorialism, the aesthetic movement in painting, the prior performances of Lady Macbeth by other actresses, new theatrical movements such as Ibsenism, her own desires to please audiences while yet imagining new interpretations, her social position and relationship to Henry Irving, and of course strong cultural ideas about the definition of Woman and Good Woman, as she immersed herself in an arduous creative process.

Over her career, which began in her childhood, Ellen Terry developed an acting style that both conformed to and challenged Victorian idealizations of women. Her voice and movements were often commented upon favorably. When she performed Lady Macbeth, she received complimentary feedback from the aesthetic artist Burne-Jones, whom she recalled modestly "was prejudiced in my favour because my acting appealed to his *eye*" (Terry 197). The famous portrait of her as Lady Macbeth by John Singer Sargent was characterized by biographer Tom Prideaux as "a theatrical eye-popper, not a penetrating study of Terry but an apotheosis of her dress" (Prideaux 178). Unlike her contemporaries, Bernhardt and Duse, Ellen Terry's uniqueness lay in her ability to make the scene come alive as painters and theatrical audiences had ideally imagined it. Terry did not overwhelm the scenery and she most certainly did not chew it. During her performances she seemed to blend into the scenery but then tantalizingly and subtly emerge from the background. Moving between static imitations of paintings and theatrical liveness, Terry's pictorial acting evoked the illicit motion beneath the Victorian construction of properly motionless femininity. Her voice was tonal and comforting, cheerful and youthful — through it she conveyed the prototypical qualities of a capable and nurturing Victorian wife. The vocal and gestural virtues that enhanced her characters with warmth and charm were honed by Terry as the primary features of a stage persona which would ultimately assure her an enduring popularity.

And yet, after three decades on stage and a well-established reputation at the Lyceum, Ellen Terry was not at all certain that she could play Lady Macbeth. At the time of its undertaking, Terry's recognized attributes were "charm and vivacity in comedy and command of feeling in pathos" (Manvell 191) not the blasting of heaths through tragic intensity. Ironically, despite her training in pictorialism which seemed to require stillness, Terry criticized herself and was later gently poked fun of by George Bernard Shaw, for failing to achieve stillness for any duration on stage. She often cited her own "nervous energy" and related it to her inability to play tragedy. Tragedy, Terry had determined, required a stillness to substantiate its emotional and dramaturgical weight. As she knew, Victorian women were supposed to be immobile, fixed for admiration and moral stability, Victorian tragediennes all the more.

This failure to be substantial and weighted is a recurrent theme of Terry's *Memoirs*. As she tells it, as a girl in 1867–68, Terry acted with the Wigans company. Leonora Wigan attempted to cure her fidgeting: "'Stand still!' she would shout from the stalls. 'Now you're of value! Motionless! Just as you are! That's right!'" (59). From early on it seems that Terry struggled with the demands of her art (dictated of course by broader social expectations) and personal impulses that spilled outside those bounded ideas of motionless value. Terry tempered but never really eliminated her habit of constant motion on stage. In a letter responding to George Bernard Shaw's friendly criticism, she responded, "Do you know, I have no weight on stage: unless I have heavy robes I cannot keep on the ground" and in relation to playing in *Cymbeline* she reflects, "Though I may seem like myself to others, I never feel like myself when I am acting, but someone else, so nice, and so young and so happy, and always in-the-air, light and bodyless" (quoted in Booth et al. 97). Perhaps her desire to keep moving was rebellious but it ultimately served to distinguish her work. Perhaps it was a means of constructing her professional self as the perfect love object — made more desirable by her constantly slipping out of the grasp of the objectifying gaze — a beautiful picture that comes alive and then transforms.

Terry also seems haunted in her *Memoirs* by the idea that she is a "woman first" and an artist second, that she has "never at any time ... been ambitious" (40). But for Victorian women, the line between art and life was somewhat blurred. Women were expected to perform socially as though they were animated art objects. It was in this period that guidebooks to the proper comportment of the public self gained enormous popularity.

In *Troping the Body: Gender, Etiquette and Performance*, Gwendolyn Audrey Foster calls her readers' attention to:

> an ideological system that was, in the nineteenth century, preoccupied with transforming the performing self, and the grotesque desires of the body into

an aestheticized version of the "natural" self, a gilded body at times indistinguishable from a decorated home [1].

The nineteenth-century actress' task might be understood as the heightened realization of a performance of the self. Such performances were promoted as methods for successful female Victorian subject formation. A number of Victorian conduct book authors conjure the figure of the stage actress as a standard of measurement for young girls. Emily Post, for example, would espouse in the early twentieth-century to the young American girl that, like an actress, she would do well to acquire a "learned self-unconsciousness" to "make herself believe that a good times exists in her own mind. If she can become possessed with the idea that she is having a good time and look as though she were, the psychological effect is astonishing" (qtd. in Foster 9). Foster goes on to observe that as a Victorian woman "one must seem 'natural' in society, lacking obvious performative gestures, yet one must simultaneously be continually conscious of rules and standards that oppressively mandate everyday social commerce. Thus, one is always on display, always striving for the real in the world of the artificial" (9). This could be a precise description of the work demanded of an actress and readily applied to Ellen Terry's project. That it may also have held true for the socially performing Victorian female subject, reemphasizes the notion that the performance of the feminine in Victorian culture was significantly constricting. What is most interesting however, is that rehearsed and repeated gestures are presumed by many etiquette *and* acting instructors to be the bases for psychological and emotional effects. In each form of training, something "real" can be experienced internally by way of behavior generated externally. By learning her role very well, practicing until gestures and attitudes are repeatable without awareness of each step, a well-conducted young woman's psychological/emotional uplift produces its own reward: a contented state of mind. This connection between gesture, repetition, attitude and experience of the self is not only the basis for performative socialization techniques based in etiquette, but can also be used, I am claiming, to disturb those same normalizing practices.

As a subject traversed by and traversing her historical context, Terry can be recognized as interiorizing the authorial voice of the nineteenth century conduct writer. As an actress whose artistic process included "conversations with herself" and enacted experimental behavior, Terry can be seen as an expert at self-transformation. Further, in relation to the practice of writing history, Terry's annotated working scripts, letters, reflections and lectures, can certainly be treated as archival documents. Analysis of such an archive reveals the intricate negotiation of a subject becoming aware of internalized limitations, current social ideologies, and the creative, even liberating potential of studying, imitating and reinventing history. Might we learn, indeed create, something new by imitating Terry's example? She studied the primary text, looked to attendant commentaries, analyzed prior performances, accounted for contemporary expectations and acquired unexpected insight by physically trying out her theories. This is what I am calling a process of critical mimesis. It involves rigorous intellectual investigation and applied, imaginative, imitation.

In what was arguably a courageous assertion of her own will, Terry reinterpreted Lady Macbeth quite apart from conventional expectations to play the character as a "monster." Lady Macbeth "was *not* a fiend" she wrote to her daughter Edith Craig, "and *did* love her husband" (Terry 197). This attitude defied contemporary critical opinion of the proper interpretation of Lady Macbeth. Victorian logic could not attribute Lady Macbeth's behavior to its construction of the female subject — no "real" woman could do such things. According to Victorian commentator Henry Giles, among Shakespeare's female characters Lady Macbeth "stands before us divested of womanly tenderness," and for his contemporary Frank Harris "It is impossible to make a woman credible to us by lending her a man's resolution and courage" (qtd. in Auerbach, 252–253). Where the character was commonly considered to be an impossibility of femininity, removed from normal social intercourse (in every sense of the word), Terry labored to bring Lady Macbeth into Victorian drawing rooms. After reading an 1844 essay by G. Fletcher of the *Westminster Review* about Sarah Siddons' mid-eighteenth century performance, Terry began formulating a conception of the character that would introduce Lyceum audiences to a "real" Lady Macbeth. Her enactment would be of an ambitious woman who became passionate in her resolve to compensate for her own husband's weakness. And most crucially, Terry insisted that Lady Macbeth (like a proper Victorian woman) loved her husband. Terry's biographers, most notably Manvell and Auerbach who quote copiously from the actress' working notes and letters, provide ample evidence of Terry's decision to motivate Lady Macbeth's behavior with wifely affection. Both include from Terry's working notes in her Lyceum script, a passage that describes Lady Macbeth as "capable of affections — she loves her husband — Ergo — she is a woman — and she knows it, and is half the time afraid whilst urging Macbeth not to be afraid as she loves a man. Women love men" (Auerbach 255).

Undeniably, Terry's counter-construction of Lady Macbeth was still grounded in terms that were acquired through largely unconscious identifications with dominant, patriarchal discourses regarding femininity. A woman's loving devotion to her husband and duty to maintain a stable home, were popular expectations to which Terry, who valued obedience, adhered. She saw the banquet scene for instance, as a social catastrophe for Lady Macbeth, who not unlike middle-class Victorians, sought after an advanced social status. Manvell describes her notes in relation to this scene:

> When Lady Macbeth says, "You have displaced the mirth, broke the good meeting,/ With most admired disorder," Ellen Terry writes "She allows the guests here to see that she reproves him — but not before. She settles that something must be done so does not return to her seat, but says goodnight to some of the guests and gets rid of them." ... "Stand not upon the order of your going/ But go at once," is said with "voice choked. Alarm. Hurry. Convulsive fear." Nevertheless, she manages to "smile and smile" as they go [361].

In the manner of a Victorian housewife, Terry's Lady Macbeth protects her own and her husband's potential social advancement. For Terry, it is Macbeth's failure to fulfill their partnership that initiates the character's "convulsive fear." What emerges in Terry's notes here, are the traces of Victorian ideologies on gender, class, and the relation between domestic and public domains. She seems to conform her thinking to conservative codes, but Terry's manipulation of received conditions dramatically expose the complex struggle of a Victorian actress and social subject toward expressivity. To suggest that the Macbeths might have occupied the home next door, or that somehow ordinary British subjects with solid values could warp and distort their own characters by following those values to an extreme, would have been a very daring assertion.

Seemingly paradoxically, Terry was inspired by Sarah Siddons, the actress whose then 100-year old interpretation of Lady Macbeth still held sway as the correct one precisely because Siddons portrayed a creature unrecognizable as a Victorian woman. Siddons had played Lady Macbeth as a "virago" a woman so apparently masculanized she "may be repulsive or heroic" as Auerbach argues, but "she is never female" (253). What was first revealed to Terry through Fletcher's *Westminster Review* essay on Siddons' performance where he quoted from that actress's working notes, was that Siddons herself had conceived a very different Lady Macbeth than she apparently acquiesced to play. Siddons described the character as "captivating in feminine loveliness" and claimed that her "feminine nature, her delicate structure, it is too evident, are soon overwhelmed by the enormous pressure of her crimes" (Manvell, 192). It was not the fragile beauty Siddons ultimately played. For unknown reasons, she was not able to risk acting out the possibility of a recognizable female treachery. But it was precisely in this space of paradoxical incongruity that Ellen Terry found inspiration to break with

Siddons's reputed performance and emulate the famous actress' imagined one. As she struggled with the notion that "Mrs Siddons shd write down one set of ideas upon the subject and carry out a totally different plan," Terry began to formulate her conviction that "sometimes nature *does* freak and put an honest eye into a villain's head" (Manvell 193). Still adhering to cultural assumptions of absolute links among nature, character and gender, Terry pushed her thinking toward an expanded definition of the feminine. In her script she notes: "Yes, Lady M. was ambitious. Her husband's letters aroused intensely the desire to be a Queeen — true to a woman's nature, even more than to a man's to crave power — and power's display" (194). Between Shakespeare's text, Siddons' contrary examples (on stage and on paper) and conventional wisdom about the role and women's nature in general, Terry was able not only to imagine a new Lady Macbeth, but to find the courage to enact such a controversial choice. And, I am claiming, such an enactment required courage, not only because it would produce controversy, but because it would challenge Terry's sense of her self.

As her work continued, Terry more and more firmly believed that Lady Macbeth must exist within the realm of knowable human possibility. Therefore the character could not be played as a monster, and Terry had to rise to the occasion by imagining a Victorian Woman who *could* commit such deeds (Terry 356). Even more dauntingly, however, she had to "make the character's thoughts her thoughts." In effect, Terry had to transform her own ego-ideal — one which she had honed and through which she had enjoyed professional success — to incorporate and express qualities she had actively suppressed. Next to Lady Macbeth's "unsexing" speech, Terry wrote: "I *must* try to do this: 2 years ago I could not *even* have tried," and then commented that during this moment Lady Macbeth "goads herself on to crime. She feels she has only a *woman's* strength and calls on 'Spirits' ... The tale of the witches fired her imagination and kindled her hopes. Under her lonely battlements she dreamed of future splendour — she did *not* realize the measure of the crime" (357). Through these notes we can observe the heightened self-consciousness of the actor. Not only does Terry try to understand Lady Macbeth's circumstances, in so doing she becomes aware of her own psychological obstacles. She actually imagines and imitates Lady Macbeth's resolve to overcome internal resistances. As Terry talks to herself about playing the role, she discovers in the role the example of a woman surmounting her own weaknesses who pushes past them.

In her notes, Terry offers herself directorial instructions that range from the somewhat transparent "Keep voice down" to the less accessible "Smile at him. Bright. Quick! Aflame! Alert" to the even more obscurely personal: "Closer in, she too plotting. Charm. Serpent" (357). Terry's decision to smile at and charm Macbeth as her means of persuasion reveals the potency of dominant discourses to limit her imaginative possibilities for character development. However, it is important to reiterate that Terry's performance schematic runs counter to accepted interpretations of Shakespeare's figure. Such an interpretation in fact, would significantly disrupt the comfort of audience members who subscribed to certain accepted middle-class mores. Within narrowly understood moral behaviors, it might have been nearly impossible to integrate the conventionally accepted signs of "womanly" behavior: tenderness, affection, loyalty for instance, with signs that were almost never ascribed to women: desire (for power), selfishness, rage.

In a complex negotiation with received wisdom, life experience and historical precedence, Ellen Terry's notes include strategies that seem to reinforce traditional gender ideas, manifest frightening impulses, or invert sets of behaviors assigned to each sex. A reflection in Terry's autobiography serves to clarify the topsy-turviness of Terry's artistic choices. In thinking back on the production of *Macbeth* and her relationship with Irving, Terry remarks that

> At this time we were able to be of the right use to each other. Henry could never have worked with a very strong woman. I might have deteriorated, in partnership with a weaker man whose ends were less fine, whose motives were less pure [Terry 195].

In their professional life, which involved their promotion of themselves as a representative Victorian couple, Irving and Terry played their gender roles well. She characterized herself as Irving's support, as any leading lady or wife would automatically have been. Irving's personality, natural to a man, demanded that he take center stage and not relinquish it. Terry acknowledges this in her *Macbeth* script when she provides for the probability that "He is sure to go on here" during the murder scene thereby ignoring the tempo she would try to establish with him on stage (Manvell 358). Yet, just as a loyal Victorian wife should, Terry praises and protects Irving's motives and intentions. Although she had built up these assessments of Irving's and her own characters, she was able to at least imagine their inversion on stage. Perhaps Henry Irving was strong, but Macbeth was weak, "A man who talks and talks and works himself up, rather in the style of an early Victorian hysterical heroine" (194). Lady Macbeth must constantly prop up her husband and during the sleepwalking scene, in Terry's interpretation of the role, "Macbeth preyed on her mind more than the deed" (362). By adhering at the core to the fundamental Victorian ideal that a woman naturally and properly supports her husband, Terry was able to justify Lady Macbeth's strength as a compensatory response to Macbeth's flaws. And Terry might herself have "deteriorated" in relation to a weak male partner, just as Lady Macbeth finally slips into madness having realized her husband's weaknesses.

Through the space of art then, Irving and Terry could enact their untried, even forbidden impulses. Both their performances were seen as controversial, even if they were dismissed as missing the mark. In the *Daily Chronicle*'s review it was wryly observed that

> without such an affectionate yet determined woman as Miss Ellen Terry makes Lady Macbeth, the newly-invested Thane of Cawdor, as illustrated by Mr. Irving, would never have laid violent hands on Duncan ... The new Lady Macbeth feels that her husband may fail at the very last, so she nerves herself to give him renewed courage [Manvell 200].

By way of conventionally accepted female tactics such as affection and even determination, Terry's Lady Macbeth renews her husband's courage. Naturally, affectionate women move men and it seems that Terry has convinced this critic that at least it is possible for a real woman, not a virago, to move a man to violence. As Nina Auerbach points out, Sara Siddons' performance that emplaced the stage tradition setting Lady Macbeth as a "blood-curdling virago, fascinating in her hybrid grandeur, unrecognizable as a woman ... thrilled audiences without implicating them in domestic evil" (252). Ellen Terry's audacity lies in her pushing Lady Macbeth into a real, imaginary, domestic Victorian relationship and space. For the critic at the *Morning Post*, this was no longer the space of Shakespeare's play. Terry's Lady Macbeth simply did not belong in *Macbeth*. Rather, "the woman who, in a quaint and indescribably beautiful costume, reading by the light of the fire the letter of her husband ... might have stood in the Court at Camelot..." Contrary to the scholarly consensus that Lady Macbeth was an "unsexed" creature whom the evil spirits she called upon had indeed answered, Ellen Terry's "is not the Lady Macbeth of tradition or of Mrs Siddons we know. It is scarcely a Lady Macbeth we realize... this was not the woman to fill Macbeth with her own resolution. It might, however, be the woman to madden him to things beyond his customary reach" (201). Despite this critic's possible frustration with the (dis)placement of what was thought to be a firmly emplaced couple in the Macbeths (and in the Lyceum stars), he seems persuaded that Terry's reconceptualization of Lady Macbeth while not the character "we realize... is, perhaps, one of which we have dreamed" (201). Here is a hint that Terry's subtle reconfiguration of the character, because it was wrought (as it could only have been) from the discourses circulating in Victorian Britain, tapped into buried fears and desires. Dreams are the underside of reality.

Might the performance Ellen Terry dreamed have been for some observers the nightmarish possibility of everyday violence? Would the possibility of a smiling, charming, loving wife persuading a husband to murderous deeds have been much more frightening than a Victorian monster from another world? Despite her usual modesty Terry admitted in her diary that

> It ("Macbeth") is a most tremendous success, and the last three days' advance booking has been greater than ever was known, even at the Lyceum. Yes, it is a success, and I am a success, which amazes me, for never did I think I should be let down so easily. Some people hate me in it; some, Henry among them, think it my best part, and the critics differ, and discuss it hotly, which in itself is my best success of all! [Terry 197].

In this private reflection, the actress can admit that her fears of not pleasing her audience have been assuaged. But the more surprising admission may be her pleasure at having ignited engaged discourse among theatre critics. She in fact, engaged particular critics in discussions of her approach both before and after they had published their reviews. Terry tried to persuade Clement Scott, who had long been devoted to her and Irving but who was among those who thought her miscast in the role, that it was possible for her to be "bad." In so doing, she also argued for the general potential of all women to disrupt Victorian standards:

> Mind you though Mr. Clement, although certainly I know I cannot do what I want to do in this part, I don't even want to be "a fiend" — & won't believe for a moment can't believe for a moment that she did "conceive" that murder — that one murder of which she is accused = Most women break the law during their lives, few women realize the consequences of that they do to day — In my memory I have facts, & I use them for ... reading women who have lived, & can't speak & tell me = I am quite top full of — (not direst cruelty I hope but) — women's secrets = (& I have my own!!! & my women — my friends — were not wicked — & you say I'm not = !!! [...] No-she was not good, but not much worse than many women you know — me for instance- My hankerings are not for blood, but I think I might kill for my child, or my love blindly — & see & regret & repent in deepest sincerity after ... [qtd. in Auerbach 257–258].

This excerpt of a letter marked "PRIVATE" to a critic who had already loved Terry but for whom her cry of despair as Lady Macbeth had been hollow (257), can be seen as another tactic to persuade men especially to consider something different about women's natures. It is my contention that Ellen Terry would not have taken on such a project had she not taken on the project of playing Lady Macbeth, at least not as forcefully. She had wanted to play Rosalind (Terry 194) and play to her strengths — comic timing, quick wit, youthful charm. Once persuaded to the role by Irving, she might have conformed to Sarah Siddons' reputed performance rather than taking inspiration from the older actress' written *ideal* of the character. As an actress Terry was uniquely prepared and willing to engage with various texts, written and performed. One result of her applying her skills, imaginative and embodied, to the task of enlivening a new Victorian image of Lady Macbeth, was that her own and her audience's expectations were challenged. Ellen Terry's performance upset basic Victorian doctrines, not only about Shakespeare and Lady Macbeth, but about women's capabilities.

In the early twentieth-century when Terry toured a series of lectures she had written on Shakespeare's female characters, the first wave of the feminist movement had provided a new discursive framework for her arguments on women's strengths. "Have you ever thought" she would ask her audience, "how much we all, and women especially, owe to Shakespeare for his vindication of women in those fearless, high-spirited, resolute and intelligent heroines?" (Manvell 203). And have we thought what we owe to the women who have embodied those characters? In taking them on, have they not changed their own thinking in order to persuade us to expand our own? The unique skills developed by an engagement in formalized performative practices may offer access to a broader freedom of subjective expressions. "Intelligence, industry and imagination" as Terry emphasized, may indeed be extremely useful tools for re-conceptualizing the gendered self.

UNIVERSITY OF MINNESOTA

Notes

1. Ellen Terry's mother was Scottish and her father Irish. Her mature career as an actress was on the English stage. I am intending my use of the term "British" as a marker of mixed descents and hybrid identities rather than to elide historical tensions.

References Cited

Auerbach, Nina. *Ellen Terry, Player in Her Time*. New York and London: W.W. Norton, 1987.

Donkin, Ellen. "Mrs. Siddons Looks Back in Anger: Feminist Historiography for Eighteenth-Century British Theater." *Critical Theory and Performance*, Janelle G. Reinelt and Joseph R. Roach, eds. Ann Arbor: University of Michigan Press, 1992.

Foster, Gwendolyn Audrey. *Troping the Body: Gender, Etiquette, and Performance*. Carbondale and Edwardsville: Southern Illinois University Press, 2000.

Manvell, Roger. *Ellen Terry*. London: Heinemann, 1968.

Prideaux, Tom. *Love or Nothing: The Life and Times of Ellen Terry*. New York: Scribner's, 1974.

Stokes, John, Michael R. Booth, and Susan Basnett, eds. *Bernhardt, Terry, Duse, The Actress in Her Time*. Cambridge: Cambridge University Press, 1988.

Terry, Ellen. *The Story of My Life*. New York: Schocken, 1982.

Terry, Ellen, Edith Craig and Christopher St. John. *Ellen Terry's Memoirs*. New York: Putnam's, 1932.

7

Spectacles in Terpsichorean Disrobing
Antecedents and Ideologies of the Striptease

Michael Schwartz

Abstract

The aim of this paper is not to "elevate" or "defend" striptease, but rather to treat it specifically as a form of dance. I will examine the "strip" in terms of choreographic and interpretive elements, and "flesh out" the characters and personae of the stripping practitioners. The paper includes an overview of the era including the burlesque of Lydia Thompson, late nineteenth to the early twentieth century "cooch" and "shimmy" dancing, and the 1920s when "burlesque" and "striptease" were practically synonymous. Anecdotal evidence from primary witnesses and practitioners illuminate what contributed to the stripper's performance style and character development. Nineteenth-century women's rights actress and activist Olive Logan described the key difference between striptease and character dancing by noting, "The nude woman of today represents nothing but herself." I would suggest, however, that the fresh-faced, winking yet unavailable girl on the burlesque stage is also a "character."

One of the unsolved mysteries of the theatrical world is who originated it [striptease]. If conjecture is dependable this spectacle in terpischorean [sic] disrobing sprang, like Venus, full-blown from infinity.
   Bernard Sobel, *A Pictorial History of Burlesque*

The leg business is a business which requires legs.
   Olive Logan, *Apropos of Women and Theatres*

Anyone can strip, but few can tease.
   Ann Corio, *This Was Burlesque*

From the perspective of dance theater history, Sobel's fanciful introduction to the striptease quoted above is in one sense accurate. His description echoes the general tone of "it came from everywhere and nowhere" that practitioners, witnesses, and biographers rely upon whenever the subject of stripping arises. Sobel's tone here is clearly tongue-in-cheek, as is a good deal of the available stripping literature, and such a tone is by no means inappropriate. The use of the distinctly highbrow phrase "terpsichorean disrobing" to describe a consummately lowbrow entertainment constitutes a neat joke on historians, intellectuals, and, of course, the strippers and their audience.

It is the mission of this paper to take Sobel's phrase, if not entirely seriously, then at least literally. In other words, while I will necessarily address the phenomenon of the strip from a cultural-historical perspective, I also intend to treat the striptease as a form of Dance Theater. I will examine the striptease in terms of choreographic and interpretive elements, and in terms of "character" dancing — in opposition to the seemingly obvious idea that the stripper is merely presenting her "naked" self. Issues of cultural value, decency, and economy, arising in the 19th century and evolving through the 1920s, impacted heavily upon the notion of character in striptease. By the 1920s, American "burlesque," as the term is commonly understood, and the striptease became practically synonymous with each other. But before we enter the old National Winter Garden Theater on 2nd Avenue and Houston (New York City), an examination of nineteenth-century striptease antecedents will serve as an introduction.

Back to The Black Crook

The influence of *The Black Crook* on vaudeville and the musical theater has been well-documented.[1] It is of particular interest here as it relates to the presentation of the female form for purposes of comic and sexual entertainment, or as Robert C. Allen puts it, "male scopic pleasure" (Allen 96).

The basic story of how the show came into being starts with the burning of the Academy of Music in 1866, leaving a French ballet company stranded in New York. It was apparently the inspired notion of William Wheatley, manager of Niblo's Gardens (a theater specializing in extravaganzas), to incorporate the scenery and ballet into a production of Charles Barras' *The Black Crook*. Barras' script, with its good fairies, evil alchemists, and elusive, magical netherworlds, is a product of the Romantic era, with room for spectacle as well as melodrama. Therefore, the insertion of ballet and scenic effects into *The Black Crook* was probably not as awkward or arbitrary as many traditional accounts describe (Allen 109). Nevertheless, it is fair to say that the "large number of female legs," in the New York *Tribune*'s words

(Allen 111), quickly became, if not the show's original *raison d'être*, then certainly its reason for success.

The most celebrated and/or notorious element of the long-running show was the "Pas de Demons" dance at the end of the second act. The dance became hugely popular for its feature of female dancers in revealing costumes: "close-fitting pantaloons, which stopped at mid-thigh, and a sleeveless bodice, both done in polka dots" (Allen 111–112). The "male scopic" appeal of this scene was not lost on Wheatley, who soon published timetables of the production specifically for a man who wished to, as the local press put it, "drop in, take a peek at his favorite scene, or dancer, or leg or something and enjoying the sight, return to the bosom of his family" (Allen 112).

The Black Crook is of critical importance in the development of striptease and American burlesque. Firstly, it provides striptease with its strongest link to the Romantic ballet popularized by Elssler and Taglioni earlier in the century. As Allen points out, *Crook* choreographer David Costa and principal dancers Marie Bonfanti and Rita Sangalli had all studied at Milan's La Scala ballet school. Under the direction of Carlo Blasis, the school stressed the Romantic ballet virtues of harmony and seemingly effortless execution (110–111). That many men went to ballets with an agenda of sexual fantasy was nothing new, of course. The vanguard of the Romantic Movement in Paris openly scoffed at the Romantic ballets as "an excuse for watching pretty, lightly clad women disporting themselves" (Jowitt 33). Indeed, the 1830s saw the sale of ballet lithographs as a thriving business, anticipating "pinup" girls by 100 years (Chazin-Bennahum 129). What distinguished *The Black Crook* was not so much its element of sex, but its open acknowledgement — not only by reviewers but also by the show's producers and its audience — that this was indeed a show that put sex front and center, complete with "a large number of female legs."

Secondly, with the publishing of the "Pas de Demons" schedule, Wheatley (and the audience) established Niblo's Gardens as an assigned place — a popular theater as opposed to a beer garden, honky-tonk, or in the slang parlance of the time, a "slab," "dump," or "free and easy"— for men to get away from "the bosom of the family" for a while and ogle beautiful girls. Wheatley had, in effect, created a space within the parameters of popular theatre for the express purpose of selling sex. The "burlesque house" of the 1920s and 1930s, as well as the later "gentlemen's clubs" and triple-X strip joints, can trace their roots to Wheatley's timetable.

The Black Crook also initiated a large-scale, ongoing public dialogue in America concerning the theatrical display of the female figure. In *The Unembarrassed Muse*, Russell Nye summarizes *Crook*'s impact: it "introduced the popular theater for the first time to the display of the female figure for its own sake, something which had little relationship to plot, theme, characterization, or any other dramatic element" (Nye 173). This notion of relatedness to a story, theme, or character became one of the key criteria in terms of determining the decency and respectability (or lack thereof) of presentations that, in Ziegfeld's words, "glorified the American girl."

The Leg Business

The Black Crook paved the way for increasingly daring (and popular) female spectacle. By the time actress and women's rights activist Olive Logan wrote *Apropos of Women and Theatres* in 1869, audiences were experiencing the plentiful scopic pleasures of Lydia Thompson's British Blondes and similar troupes.

Logan's views on feminine display are interesting on a number of levels. While her writing in many respects represents a highly individual and idiosyncratic opinion, Logan does reflect the prevailing view that a ballet dancer, while deserving of "some respect" (110), should not be placed "in the same rank with an intellectual player" (112). In a particularly telling quote, Logan writes,

> In this country, the ballet proper has had little illustration. Yet it is a branch of art,— not the noblest art, it is true; but by the side of the jigging woman, almost rising to dignity [132].

Although Logan defends the innocence of those girls "whose whole heart was ... lovingly given over to Terpischore [sic]" (113), the ballet dancers are nonetheless at least partially responsible for attracting many of the same "bad" audiences who cheer for those who were "neither fish, flesh, nor fowl of the theatrical creation" (114).

Moreover, Logan sets forth the distinctions between art and vulgarity that would simultaneously help burlesque and striptease thrive, and ultimately bring about their demise. While Logan by no means embraces *The Black Crook* with any enthusiasm, she writes in their (partial) defense that the women involved "were ballet-dancers from France and Italy, and they represented in their nudity imps and demons. In silence they whirled about the stage, in silence they trooped off. Some faint odor of ideality and poetry rested over them" (135). In stark contrast, she describes the "leg business" entertainer in withering terms:

> The nude woman of to-day represents nothing but herself. She runs upon the stage giggling; trots down to the foot-lights, winks at the audience, rattles

off from her tongue some stupid attempts at wit, some twaddling allusions to ... [a] subject prominent in the public eye, and is always peculiarly and emphatically herself [135].

What made *The Black Crook* tolerable as entertainment for Logan and her supporters, as compared to the burgeoning American burlesque, touches on a number of cultural and performative factors. In the first place, there was the fact that *Crook* used ballet dancers — if not, as Logan tells us, a "high" art, certainly a discipline requiring years of study, devotion, and sacrifice, as opposed to the "few weeks" it would take the typical "nude woman" to learn a jig (131–132). Another important distinction here is the fact that the ballet dancers came "from France and Italy"— by 1869, an important signifier in American popular discourse that conveyed cultural superiority.[2] Most intriguing, however, are the distinctions concerning character and presentation. A "nude" ballet dancer — silent and in some way portraying a "character," be it a demon, imp, or sylph — was far preferable to the "nude woman of to-day," who seemed to portray nothing more than her (vulgar and obscene) self. "Hence," Logan wrote, "the nude woman of today ... out-strips [the ballet dancer] in the broadest sense" (132). (It would seem that even the most morally indignant critics of stripping could not avoid puns.) The issues that fueled Logan's attacks on "the leg business"— class, culture, character, and presentation — would continue to fan the fires of moral outrage that plagued (and generated tremendous publicity for) the burlesque and striptease of the 1920s.

Logan opined, somewhat prematurely, that the "leg business" was a "style of performance which is already fluttering in the last agonies of death" (115). In fact, burlesque at this time was beginning to refresh the feminine display through the increased use of dance and comedy. By the 1890s, even burlesque pioneer Lydia Thompson declared the current brand of burlesque to be "unrecognizable" from the entertainment of her heyday (Allen 30).

Enter the Cooch

Whether the dance was referred to as "hootchie-kootchie," "cooch," "Oriental," "nautch," "harem," "belly," "shimmy," "tassle," or any of numerous other names, the "daring" or "exotic" dance soon became a staple of American burlesque (Nye 173–174). Tradition credits Little Egypt's appearance at the 1893 Chicago World's Fair as the introduction of the hootchie-kootchie to the American public. Bernard Sobel offers the following description of Little Egypt's appearance: "Her costume was always strictly Oriental: a short bolero with coin decorations, a white chemise, harem pantaloons and a wide sash. Her hair hung loose over her shoulders, an outward indication of abandon that was somewhat startling in the nineties" (Sobel 57). The condition of hair is a key character signifier in dance theatre. As an example, in *Giselle,* one of the most prominent Romantic-era ballets, Giselle pulls her neatly arranged hair until it hangs down loose as she goes mad. Whether or not, as Sobel writes, Little Egypt singlehandedly saved the Chicago World's Fair from financial ruin (56–57), her success was indisputable, and quickly spawned a large number of "Fatimas, Cleos, Zazas, and Fifis" (Nye 174) who spread the gospel of the exotic dance.

With the cooch dance, we can see not only an increased and more concentrated effort to commercialize sex, but also the creation of an exotic persona — complete with fabricated name, place of origin, and "native" music. Sobel tells us that Little Egypt's "real name was supposed to be Fahreda Mahzar Spyropolos. A native, according to her own story, of Armenia" (Sobel 55). As for the exotic "Oriental" music, Sobel notes that the *"danse du ventre"* had its origins in the Balkans, and the principal motif had previously appeared in German and Russian dances in the early part of the century (60). The dancers themselves, with the help of savvy producers, were clearly creating and portraying characters, and not merely themselves. Onstage, they were "peculiarly and emphatically" Little Egypt, Fatima, Cleo, Zaza, and Fifi.

Concerning the dances themselves, as several of their slang names suggest, the emphasis was on shaking, gyrating, and shimmying. Sobel reproduces the following barker's spiel for either Little Egypt or one of her many imitators: "When she dances, every fiber and every tissue in her entire anatomy shakes like a jar of jelly from your grandmother's Thanksgiving dinner" (57–59). The Philadelphia *North American*, reporting on exotic dancer Milly De Leon in 1909, described her as seizing the attention of audiences by "agitating the muscles of her body in a wavelike motion" (Nye 174). As Nye points out, the progression toward increased agitation with decreased costume was both logical and inevitable (174).

Take Off a Little Bit More

Understandably, the date of the first striptease in the modern sense is not agreed upon. Russell Nye, for example, dates the stripper's first appearance as "about 1917," somewhat earlier than most witnesses and historians (Nye 174). Robert C. Allen notes that "[i]ronically, the one feature with which burlesque is most closely associated, the striptease, did not become a standard feature of burlesque until the mid–1920s. This timeframe is supported by Morton Minsky's first-hand account of introducing the striptease into the Minsky burlesque show. He describes the 1924 season: "we began slowly to introduce the striptease, which still had not come to dominate burlesque as it later did" (Minsky 60). To give credibility to Nye's earlier date, we have the following Irving Berlin lyrics from the 1915 show *Stop, Look and Listen*: "Take off a little bit/ If that don't make a hit/ Take off a little bit more" (Sobel 125). Nevertheless, the removal of costume is not necessarily synonymous with the striptease as we now know it.

Fashion in the 1920s was another notable influence on stripping. As short skirts were now in style, "a large number of female legs" no longer qualified as a novelty. Consequently, practically all female burlesque performers had to raise the bar, as it were, in order to provide higher degrees of titillation. This meant a large number of bare breasts (Nye 174).

To further complicate the issue, the oral tradition generally ascribes the first striptease to accident. Burlesque had already featured "quick-change" acts in which the women changed costumes in varying degrees of audience view (Nye 174). Further, as practitioner Ann Corio writes in her informal and anecdotal overview, "It was inevitable that sooner or later with the constant quiver of the anatomy, somebody was going to lose a part of the costume she was wearing" (Corio 72).

Corio's choice as the first modern striptease artist is Carrie Finnell, whose career dated back to the late teens and who thrived throughout the 20s as a specialist in tassel twirling. "Carrie was the first one to deliberately 'tease' the audience," Corio wrote. In an unidentified quote, a reviewer describes one of Finnell's performances: "She has trained each gorgeous bust to twitch on cue, jump to attention, and do just about everything except sing 'April Showers' in Swahili" (Corio 74). Irving Zeidman offers this additional view:

> A versatile cooch, she perfected her specialty of popping up her breasts, to the tune of "Pop Goes the Weasel," singly and in unison, by purely muscular action, with no strings attached. As she grew older and even fatter, this specialty was tolerated as a "comic" interlude in respectable theatres ... [Zeidman 115].

What is notable here is the comic element of the striptease performance. Comedy played a great role in "Thompsonian" burlesque, where the women told jokes and sang bawdy songs. The comedy was notably missing from the "cooch" era, as the dancers focused squarely on (unspoken) forbidden sexual abandonment. As the striptease entered its modern phase, the comic element was back in place, playing on the expectations of the audience to see that which was forbidden, and on the implicit promise from the performer that the hidden would be revealed. To be sure, this joke was not always particularly subtle (as the above descriptions of Carrie Finnell's act attest), but until the end of the modern burlesque era, both audiences and performers were in on the joke together. This shared comic understanding between audience and stripper became the key element in establishing the "character" of the stripper as burlesque shimmied its way into the mid to late 1920s.

"Pelvic Contortions Such as What?"— Class, Vice and Morality

The issues that Olive Logan had raised back in 1869 regarding ballet versus the "leg business" were still very much on the minds of authorities as well as religious leaders in the 1920s. The question of what constituted the difference(s) between the artistic and the obscene permeated the entire burlesque production, and informed the striptease performance as well.

"What exactly *was* burlesque?" Morton Minsky asks in *Minsky's Burlesque*. "Some people called it the poor man's *Follies*. It was a popular and inexpensive form of entertainment whose basic ingredients were girls, gags, and music" (Minsky 26). The key terms here are "poor" and "inexpensive." The burlesque shows did, of course, push (and often exceed) the boundaries of vice laws, not only because of the increasing use of strippers, but because of the off-color jokes and skits that rounded out the program. Even more than the content of the shows, however, class distinctions — uptown versus downtown, highbrow versus lowbrow, expensive versus inexpensive put the burlesque show and the striptease artist on the wrong side of the authorities time and time again. A brief look at Florenz Ziegfeld's *Follies* will illustrate this dichotomy.

By the mid–1920s, roughly the same time the strippers began to dominate burlesque downtown, Ziegfeld's revues (and those of his competitors) regularly featured chorus girls in tableaux, topless or nearly so. As Allen points out:

> What would have been immediately suppressed by municipal authorities had it been innovated for working-class audiences in burlesque was tolerated when produced for the pleasure of middle-class audiences in cabarets and revues. Ziegfeld and his imitators cloaked their shows' sexuality in the trappings of art and glamour [Allen 246].

Minsky adds,

> Billy [Minsky] figured that if it was permissible to expose the attractions of sixty gals at Ziegfeld's at $4.40, it was equally permissible to offer a dozen

similarly clad girls at one-sixth the price. But Minsky's seemed to offend the Legion of Decency, and Ziegfeld didn't [Minsky 43].

In her attack on the "leg business," Olive Logan primarily drew her distinctions between art and vulgarity based on talent, dedication to craft, and the context (or lack thereof) of characterization and theme. Some 55 years later, the distinctions had become more overtly economic. The *Follies* qualified as art because these were expensive productions with elaborate scenery, presented in uptown theatres at prices that prohibited the attendance of anybody who was not, at the very least, securely ensconced in the middle class.

Naturally, the Minskys and their competitors often used the ever-present charges of immorality to their advantage, just as Wheatley had done with *The Black Crook* years before. Public charges against the burlesque shows, arrests, and trials generated valuable publicity. One decency trial in 1925 that Minsky describes in detail with infectious glee illustrates the difficulties in 1) defining the striptease in terms of dance and performance and 2) making objective legal rulings based on highly subjective notions of decency. In this particular trial against the Minskys and Mademoiselle Fifi, John Sumner, then Secretary of the New York Society for the Suppression of Vice, declared that "Miss Fifi's pelvic contortions during the dance ... 'The Shame of La Bohème' were such as to be lewdly suggestive, of lascivious import, and therefore indecent and immoral" (Minsky 81–82). When the judge asked what Sumner meant by "pelvic contortions," Sumner had understandable difficulty in providing a suitable definition. The judge lost patience:

> "I said pelvic contortions such as what? If you lack the powers of speech to deliver a clear answer to my question, I suggest that you call upon your powers of locomotion."
>
> "Meaning what, Your Honor?"
>
> "Meaning, Mr. Secretary, that you step down here, before the bench, and demonstrate with your own anatomy exactly what you saw the defendant perform on the night of April 20, 1925, and which did so offend your sensibilities that you drew up a complaint of violation of Section 1140 A of the Penal Law. That's what I mean" [Minsky 82].

The complaint was dismissed. Sumner, it might be said, found himself the victim of reception theory.

Striptease as Dance: Interpretation and Character

Following an informative and comprehensive overview of the most notable striptease practitioners, Irving Zeidman closes with this rather cold summation: "Notwithstanding all their differences, the strippers could meet on one common ground — they were all, or nearly all, devoid of any authentic talent" (Zeidman 158). It is an opinion at least as old as *Apropos of Women and Theatres*, and it is not without validity. The fact that the vocabulary of burlesque always consisted of feminine display and bawdy comedy led all too easily to repetition and lack of innovation. "When burlesque was too good, it was no longer burlesque; when its performers were too talented, they left it," as Russell Nye has noted (174). With this overriding opinion of burlesque in general, and striptease in particular, it is small wonder that comparatively little has been written about striptease and its elements of dance.

If historians tend to dismiss the performative elements of striptease, the witnesses and practitioners who have written about burlesque tend to overcompensate by romanticizing the era. Nevertheless, while Ann Corio, for example, seems to have nothing but the most glowing praise for all her sister strippers, she does provide some interesting concrete information concerning costume and technique:

> ...they [the costumes] were elaborate. Some were slinky gowns of satin with mink stoles casually tossed around the shoulders. Some were full-hooped dresses of the Southern belle era. Usually, when the girls had shed this outer garment, they would be dressed underneath in a bra and a panel dress. A panel dress consisted of two panels, one in front and one in back secured low around the waist. These the stripper could swirl, or pick up, to show a bit of dazzling leg as she went through the dance. Then, at long last, the bra would come off revealing pasties [Corio 76].

She also touches on the musical component of the striptease performance. The strip was originally accompanied by singers — "cracked-voice tenors," in Corio's words — and then music without singing. The most important component was the drummer, who set the tempo for the stripper's act. "He controls her movements," Corio wrote, "like a Drill Sergeant" (75–76).

In fact, pace was one of several "general rules" that the Minskys developed in terms of working with strip acts. "A stripper has to maintain and sustain a definite pace, a tempo, from the time she appears until she exits," Morton Minsky wrote, supporting the Drill Sergeant-like status of the drummer. Closely related to pace was a sense of timing — knowing what to take off, when to do so, "and what to do for an encore." Hair and makeup were essential to take full advantage of the theatrical lighting. Strippers dyed their hair red, yellow, or black — it was usually Billy Minsky who gave initial orders regarding hair and costume. Neither the Minskys nor their competitors provided makeup artists for the girls, so it was up to the strippers themselves to learn what worked. In terms of character, perhaps the most important element was the walk. Depending upon whether the stripper's persona was demure, "hot," or "girl-next-door," the girls, who developed their own routines, would perfect the appropriate stage walk (Minsky 114). The development of the stripper package, therefore, was a carefully guided project that combined the savvy of the producers, the instincts of the stripper, and, of course, audience response.

The strippers who garnered the greatest fame (or at least, the greatest publicity) each developed a unique persona, which was something more than (although it might very well include) an interesting "gimmick." Gypsy Rose Lee, who remains the most well known of strippers thanks to the popular musical *Gypsy,* was the ultimate sophisticated "teaser," restoring verbal comedy to the feminine sexual display that had been missing since the Thompson era. Irving Zeidman writes of her disrobing technique: "She discarded the pins on her trick costumes, one by one, each with the aplomb of an historic event" (Zeidman 151). By simultaneously fulfilling the unspoken contract between audience and stripper (i.e., disrobing), and commenting on the inherent ridiculousness of such a contract by reciting racy poetry and italicizing her gestures, Gypsy Rose Lee was the most alienating and metatheatrical of strippers. Robert C. Allen makes the observation that the female burlesque performer from the 1890s onward was silenced and objectified: "As the burlesque performer's mouth became the only part of her body that did *not* move in the cooch dance, the shimmy, and the striptease, she literally and figuratively lost her voice" (Allen 240, author's emphasis). Gypsy Rose Lee proved to be the hugely successful exception.

Ann Corio, Gypsy Rose Lee's nearest competitor in terms of long-term popularity, owing largely to her series of successful burlesque revival shows, was in many ways a throwback to the extravaganza-spectacle era of *The Black Crook.* Corio's most successful disrobing was deep in character — in one show, a lovelorn Indian maiden dancing wildly with grief as her boyfriend is assassinated; in another, an angel revealing her heavenly form for male scopic pleasure. In a preemptive strike on potential charges of indecency, Corio apparently announced that her three-year-old nephew would play the violin during the performance (Zeidman 148). It is notable that the two most successful strippers, Corio and Gypsy Rose Lee, seldom revealed anything more than a flash of breast. "A girl looks sexier in panties than she does nude," Corio wrote (76). While it is difficult to say whether or not Corio was fully aware of the highbrow/lowbrow conflation she brought to the burlesque stage, her act, like Gypsy Rose Lee's, brought her enormous financial success.

By contrast, Hinda Wassau was a stripper who specifically identified herself as a dancer. She made her mark by consciously integrating specialized dance into her routine — she was billed as a "classic dancing specialist." Her dance apparently consisted of "a maze of head jerks, arm swinging and deep breathing spells." She also introduced one of the most salient features of the modern strip — the lingering, self-caressing movements of the hands. According to one critic, "She pants, darts spasmodically, lets her hand glide over her body; she exerts herself, full of sex movement." Wassau, of the major strippers, also seemed to have the keenest flair for the dramatic. After letting the audience surmise that absolutely nothing was beneath her dress, Wasssau would caress herself, execute some "sex movement," and with one pull of the arm rip the dress off entirely as the lights went out (Zeidman 155–156).

Margie Hart and Georgia Sothern were two strippers who at one time or another directly addressed the issue of presentation of "self" as "character." Hart's most notable contribution to the world of striptease was her "daring"— she performed without a visible G-string. A typical performance consisted primarily of slinking from one side of the stage to the other, while her hands, with seeming carelessness, would casually brush at the taffeta that separated the audience from the lack of G-string. While Gypsy Rose Lee and Ann Corio scored crossover successes with the tourist trade, it was Hart who was the darling of the veteran burlesque-goer. When queried as to the reason for her success, Hart was quoted in the July 1941 *Collier's Magazine*: "Maybe ... it's because I'm just a wholesome, clean American girl trying to get along" (Zeidman 151–155). Whether or not Hart was being ironic, it is fair to say that the daring, redheaded American girl who consistently gave the men what they wanted to see (but could never touch) was absolutely a character in her own right.

David Scott's thoughtful study of present-day "gentleman's club" dancers, *Behind the G-String*, further explores the levels of characterization inherent in strip performance. As mentioned earlier, makeup was a key component in fixing the character of the Minsky stripper. Scott quotes an anecdote from H. Allen Smith's *Low Man on a Totem Pole* concerning celebrated fan dancer Sally Rand:

> When a reporter for the New York *World Telegram* dropped in on her for an interview, he caught her in the middle of making herself up. Suddenly self-conscious, she said to him, "I'm sorry you came in on me like this, with my face bare of makeup. I don't mind if you see any other part of me bare, but not my face" [Scott 63].

In a world whose entire vocabulary would seem to consist of full exposure and disclosure, the simple application of makeup, which might not even read as makeup from the audience's view, is often enough to provide the necessary performance mask.

In conclusion, the stripper and the striptease evoked, and continue to evoke, wildly divergent responses in terms of its merits and faults. Depending upon whom one reads or listens to, striptease was essentially innocent, or it was thoroughly salacious. The strippers were voiceless, ruthlessly exploited victims of the male-operated sex business. Or they were clever women, always in control, who were in fact making the joke on men. Strippers thoroughly lacked talent. Or they had the grace and beauty to personify an unattainable ideal — sylphs for the 20th century. To be sure, where the individual stripper landed on this spectrum depended largely on the degree of success, and the success depended largely on canny publicity. If, in the end, the strippers, coochers, and "nude women" did not contribute so much as take from the world of dance theater, it would nevertheless be remiss to omit "Terpsichorean disrobing" from the ongoing dialogue altogether.

UNIVERSITY OF PITTSBURGH

Notes

1. Just a few examples include Robert C. Allen, *Horrible Prettiness: Burlesque and American Culture*; Irving Zeidman, *The American Burlesque Show*; and Russell Nye, *The Unembarrassed Muse* (see Works Cited).

2. See especially Lawrence Levine, *Highbrow/Lowbrow: The Emergence of Cultural Hierarchy in America*. Cambridge, MA: Harvard University Press, 1988.

3. Roughly speaking, 1942, when New York City License Commissioner Paul Moss unconditionally and finally refused to renew any licenses for the remaining burlesque theatres (Zeidman 235).

References Cited

Allen, Robert C. *Horrible Prettiness: Burlesque and American Culture*. Chapel Hill: University of North Carolina Press, 1991.

Chazin-Bennahum, Judith. "Women of Faint Heart and Steel Toes." In *Re-Thinking the Slyph: New Perspectives on the Romantic Ballet*, ed. Lynn Garafola. Hanover, Wesleyan University Press, 1997.

Cohen, Selma Jean, ed. *Dance as a Theatre Art: Source Readings in Dance History from 1581 to the Present*. 2nd ed. Hightstown, NJ: Princeton Book, 1992.

Corio, Ann, with Joseph DiMona. *This Was Burlesque*. New York: Madison Square Press, 1968.

Jowitt, Deborah. *Time and the Dancing Image*. Berkeley, CA: University of California Press, 1989.

Levine, Lawrence W. *Highbrow/Lowbrow: The Emergence of Cultural Hierarchy in America*. Cambridge, MA: Harvard University Press, 1988.

Logan, Olive. *Apropos of Women and Theatres*. New York: Carleton, 1869.

Minsky, Morton, and Machlin, Milt. *Minsky's Burlesque: A Fast and Funny Look at America's Bawdiest Era*. New York: Arbor House, 1986.

Nye, Russell. *The Unembarrassed Muse: The Popular Arts in America*. New York: The Dial Press, 1970.

Scott, David A. *Behind the G-String: An Exploration of the Stripper's Image, Her Person and Her Meaning*. Jefferson, NC: McFarland, 1996.

Sobel, Bernard. *A Pictorial History of Burlesque*. New York: Bonanza Books, 1956.

Zeidman, Irving. *The American Burlesque Show*. New York: Hawthorn Books, 1967.

Menagerie à Trois
Surrogate Love in
The Glass Menagerie

Graley Herren

Abstract

As Tom Wingfield famously confesses in the prologue of The Glass
Menagerie, *"The play is memory." This admission dictates a certain
critical approach to the action which follows. The play should be
regarded as a re-enactment of certain past events, selected and introduced by Tom, and filtered through his biased perspective. The "gentleman caller scene" (Scene Seven), however, requires still more special
consideration. Tom positions this encounter between Jim and Laura
as the climax of the play, yet Tom himself remains conspicuously
absent from this scene. In other words, the climactic scene of his
"memory play" is not his first-hand memory at all, but an act of
fiction, an exercise in imaginative conjecture. In this paper I will
interrogate the authorial choices and the psychological motives behind
Tom's staging of the gentleman caller scene, emphasizing Jim's function as a surrogate for Tom's own incestuous desires for Laura.*

In an interview with Stewart Stern about his film adaptation of *The Glass
Menagerie*, Paul Newman confided, "I want to see Tom witness the Gentleman
Caller scene, I want to see him watching when Laura and the gentleman caller
think they're alone. In the play he never watches, but I don't see any reason for
that scene unless he witnesses it. How can it be his memory if he wasn't there?"
(Stern 14). That is actually a very good question: How can the gentleman caller
scene rightly be considered a memory when Tom was not even present for the
bulk of the scene? Newman concludes that Tom must have been eavesdropping,
and so he proposes to correct the playwright's omission by physically reinsert-
ing Tom. On the contrary, I propose that Tom's real absence from this "memory" is vital to an understanding of the scene. For only through his literal absence
is Tom able to figuratively reinsert himself into the scene, telling Laura the things
he could never tell her otherwise through the surrogate of Jim O'Connor.

Tom announces in his opening monologue that "The play is memory" (4), so we know from the beginning that we must regard each scene with some skepticism. We know that if we were witnessing Amanda or Laura's version of events, each scene might unfold differently. What we see enacted on stage must then be regarded as a reenactment, filtered through time and Tom's consciousness and potentially manipulated for his purposes. As Thomas L. King allusively notes, "Tom is the Prospero of *The Glass Menagerie*, and its world is the world of Tom's mind even more than *Death of a Salesman* is the world of Willy Loman's mind" (King 76). But what are we then to make of the gentleman caller scene, that private encounter between Jim and Laura which serves as both "the climax of her secret life" (*Menagerie* 70) and the climax of the play, but a scene from which Tom is conspicuously absent? Newman is right: this cannot be Tom's memory, so what is it? Surely this scene is forged in a different part of his mind through an alchemical fusion of memory and imagination. I contend that the crux of Scene Seven must be understood as fiction, as Tom's imaginative reconstruction of what might have transpired between Jim and Laura. Here his "poet's weakness for symbols" (*Menagerie* 5) is given full reign. As a fiction, the scene is also subject to different sorts of questions: Why does Tom imagine the scene as he does? What symbolic use does he make of Jim and Laura's encounter? What is revealed about Tom through his imaginative reconstruction? And why does Tom position this scene, from which he was absent, as the climax of his "memory play"? The following essay will attempt to answer these questions, showing how Tom sublimates his feelings for Laura by surreptitiously re-channeling them through Jim.

Williams outlines his theatrical platform in the prefatory Production Notes to the play. He counsels,

> Everyone should know nowadays the unimportance of the photographic in art: that truth, life, or reality is an organic thing which the poetic imagination can represent or suggest, in essence, only through transformation, through changing into other forms than those which were merely present in appearance [xix].

Accordingly, Williams' authorial representative in the play, Tom, owns up to his own poetic manipulation of the material. He opens the play by confessing, "Yes, I have tricks in my pocket, I have things up my sleeve. But I am the opposite of a stage magician. He gives you illusion that has the appearance of truth. I give you truth in the pleasant disguise of illusion" (4). Disguising the truth and retreating into a world of illusion are old family traditions for the Wingfields, and Tom has clearly taken full possession of this inheritance. Tom's opening soliloquy sets the solipsistic parameters of the play. The stage is Tom's mind, and he will animate it with illusions based on real people and real events. This is not to say that Tom's "memory play" is untrue. Thomas P. Adler notes that baring the poetic device of the play "challenges its audience to revel in the conventions of make-believe; yet, at the same time, to recognize that illumination *about* life can come clothed in an illusion not necessarily true *to* life" ("Lyricism" 173). In other words, Tom's tricks, masks, and illusions are capable of revealing even more of the truth about life in the Wingfield home than an exact transcript or photographic reproduction of events could have done.

A telling case in point is Tom's rendering of Jim. "He is the most realistic character in the play," Tom explains, "being an emissary from a world of reality that we were somehow set apart from" (5). Jim is one of those rare, bewildering creatures who occasionally wander into a Williams play: the well-adjusted man. Jim lives in the "real world," and though he does not exactly thrive there, he still believes in its tenets and does not seek to escape. However, there is a difference between the real Jim and the character "Jim," as Tom goes on to explain: "But since I have a poet's weakness for symbols, I am using this character as a symbol; he is the long-delayed but always expected something that we live for" (5). Tom openly admits that he is enlisting Jim for an artistic function greater than his real dimensions as a person. For Amanda, Jim symbolizes "the long-delayed but always expected" Savior, who will fill the family's patriarchal void and restore them to their rightful position of respectability. For Laura, Jim symbolizes "the long-delayed but always expected" Lover, who will appreciate her despite her handicap and who will replace her dependence on glass animals and phonograph records with something more substantial. But what "long-delayed but always expected" desire does Jim represent for Tom? That answer is more complicated, but hints can be found inside the carefully crafted illusion of Scene Seven.

In this scene Tom, a disgruntled factory worker and would-be poet, has invited fellow laborer and former high school wonder-boy Jim over for dinner. The invitation, however, is simply a ruse, designed by mother Amanda and reluctantly executed by son Tom, in hopes of luring a suitor for the physically and emotionally crippled daughter Laura. The dinner proves a disaster. The terminally shy Laura cannot even muster up the courage to sit at the table with Jim, whom she had worshiped from afar in high school. Furthermore, dinner ends with the household plunged into darkness, the consequence of Tom's negligence in paying the light bill (secretly paying his Merchant Marine dues instead so he can escape the family). Nevertheless, Amanda bravely perseveres, salvaging what she can of the dinner while waxing sentimental and fawning over Jim. In fact, by dinner's end, she has successfully managed to choreograph a private interlude between Laura and her gentleman caller. She summons Tom into the kitchen to help with the dishes, and sends Jim with a candelabrum into the dark parlor to tend to Laura.

Here Amanda's direction of the scene ends and Tom's direction begins. Safely sequestered in the kitchen, Tom can have no first-hand recollection of this scene; nor is there reason to believe that he subsequently received much second-hand information, given Amanda's subsequent anger, Laura's subsequent withdrawal, and Tom's own subsequent escape from the family. No, the only reasonable conclusion is that the climactic scene between Jim and Laura is [im]pure speculation. Of course, Scene Seven is not the only instance where Tom "recalls" dialogue and action for which he was not physically present. Scene Two and the conclusion of Scene Five also require some speculation on his part. However, in these cases the only "players" in his reconstruction are Amanda and Laura, whose speech patterns, physical mannerisms, and interpersonal chemistry he is all too familiar with. On the other hand, Laura's un-witnessed episode with Jim marks a brand of encounter utterly unprecedented in the Wingfield household. Tom has no dependable, ready-made frame of reference for knowing how such a scene would develop — but this does not prevent him from staging the scene anyway. Tom knows first-hand how the scene begins and ends; those are given. His job as author is then to reconstruct a dramatic through line, connecting the known facts with a plausible bridge of fiction. That is his *artistic* mission; but the bridge he constructs also ends up revealing much about the deeper hidden drives of its architect.

Tom's direction of the scene picks up where Amanda's left off, setting the stage for romance. Amanda and Tom have both conspired to produce the romantic mood lighting of the scene, and Jim enhances the ambiance when he suggests the couple move to pillows on the floor. He is the mock–Prometheus, bearing candle-light into the parlor, but she is the one who has been carrying a torch for years. She gradually reminds Jim of their former high school acquaintance, even producing their high school yearbook (literally called *The Torch*) to help rekindle his former glory. As this scene develops, we can also indirectly observe Tom's artistic handiwork in practice. Like a dutiful playwright, he is filling in valuable exposition and fleshing out his characters. This scene represents the only extended look the audience receives into the character of Jim, so his portrayal here is of special interest. Of course, what we are really seeing here is not simply Jim but Tom's perspective on Jim. Refracted through that lens, Jim emerges in the early part of the scene as vain, shallow, intrusive, egocentric, and self-deluded — a gum-smacking caricature of the well-adjusted American man. Jim's shortcomings are obvious to Tom, and he communicates these flaws to the audience. But he also shows us the deified image of Jim worshipped by Laura. She sees only his glory, and her hagiography of his past begins to embolden him in the present.

Amanda may have set the scene for light romance, but under Tom's direction the encounter soon heats up with latent sexuality. This is Tom's sister he is thinking about, however, and he does retain some brotherly scruples about contemplating this subject directly. He also harbors a self-confessed "poet's weakness for symbols." The result therefore is a seduction scene which develops through misprision and metaphor. Two extended (and eroticized) metaphors dominate the scene: the glass unicorn and the dance.

Eager to impress Jim, Laura shows off her glass collection, with special emphasis on her favorite glass unicorn. Jim is reluctant to handle this delicate creature, but Laura insists. The glass unicorn is blatantly symbolic of Laura herself: fragile, rare, transparent, lonesome. Therefore, in handling the unicorn Jim is in effect handling Laura, bringing him one step closer to "bagging his exotic prey" in the symbolic language of this scene. But notice that Laura is the one who initiates contact. She offers up the most precious and fragile piece in her collection and willingly places it in Jim's hands. She recognizes the danger, but she too is becoming bolder, and she apparently accepts the risk of damage in exchange for a closer connection with Jim.

The sexual tension mounts and physical contact between the couple increases when Jim asks Laura to dance. In the symbolic language of this scene, the waltzing initiation sparks with highly charged eroticism:

> Laura: Like this?
> Jim: [*taking her in his arms*] A little bit higher. Right. Now don't tighten up, that's the main thing about it — relax.
> Laura: [*laughing breathlessly*] It's hard not to....
> Jim: Let yourself go now, Laura, just let yourself go.
> Laura: I'm —
> Jim: Come on!
> Laura: — trying!
> Jim: Not so stiff — easy does it!
> Laura: I know but I'm —
> Jim: Loosen th' backbone! There now, that's a lot better.
> Laura: Am I?
> Jim: Lots, lots better! [*He moves her about the room in a clumsy waltz.*]
> Laura: Oh, my!
> Jim: Ha-ha!
> Laura: Oh, my goodness!
> Jim: Ha-ha-ha! [85].

One hardly needs to be a trained analyst to intuit the sexual subtext beneath this dance. Moments earlier Laura had surrendered control of her symbolic self when she allowed Jim to handle her unicorn. Now she has surrendered control of her actual body to Jim's able tutelage. The results sound rapturous for them both.

Tom's reconstruction of this scene indulges Jim and Laura's virtual consummation, only to interrupt the climax with a crisis. As the couple dances, they bump into the table and send the unicorn crashing to the ground, breaking off its horn. In the wake of the rapture which precedes it, the rupture of the unicorn lends itself to multiple interpretations. In psychological terms, the snapped off horn would seem to represent castration. But that connotation seems utterly inconsistent with the sexual potency of the scene. If phallic symbolism does pertain here *vis-à-vis* Jim, then post-coital detumescence seems a more valid reading. However, the glass unicorn has heretofore served as a symbol, not for Jim, but for Laura. One would then expect the unicorn's injury to have a shattering effect on her, but not so. In fact, she celebrates the rupture. "Maybe it's a blessing in disguise," she reassures the apologetic Jim. "I'll just imagine he had an operation. The horn was removed to make him feel less — freakish!" (86). Jim fell down and broke the unicorn's crown, but Laura came tumbling after — and she counts it a fortunate fall.

The broken unicorn becomes still more intriguing once Tom is factored into the equation. Remember, Tom has no transcript of Jim and Laura's encounter in the parlor. The scene is neither documentary nor memory but imaginative reconstruction, so the double entendre above should more accurately be attributed to Tom. He is implicated artistically in the scene, but he gradually becomes implicated psychologically as well. The castration imagery of the broken unicorn is more compelling if associated with Tom rather than Jim. Adler, for one, detects an undertone of sexual jealousy in Scene Seven. He asserts that Tom feels threatened by any gentleman caller's pursuit of his sister and therefore seeks to forestall any such union by matching her up with a spectacularly ineligible bachelor. He concludes that "Tom demands, in short, that Laura remain virginal for him" ("Ghosts" 178). Adler is not the first critic to identify incestuous drives in Williams' plays, nor is he the first to suggest that this incest motif may be rooted in the playwright's relationship with his sister, Rose. Indeed, the play is nakedly autobiographical in parts, leading Williams' biographer Lyle Leverich to assert that, "For the first thirty years of his life, he was living *The Glass Menagerie*" (xxiii). Many of the suspicions about Tom Williams' relationship with Rose are fuelled by Tennessee's memoirs. There he cautions, "My sister and I had a close relationship, quite unsullied by any carnal knowledge. As a matter of fact, we were rather shy of each other, physically, there was no casual physical intimacy." However, he adds, "And yet our love was, and is, the deepest in our lives and was, perhaps, very pertinent to our withdrawal from extrafamilial attachments." He also whets the critical appetite by conceding, "Some perceptive critic of the theatre made the observation that the true theme of my work is 'incest'" (*Memoirs* 119–20).

Beguiling as this corroborating evidence may be, one need not look outside the play to find ample signs of the incest motif. Though the sexual undertones of Scene Seven are pervasive from the beginning, the incestuous tenor of that sexuality only begins to sound after the breaking of the unicorn. From that point on, Tom's vested self-interest in the scene becomes more acute, and his identification with — even appropriation of — Jim becomes more pronounced. Again, the catalyst for this shift is the breaking of the glass. This "gestus interruptus" apparently prompts an important association in Tom's poetic, symbolic mind, for we have seen virtually the same image on stage once before. In Scene Three, Amanda and Tom have an explosive argument. She accuses Tom of lying about how he spends his evenings at the movies and charges, "I think you've been doing things that you're ashamed of." He counters with a mock-confession, imaginatively admitting to a secret "double-life" as Killer Wingfield, a drug fiend and hired assassin. In a fury, Tom then grabs his coat and attempts to flee the apartment, accidentally upsetting Laura's glass collection in the process. "Laura cries out as if wounded," and Amanda exits in disgust. The stage directions continue,

> Tom is left with Laura. Laura clings weakly to the mantel with her face averted. Tom stares at her stupidly for a moment. Then he crosses to the shelf. He drops awkwardly on his knees to collect the fallen glass, glancing at Laura as if he would speak but couldn't [24–25].

The *tableau vivant* at the close of Scene Three prefigures the crisis moment in Scene Seven in some obvious ways: two stooped figures, a man and woman, silently address a shattered glass figurine. It is reasonable to surmise that Tom uses this former experience for source material in imagining the latter scene. Yet these stage moments differ notably in at least two respects. First, Laura is "wounded" by the earlier accident, whereas she regards the latter as a good omen, a *felix culpa*. Secondly, the subsequent behavior of the two respective male figures is in marked contrast. In Scene Three, Tom is too paralyzed to move or speak after breaking Laura's glass. When he imagines an analogous scenario in Scene Seven, however, Jim's response is far more expressive and assured. Tom takes a memory which had been emblematic of his own inarticulate frustration and transforms it imaginatively into Jim's confident declaration of affection for Laura. In short, the breaking of the unicorn emancipates all three characters involved. For Laura, it represents freedom from her former social freakishness. For Jim, emboldened by her validation, it constitutes a green-light to proceed with even more intimate advances. And for Tom, who has recognized the potential for eliminating Jim as a rival by recasting him as surrogate spokesman, it introduces an opportunity finally to express his true feelings for Laura.

After Jim and Laura share a laugh over the broken unicorn, Jim unequivocally shifts gears into seduction mode. He tells her that she is different (in a good way) and pretty. As the latent sexuality becomes more manifest, Jim's demeanor alters significantly. He is no longer the shallow, vainglorious cad who blurts out the first thing which pops into his head. He is becoming more serious, more sensuous, more reflective — in short, he is becoming more like Tom. In fact, Tom all but announces himself as the ventriloquist behind the scene when Jim presses forward:

> Jim: [*His voice becomes low and husky. Laura turns away, nearly faint with the novelty of her emotions.*] I wish that you were my sister. I'd teach you to have some confidence in yourself [87].

"I wish you were my sister" indeed! Why would Jim say this? Why, in the rising heat of passion, as he is actively wooing this woman, would he suddenly profess his desire to be her brother? This is more than a Freudian slip, it is a Freudian pratfall; but it does provide a telling glimpse behind the mask. Within the world of *The Glass Menagerie*, there is a real Jim O'Connor, and that Jim really did come to dinner, and afterwards he really did have an encounter with Laura which overwhelmed her. But that real encounter is *not* what we see on stage. What we see is Tom's imaginative recreation, and what we hear are Tom's words to Laura delivered via the fictional mouthpiece of Jim. Tom and Jim's words and agendas are so thoroughly intertwined in the seduction sequence as to be indistinguishable, synonymous. Jim says he wishes he were Tom, but what we see in Scene Seven is that Tom wishes he were Jim. His motives extend well beyond the fraternal; and, when Jim finally does kiss Laura, Tom has achieved a vicarious consummation of sorts which would have been impossible otherwise.

The incest taboo has been temporarily breached with the kiss, but the strictures against forbidden love are quickly reinstated. As soon as Jim kisses Laura, he begins to regret it. "Stumblejohn!" he quaintly admonishes himself. "I shouldn't have done that — that was way off the beam" (88). He clearly feels he has overstepped some bounds, and the language he uses to account for this transgression is once again telling:

> Jim: …Laura, you know, if I had a sister like you, I'd do the same thing as Tom. I'd bring out fellows and — introduce her to them. The right type

of boys — of a type to — appreciate her. Only — well — he made a mistake about me. Maybe I've got no call to be saying this. That may not have been the idea in having me over. But what if it was? There's nothing wrong about that. The only trouble is that in my case — I'm not in a situation to — do the right thing [89].

As it turns out, he is not in a position to do the right thing by her because he is engaged to another woman, a fact which apparently slipped Jim's mind as he was seducing Laura but which conveniently recurs to him immediately after kissing her. "[I]f I had a sister like you, I'd do the same thing as Tom" indeed! In the aftermath of the most moving experience in Laura's life, Jim's admission that he is not the "right type of boy" for her is both excruciating and laughably understated. For Tom's purposes, however, Jim proves to be exactly the right type of gentleman caller — the type who will not be calling again. Tom uses the fictional Jim to sublimate his own secret desires for Laura without a threat that the real Jim will ever displace him. Jim, like Tom, is off limits, and both choose to flee from any further entanglements with Laura by the end of Scene Seven.

Jim exercises his escape clause with relative ease. Tom's escape is more difficult and less complete. He has never managed to escape the memory of his home life, and he is particularly haunted by regret over Laura. Tom's closing soliloquy rightly remains one of the most famous in twentieth-century drama; yet, without recourse to his deeper psychosexual connection with Laura, one is hard pressed to account for the depth of his pathos. He movingly recounts his aimless existence after leaving the family:

Tom: …The cities swept about me like dead leaves, leaves that were brightly colored but torn away from the branches. I would have stopped, but I was pursued by something. It always came upon me unawares, taking me altogether by surprise. Perhaps it was a familiar bit of music. Perhaps it was only a piece of transparent glass. Perhaps I am walking along a street at night, in some strange city, before I have found companions. I pass the lighted window of a shop where perfume is sold. The window is filled with pieces of colored glass, tiny transparent bottles in delicate colors, like bits of a shattered rainbow. Then all at once my sister touches my shoulder. I turn around and look into her eyes. Oh Laura, Laura, I tried to leave you behind me, but I am more faithful than I intended to be! [97].

Tom is clearly devastated by the memory of Laura, but why? After all, Tom and Laura spend relatively little stage time interacting directly with one another in this "memory play"; and those few memories where they are alone together — including the inarticulate paralysis of Scene Three and the drunken stammering of Scene Four—do not reveal an unusually close sibling bond. The closing soliloquy seems suffused by guilt, but guilt over what? Tom no doubt feels bad that Laura's heart was broken by the man he brought home for her; but it was Jim who did the heartbreaking (Tom did not make that part up), and Tom only played matchmaker in the first place at Amanda's insistence. He might feel well-deserved guilt for abandoning the family without any means of financial support, and surely some of his remorse is anchored in that selfish decision. If his abandonment were the sole source of regret, however, then one would expect him to be haunted as much by the mother he abandoned as by the sister. But the final soliloquy locates Laura exclusively at the epicenter of his regret.

I contend that our clearest insight into Tom's bond with Laura comes not through his memories in Scenes One through Six, but through his fiction in Scene Seven. Furthermore, I contend that the full spectrum of his feelings for her encompass not only sympathy, protectiveness, and fraternal affection, but also sexual desire. Even in the final soliloquy, which is generally received as an expression of heart-breaking nostalgia, echoes of latent sexuality can still be heard. For what prompts Laura's disturbing intrusions into Tom's thoughts? "Perhaps it was a familiar bit of music. Perhaps it was only a piece of transparent glass. Perhaps I am walking along a street at night, in some strange city, before I have found companions." What sort of companions would those be? Tom is almost certainly referring to his pursuit of sexual partners. It is not clear if these lovers are male or female, if he pays prostitutes or merely depends upon the kindness of strangers, but these are secondary concerns here. The point is that, along with hearing music and seeing glass, cruising for sex tends to conjure up images of his sister for Tom. Hooking up with strangers also seems to be one of the palliatives for dispelling her ghost:

> Oh Laura, Laura, I tried to leave you behind me, but I am more faithful than I intended to be! I reach for a cigarette, I cross the street, I run into the movies or a bar, I buy a drink, I speak to the nearest stranger—anything that can blow your candles out! [97].

Tom has apparently been prodigiously unfaithful to Laura in terms of sexual fidelity. However, in his mind—which is what really counts in this solipsistic play—he always returns to his *ur*-Taboo-Lover. Or, more precisely, she returns to him, carrying the torch of loyalty—and the flame of passion—which he perpetually implores her to extinguish.

Tom ends the play by bidding Laura to blow out her candle, and she complies. While this poignant final image is often perceived as a signal of closure, R.B. Parker astutely observes that the entire play "can just as accurately be seen as repetition" (418). Indeed, this "memory play" represents only one performance in a long-running revival on the stage of Tom's mind. He has no apparent control over his compulsion to repeat, but he does exercise considerable control over the form which these reenactments take. Fictional recreation again plays a crucial role in the closing moments of the play. Remember that Tom had already stormed out of the apartment before Laura extinguishes the candle, meaning that even this clinching gesture is drawn from Tom's imagination rather than his memory. As Adler puts it, "...Laura's blowing out the candles is not part of Tom's memory of things past but pure projection, a figment forged in the solipsistic world of a guilty imagination that refuses to speak its real guilt" ("Ghosts" 178). That "real guilt" is Tom's incestuous desire for Laura, and his attempt to disguise that desire behind the mask of Jim only ends up further confirming its existence.

Even the sequence of the play reinforces the root cause of Tom's lingering distress. He is the narrator reconstructing his story for us, and he chooses to position the Jim-Laura scene as the climax of his recitation and the *raison d'être* for his guilt. Yet notice some of the scenes he chooses not to include. He does not provide us with the scene in which he finally leaves the Wingfield home for good. Nor does he marshal his fictional powers of speculation to provide any examples of Amanda and Laura's troubled life after he leaves them. These omissions certify that his abandonment is not the true source of his guilt. Instead, he locates his personal epiphany in a scene which physically excludes him. Nothing in Tom's past matters so much as the gentleman caller scene, and nothing after it seems to matter at all. This means of course that Tom was absent from the most important "memory" of his life. Nevertheless, his physical absence allows him to give voice to his deepest desires for Laura through the fictional surrogate of Jim. The stage direction leading into Jim and Laura's momentous encounter forewarns, "While the incident is apparently unimportant, it is to Laura the climax of her secret life" (70). However, through Tom's imaginative reassembling of events and his creative recasting of parts, the incident emerges as the climax of his own secret life as well.

XAVIER UNIVERSITY

References Cited

Adler, Thomas P. "Tennessee Williams's 'Personal Lyricism': Toward an Androgynous Form." *Realism and the American Dramatic Tradition.* Ed. Welliam W. Demastes. Tuscaloosa: University of Alabama Press, 1996.

_____. "When Ghosts Supplant Memories: Tennessee Williams' *Clothes for a Summer Hotel.*" *Critical Essays on Tennessee Williams.* Ed. Robert A. Martin. New York: G.K. Hall, 1997.

King, Thomas L. "Irony and Distance in *The Glass Menagerie.*" *Twentieth Century Interpretations of* The Glass Menagerie. Ed. R.B. Parker. Englewood Cliffs, NJ: Prentice-Hall, 1983.

Leverich, Lyle. *Tom: The Unknown Tennessee Williams.* New York: Crown, 1995.

Parker, R.B. "The Composition of *The Glass Menagerie*: An Argument for Complexity." *Modern Drama* 25.8 (1982): 409–22.

Stern, Stewart. *No Tricks in My Pocket: Paul Newman Directs.* New York: Grove Press, 1989.

Williams, Tennessee. *The Glass Menagerie.* 1945. Ed. Robert Bray. New York: New Directions, 1999.

_____. *Memoirs.* Garden City, NY: Doubleday, 1975.

9

Reconsidering Surrealist Drama
The Case of Nanos Valaoritis'
Round Tables

Vassiliki Rapti

Abstract

*Theatre has never been fully developed within Surrealism and sur-
realist theatre is often dismissed as nonsense. Greek avant-garde
author Nanos Valaoritis challenged this view by experimenting with
surrealist games in the theatrical realm. His forty-odd unpublished
plays, culminating in* Round Tables *(Les Tables rondes, 1957),
which is the focus of this paper, all are marked by a creative ludic
spirit that is characteristic of Surrealism, and offer a solid corpus for
reconsidering the poetics of Surrealist theatre in the context of ludics.
In light of game theory as applied to the wide gamut of Surrealist
ludics, I argue that Valaoritis experimented with surrealist games in
terms of both theme and form for two reasons: first, to prove to André
Breton that surrealist theatre could exist without betraying the principles of Surrealism, and second, to show that the "logic" of surrealist games may lead to a fruitful reconsideration of surrealist theatre.*

The last Greek surrealist Nanos Valaoritis and his French play *Les Tables
rondes* (*Round Tables*) are the focus of this paper.[1] Born in Lausanne, Switzerland in 1921, Valaoritis represents a rare case of a multi-lingual avant-garde
writer who experiments with all genres in three languages — namely, English
and his two mother tongues, Greek and French. Author of about thirty books
of poetry and fiction and more than 43 mostly unpublished plays and skits,
Valaoritis received numerous awards in Greece, France and the United States.
Part of his work is now archived at Princeton University.

His three-act play *Round Tables* was written in 1957 and has never been
performed. He wrote it when he participated in the last phase of ludic activities by André Breton's surrealist group in Paris from 1954 to 1960.[2] This

110

group performed many dialogue games, which were at the heart of surrealist writing. The word "ludic," more common in French than English, is associated with the activity of playing games. I show that *Round Tables* was created out of rules that guided surrealist ludic activities, making a case for surrealist theatre as something worthy of study because it ingeniously places the inherent logic of the games in the service of the irrational.[3]

This project began when I interviewed Valaoritis, and he commented that many surrealist dialogues were generated by playing surrealist games. The games have rules, so the seeming incoherence of surrealist texts was in fact produced according to rational standards. These standards fascinated him, particularly when he compared surrealist dialogues with Plato's dialogues which displayed a coherent logic. Intrigued by the apparent incoherence of surrealist dialogues, Valaoritis told me that he had used surrealist games to write plays. He added that an audience might enjoy his plays if it had a grasp of the game rules employed for their composition. The same precondition, I believe, applies to all surrealist texts. Understanding that seemingly incoherent contradictions in surrealist texts are rule-generated can only make surrealist texts interesting.

For the surrealists, who were deliberately anti-literary, playing games guaranteed the marvelous, which, in Anna Balakian's words, is "the sacred both sublime and terrifying" that opens the path to the supreme aesthetic category of "surreality" (qtd. in Feman-Orenstein xiv). According to Breton, "surreality" is "a kind of absolute reality" that fuses all contradictions (*Manifestoes* 14). Surrealist games work in exactly the same way — Breton explained — as a free activity *par excellence* that expresses the Surrealists' desire "to break with all obsolete antinomies such as action versus dream, past versus future, reason versus folly, high versus low, etc." (qtd. in Garrigues 217; the translation is mine). Surrealist games, Breton added, support Johan Huizinga's conclusion about the "standing supra-logical (*supralogique*) character of our situation within the world" in his study *Homo Ludens* (qtd. in Garrigues 218; the translation is mine). Surrealist games thus put into practice a new concept of dialogue that enables them to enact "surreality" as they put together the most arbitrary images that could fascinate an audience. Breton compared the mysterious effects and the particular pleasure deriving from such images to the effects of "the opium" that enrapture people (*Manifestoes* 36).

Although the first surrealist game called "Liquidation," published in *Littérature* in March 1921, was based on Breton's concept of dialogue as two simultaneous monologues, it was only in March 1928 that Surrealists decided to name explicitly their games a "dialogue." Their games became a dialogue in progress. Both the rules and the texts they produced were published under the name "Dialogue in 1928" in *La Revolution Surréaliste* of the same year. Other games were published in subsequent issues until September 1962 and were collected in a volume edited by Emmanuel Garrigues in 1995.[4] "Dialogue" consisted of questions and responses written on a circulating piece of paper by the participants, seated around a table without looking at their neighbors. Their various sentences were then assembled and the result was always funny and puzzling.

Valaoritis saw that these linguistic games produced a dialogue that generated surprise and a disorientation of the senses. He argues that dialogue, rather than plot — as Aristotle thought — is the essence of drama. Ludics is what I call the dialogue that is produced through the techniques of the surrealist games.[5] Valaoritis inscribed *Round Tables* in its surrealist context by placing two epigrams in its beginning: 1) Breton's definition of surrealist dialogue as two simultaneous monologues that free the speakers from the obligations of politeness; and 2) Breton's phrase "these un-prejudiced interlocutors" which emphasizes the interlocutors' free imagination (*Manifestoes* 35). Both epigraphs introduce the reader to the ludics of the play and set the frame within which the *Round Tables* unfolds.[6] The frame is that of a frantic game conceived by some child-like interlocutors-players. The game from an innocent joke (in response to a chance happening) to a tragic farce. This protean game that takes shape through dialogue, as opposed to action, organizes the "tragic comedy" *Round Tables*.

Round Tables is about three young men who hang out in a cafeteria. There they play tricks on two strangers whom only chance procures for their entertainment. Their first victim is a country girl, Anabelle. Her name alludes to "la Belle Hélène," i.e., Helen of Troy, and it immediately marks her as a target to be conquered. Their second victim is a robust, strange man, called Nero. He is endowed with the prophetic power of a medium at best, but also with insanity like his namesake, the Roman emperor, a link that is strengthened by Nero's self-appellation as "august" (17). The young men weave the romance of the two victims and entangle themselves in an endless game, the rules of which are constantly shifting and, in the end, are turned against those who started the game.

Round Tables, in sum, is about trivial events. Action is simulated because nothing really happens except for the constant talk about action. This simulated action unfolds in a café which is referred to as "Two Pearls," or "Three Peals," or "Two Laurels," or "Little Babylon." The constant name changes and the incongruent time references confuse the reader and function as a reminder of the surrealist setting where all contradictions are absorbed and where there are no boundaries between reality and dream, or life and death.

The first Surrealist game that Valaoritis explicitly employs in *Round*

Tables is modeled after the metaphor game of "one into another," introduced in 1954 and played according to the following rules, as Mel Gooding explains:

> one player withdraws from the room, and chooses for himself an object (or a person, an idea, etc.). While he is absent the rest of the players also choose an object. When the first player returns he is told what object they have chosen. He must now describe his own object in terms of the properties of the object chosen by the others, making the comparison more and more obvious as he proceeds, until they are able to guess its identity. The first player begins with a sentence, such as, "I am an (object) ..." [31].

This game that draws on the notion of the surrealist object is at work when Anabelle's limbs erotically excite the imagination of Anastase and André as follows:

> Anastase: Her leg is a fan!
> André: And her ear is tiny!
> Anastase: Her hands are mushrooms!
> André: Her hair is the hair of a coach! [6].

Soon the "one into another" surrealist game shifts to a childish mimicry that simulates all possible sounds emitted by means of transportation such as the sirens of boats, the whistles of train, and the horns of cars. Anastase and André imitate these sounds to irritate Anabelle. Jazz music played on a phonograph plays only as long as they feed it with coin — stressing the improvisational nature of their game. Valaoritis alludes here to the raw material available for poetic composition in terms of rhythm and sound patterns. At this point the two young men regress to puerility as though convinced that if one game does not work, another might. They continue to talk simultaneously when they are trying to guess who it is that Anabelle is expecting:

> Anastase: It's the Emperor of China she is waiting for!
> André: No. It's the King of Eskimos!
> Anastase: The Aurora Borealis in person!
> André: Dalai-Lama in person!
> Anastase: No, she is waiting for the bus!
> André: You're mistaken! The tramway!
> Anastase: There are no tramways, Miss! No buses either!
> André: Let's see, she's waiting for the plane!
> Anastase: The train!
> André: The boat! [9–10].

The ironic juxtaposition of well-known real and fictionalized persons with means of transportation suggests Valaoritis' effort to apply Breton's premise —

namely, the more arbitrary the juxtaposition of images becomes, the more effective it is. In fact, the above example is not a pure dialogue, as no communication at all is achieved between the two interlocutors. Instead, each character's words are repeated by the other character, slightly modified, only to function as springboards to the most audacious images for Anabelle as well as for the audience.

The appearance of Nero, who has a muscular body and a suspect self-absorption, calls for the three young men's change of game plan. Nonetheless, Nero is entrapped in their malicious plan which attempts a more sophisticated make-believe as all of them make up a story about Anabelle. They pretend that they are ready to save her from suicide. This is yet another reference to the scene "Is Suicide a solution?" in "Dialogue in 1928." Nero falls into their trap when he decides to save the girl.

Protracted convulsive laughter seals the triumph of the three young men who end this part of their game by writing a love letter, supposedly from Anabelle to Nero, to be delivered by a waiter. The message, a parody of romantic literature, marks a turning point in the game. Writing and reading have become part of the game. The three young men momentarily feel guilty, but their game has acquired a kind of autonomy that makes it impossible for them to end it. They are all under Anabelle's spell. When she "confesses" that she desires all of them at once because they satisfy her standard of masculinity, they feel that their masculinity is threatened and want to withdraw from the game. Anabelle dismembers each young man in her imagination and creates, from their limbs, a "perfect man" who is suitable to her tastes. Whether Anabelle makes fun of the three young men or tells them the truth is left vague. She may indeed be a liberated woman, like Breton's Nadja. Anabelle later explains to one of them that she is a creature of chance:

> Anabelle: I've always been the creature of the second. I am a creature of a crossroads ... I knock at all doors. I feel good. Everybody suits me provided that the affair with him does not last long. I am not tough, but I become tough against everything that tends to be permanent. I like changing. Even changing a train [95].

Anabelle is no ordinary woman, but the personification of freedom itself. Her freedom propels her desire to play with all these men. Her involvement with their game does not come from a mere desire to get revenge for having been the target of their mockery, but also from a feeling of self-indulgence that justifies her existence. Her desire to be desired and, at the same time, remain unattainable, appears in the wordplay that constitutes her name (An/Ana/Belle/Elle). In Greek and French in succession, her name means

"If/Again/Beautiful/She," reminiscent of another surrealist game called "The Game of Syllogisms." According to this game, sentences beginning with either "If" or "When" were circulated among the surrealist players around a table. It would not be an exaggeration then to claim that Anabelle stands as an allegory for writing itself—one that ultimately defeats anyone who makes the effort, just as Anabelle remains unconquerable.

A "Hide-and-Seek" follows along with a strange incident. A woman appears and disappears three times on the top of the music box when the waiter rings a bell. The waiter says:

> It's a hide-and-seek game! One is hidden, one is found. We hide ourselves, we find ourselves. You hide yourself, we find you! [40].

This is perhaps the most surrealistic scene in the play, and its significance is of critical importance. It evokes the permanent concern of Surrealists to bridge the gap between reality and imagination by inventing a supreme reality, and its application in the surrealist game "Ouvrez-vous?" (Would you Open?) which appeared in 1953 in the French review *Médium*. According to this game the participants recorded their reactions each time they imagined that a famous person suddenly appeared asking them to open the door. The originality of this game in Garrigues' view, lies in "the effect of surprise and the free interplay between the real and the imaginary, as well as in the degree to which each one of the participants is willing to reveal himself" (35; the translation is mine). The play ends with a switch to a vertiginous game that Nero plans in order to entrap all the other characters by pretending that he knows where one can find a secret treasure. After having marked the whole parquet of the café with various signs, Nero gives a message to the waiter who first reads it and then tears it into small pieces. The five men frantically pick up the pieces to reassemble it in order to find the hidden treasure to no avail. The vertigo game reaches its peak at this moment, when exactly the curtain falls leaving all of them breathing heavily.

This last episode combines three of the four types of games classified by the mid–twentieth-century French sociologist Roger Caillois as *agon* (competitive games), *alea* (games of chance), *mimicry* (simulacrum and mimesis devoted to make-believe games) and *ilinx* (vertigo such as carnival rides or roller coasters). All these types of games, as Caillois understood them, may appear in combination. Throughout *Round Tables* a number of various combinations are evident. Caillois argues moreover that games in any of these categories stretch along "a continuum between two attitudinal poles: *paidia* or infancy, characterized by free improvisation and fantasy, and *ludus*, characterized by constraint, arbitrary rules, and effort" (Motte 7).

As I have shown, the games in Valaoritis' play exemplify this entire continuum. For Valaoritis, the power of the game is a protean process of transformation that stretches from the pole of free improvisation to the more sophisticated pole of games structured by rules that generate new forms of dialogue. Valaoritis attempted to write *Round Tables* as a purposeful exercise of style based on such a definition of surrealist dialogue and its magic that takes the form of a maze in terms of both structure and theme to guide the audience to experience the marvelous. By so doing, Valaoritis pays homage to Breton, while challenging Breton's idea that poetry and even the novel were better adapted than drama to expressing "surreality" as generated by juxtapositions.[7]

The creative process in *Round Tables* was governed by the rules that guided surrealist ludic activities and these games explain how their hidden logic permeated surrealist theatrical writing, endowing it with something that is not entirely nonsense and yet passionately seeks the irrational. In sum, Valaoritis' plays and ideas about playwriting show how well the largely dialogic surrealist games can be rendered on the stage. For Breton, the purpose of the surrealist juxtapositions was to create for readers and audiences a sense of the marvelous. Valaoritis, in contrast, wants his readers and audiences to recognize that the seeming irrationality of his characters' dialogues is generated through rational means (games), and that an awareness of the rules of the games can only reinforce their experience of the marvelous. Valaoritis is convinced that if audiences can understand the rules of the games that generate these texts, they will be able to grasp the inner logic of the texts by reassembling it step by step, scene by scene in the manner of the characters that reassemble the pieces of the text in the last scene of *Round Tables*. By understanding how *Round Tables* echoes the rules that guided surrealist ludic activity, actors and audiences may also find a guide about how to approach any surrealist theatrical text. Valaoritis' experiment with surrealist games sets forth a poetics of surrealist theatre based on a game-theory that may lead to a reevaluation of surrealist theatre.

WASHINGTON UNIVERSITY IN SAINT LOUIS

Notes

1. Hereafter referred to as *Round Tables*. All quotes from this play have been translated by the author of this article and have been approved by the playwright to whom I address my warmest thanks for his advice and for kindly offering me access to his archive. My thanks also go to Professors Emma Kafalenos, Stamos Metzidakis and Robert Henke for advising me on this topic.

2. Nanos Valaoritis stayed in Paris during the years 1954–1960. In 1954 he joined André Breton's Surrealist circle along with the Surrealist painter Marie Wilson, later his wife. During these years he wrote more than 40 plays and skits in French and Greek, both of them being his mother tongues, since he was born in Lausanne, Switzerland and both languages were spoken at his home all the time. Later on, when the author moved to the United States he also wrote plays in English.

3. I make here the same assumption as Elizabeth Sewell does in *The Field of Nonsense* (1975). According to her, "Nonsense is not merely the denial of sense, a random reversal of ordinary experience and an escape from the limitations of everyday life into a haphazard infinity, but is on the contrary a carefully limited world, controlled and directed by reason, a construction subject to its own laws" (5).

4. In addition to the "Dialogue in 1928" the following forms of this game appeared in various journals: "The Dialogue in 1929" (*Variétés*, June 1929), "The Dialogue in 1934" (*Documents*, Special Issue, June 1934). These were published by Emmanuel Garrigues along with "The Dialogue in 1952–1954" and "The Game of Syllogisms."

5. This term is borrowed from Warren F. Jr. Motte in his book *Playtexts: Ludics in Contemporary Literature* (Lincoln & London, 1995). This book is a collection of essays that explore the concept of play as "necessarily and fundamentally creative," and therefore, as inseparable from writing itself, a statement made since Plato's time (Motte 15).

6. Part of such advance information offered to the audience is the allusion to another game most cherished by Surrealists, the so-called "Who is medium?" inherited by the Romantic tradition. Victor Hugo's account of spiritualism in "Les Tables Tournantes de Jersey (1853–55)," an account of Hugo's experiments with medium sessions after the death of his daughter Léopoldine, offers a detailed description of the mission of these medium sessions. During these sessions people were seated around a table and were invoking spirits in order to cross another world and achieve a sense of unification with the cosmos. For more details see Francis Lacassin's edition *Les Fantômes de Jersey* (Monaco: Rocher, 1991). Another inter-textual reference is the medieval fellowship of the Round Table in the King Arthur legend, where all the knights have an equal status around the egalitarian round table. Cf. Richard Barber. *King Arthur: Hero and Legend* (New York: Saint Martin's) 39–40. The well-educated Valaoritis (particularly in the field of French literature) was familiar with both Victor Hugo's work and the Arthurian tradition. His overwhelming erudition is present in all of his works, including his plays and has been considered as a shortcoming for staging his plays. Marcelle Capron (*Le Combat*, April 29, 1959), for instance, as Valaoritis admits, saw his erudition as an obstacle apropos of the staging of his play *L'Hôtel de la nuit qui tombe* (*The Hotel of The Falling Night*) in Paris in 1959 (Personal Interview).

7. André Breton explicitly showed contempt for the medium of theatre. His disapproval of the theatre as incompatible with poetry — the form he cherished above all — is notorious, although he himself began his writings as a playwright. In his *Nadja* (1928), Breton admitted that the only play written for the stage worth of recollection was Pierre Palau's *Les Détraquées*, performed by Le Théâtre des Deux Masques on February 1921. See André Breton. *Œuvres Complètes*. Vol. I (Paris: Gallimard, 1988) 669–73 and 1535. Also, his first writings were short skits which he

performed himself with his friends. I refer to his dadaist experiments *S'il vous plaît* (*If You Please*, 1919) and *Vous m'oublierez (You Will Forget Me*, 1920), both later included in his famous *Les Champs Magnetiques* (*Magnetic Fields*, 1920*)*, a collection of texts written in collaboration with Philippe Soupault by means of automatic writing, included in the first volume of the Gallimard edition of Breton's complete works. Also, his later work including many of his poems abound in references to the stage and its magic. For a more detailed discussion of this issue, see Henri Béhar's *Étude sur le théâtre dada et surréaliste* (Paris: Gallimard, 1967) 30. In a way then Breton is responsible for the negative reception of Surrealist theatre. For more details about this issue see Martin John Bennison. *Aesthetic Principles in Representative Surrealist Plays*. Diss. (U of Missouri–Columbia, 1971) 4–5.

References Cited

Barber, Richard W. *King Arthur: Hero and Legend*. New York: Saint Martin's, 1986.

Béhar, Henri. *Étude sur le théâtre dada et surréaliste*. Paris: Gallimard, 1967.

Bennison, Martin John. *Aesthetic Principles in Representative Surrealist Plays*. Diss. University of Missouri-Columbia, 1971.

Breton, André. *Œuvres Complètes*. Vol. I. Paris: Gallimard, 1988.

_____. *Manifestoes of Surrealism*. Trans. Richard Seaver and Helen. R. Lane. Ann Arbor: University of Michigan Press, 1972.

_____. *Nadja*. Paris: Gallimard, 1964.

Capron, Marcelle. *Le Combat*, April 29, 1959.

Caillois, Roger. *Man, Play, and Game*. Trans. Barash Meyer. New York: The Free Press, 1961.

Garrigues, Emmanuel. *Archives du surréalisme: Les jeux surréalistes. Mars 1921–Septembre 1962)*. Paris: Gallimard, 1995.

Gooding, Mel. *Surrealist Games*. Boston: Shambhala Redstone, 2001.

Hugo, Victor. "Les tables tournantes de Jersey: 1853–1855." *Œuvres dramatiques complètes*. Ed. Jean-Jacques Pauvert. Paris: Société française des presses suisses, 1963: 1619–1713.

_____. *Les Fantômes de Jersey*. Ed. Francis Lacassin. Monaco: Rocher, 1991.

Huizinga, Johan. *Homo Ludens*. 1939. Boston: Beacon, 1955.

Motte, Warren F., Jr. *Playtexts: Ludics in Contemporary Literature*. Lincoln & London: University of Nebraska Press, 1995.

Orenstein-Feman, Gloria. *The Theater of the Marvelous: Surrealism and the Contemporary Stage*. New York: New York University Press, 1975.

Plato. *The Laws of Plato*. Trans. Thomas L. Pangle. New York: Basic Books, 1980.

Sewell, Elizabeth. *The Field of Nonsense*. London: Chatto & Windus, 1952.

Valaoritis, Nanos. *Les Tables Rondes*. Unpublished.

_____. Personal Interview. 20 May 2001.

Narrative Discontinuity and Identity in Greek Old Comedy and the American Concept Musical

John Given

Abstract

The formal structures of Greek old comedy and the American concept musical are strikingly similar. Both utilize an episodic organization in lieu of the cause-and-effect narrative so prevalent in Greek tragedy and in musicals in the tradition of Rodgers and Hammerstein. This paper argues that, while neither genre fully abandons a linear plot, each takes advantage of narrative discontinuities to construct character identity against audience expectations for coherence. Yet the effects of discontinuous narration and characterization in each genre differ because of the way in which Greek and American dramas conceived of identity. The concept musicals present characters as underdetermined insofar as their actions are not consistently motivated by their previous actions on a psychological level. The Greek comedies, on the other hand, use narrative discontinuity to reveal overdetermined characters, individuals who have too much identity insofar as their behaviors do not reveal a logical orientation toward a coherent goal in life.

In the *Poetics*, Aristotle prescribes characterization and plots that proceed by a logic of probable or necessary cause (1451a 13–14). It is much better to have a story, he says, in which one event takes place *because of*, rather than merely *after*, another (1452a 20–21). Aristotle is thinking primarily of Tragedy, and the majority of Western drama since Aristotle has adhered to his ideal. The two genres that I want to consider, however, Greek Old Comedy and the American concept musical, significantly depart from the model practiced by ancient Tragedy and theorized by Aristotle. "Old Comedy" is the ancient term for the Athenian comedies produced in the fifth century B.C.; the only

119

surviving examples are the plays of Aristophanes.[1] The term "concept musical" was coined in the 1970s to describe musical plays that were organized around a governing idea rather than a plot; examples include *Lady in the Dark, Cabaret, Company, Follies, Pippin, A Chorus Line, Pacific Overtures* and *Assassins*.[2] The two genres are often structured episodically so that events follow one another sequentially rather than consequentially. I study here how this structure of narrative discontinuity impacts the plays' representations of characters' identities. Although the narrative structures are similarly episodic, I argue that, in the two genres, their effects are quite different. The musicals use narrative discontinuity to present protagonists that do not receive full characterization. They seem underdeveloped. The Greek comedies, on the other hand, use narrative discontinuity to give characters too much identity. The comedies' shifting narrative structure enables the protagonists to change with little or no motivation and thus to pile one incongruous identity upon another.

In order for playwrights to manipulate characters' identities, there needs to be some stable expectation regarding identity on the part of the audience. I do not have the space to explore the complexities of Athenian and American identity, but some general remarks should serve my purpose. For a twentieth or twenty-first century audience of musical theatre, strongly accustomed to the (very Aristotelian) style of Rodgers and Hammerstein, characters ought to possess a coherent subjectivity. Modern audiences expect a character to be an autonomous agent, who makes decisions rationally. They assume that changes in character (taking into account, of course, that the character is fictional and does not 'really' have a mind) are actually changes in psychological makeup. A character is recognizable as a person because he or she possesses a coherent psychology.[3] Ancient Greek conceptions of identity are more concerned with external behavior than with psychology. What brings unity to a person's life is his or her behavioral orientation toward a successful life (where success can have many possible definitions), an orientation that exists prior to psychological desire. A character changes in a Greek play when his or her orientation toward that goal changes, whether through the agent's decision or because of external contingencies. Thus, Oedipus, in Sophocles' *Oedipus Tyrannus*, changes, insofar as his life is at first oriented toward intellectual discovery and political power, but, against his wishes, becomes oriented toward darkness and powerlessness. Psychological developments, such as Oedipus's desire for knowledge and distress upon learning the truth of his past, while not non-existent, are secondary in terms of character and identity.[4]

The concept musicals that I will discuss frustrate modern audience expectations for a coherent self by presenting characters who do not significantly alter. Most of these plays contain a series of episodes set within a controlling interpretive frame. This is clear, for example, in *A Chorus Line* (1975), by Nicholas Dante, James Kirkwood, Edward Kleban and Marvin Hamlisch, where the dancers' contest frames the action. The contest is foregrounded primarily in the opening and closing scenes, but, in the context of the entire show, exists only as a pretense for the intervening episodes, the individual dancers' stories, which are the play's *raison d'être*.[5] *Company* (1970), by George Furth and Stephen Sondheim, has a similar structure.[6] The play is organized as a series of vignettes about married couples. The main character, Robert, is an unmarried friend of each couple, a detached observer through each vignette. As an observer, he does not alter significantly until the final scene, the song "Being Alive." It is not clear how any given scene relates temporally to the scenes around it.[7] One episode clearly does not take place *because of* the episode that preceded it. It is not even clear that one episode takes place *after* the one that preceded it.

The temporal structure of *Company* is particularly ambiguous in the four birthday parties that Robert's friends throw for him, which serve the same framing function as *A Chorus Line*'s dance contest. The play opens with the first party, for Robert's thirty-fifth birthday. The party scene is repeated at the end of the first act, at the beginning of the second act and at the end of the second act. Though each party differs with respect to the dialogue and Robert's ability to blow out the candles, it seems that the four birthday parties all represent a party for Robert's thirty-fifth birthday. The repeated, yet changed, scene has led some writers and directors to assume that the parties and indeed the entire play happen within Robert's head (e.g., Miller *Director's Guide* 57). This explanation attempts to provide a rationale for the unusual temporal sequence, by attributing the seemingly illogical sequences to the illogical unconscious. To understand *Company*'s structure in this way, though, is to try to fit it into a false narrative continuity, to try to provide a rationale when there is no need for one. The concept musical seeks to undermine such expectations of coherence; the sequences simply are illogical. The four birthday parties — each the same as, yet different from, the others — exist in an extra-temporal, even a ritual, space (Bristow and Butler 250). They represent a temporal paradox. By framing each act, the birthday parties point out that all the scenes exist in this illogical, discontinuous space. During the third party scene, Sarah even says to Robert, "Stay exactly the same. You may be the one constant in this world of variables" (76).[8]

The development of Robert's identity is greatly inhibited by this discontinuity. While we certainly come to know him as a character, we never see how one action leads to another. In the opening song, Robert sings along with the entire cast, "Love is company" (20). At the end of Act I, in a song interpolated into the revised *Company*, he claims that he is ready for marriage so that he will have someone to "keep me company" (70). When asked toward the end of the play why he or anyone should get married, his answer is the same: "for company" (109). Until the middle of "Being Alive," he maintains this same, immature view of marriage as existing for the sake of "company," insofar as he fails to understand — a failure that is marked in the play by the frequent underscoring of the "Bobby Baby" musical motif— the nature of marriage as it appears in the play's many episodes. In Act I Scene 2, when Sarah and Harry deceive one another about their diets and then wrestle with seeming violence, Robert can only mutter "Wow" (underscored with "Bobby Baby") in disbelief that this is a functional marriage (32). In Scene 4, Robert repeats the same reaction (with the same underscoring) when David tries to explain how his marriage with Jenny works. Scene 6 presents Amy's wavering whether to marry Paul; when she hesitates, Robert rashly (with the familiar underscoring) asks Amy to marry *him*. When Amy points out his immaturity, he soliloquizes the self-deceiving song, "Marry Me a Little," which is framed by the "Bobby Baby" motif.[9] The motif appears again in Act II, Scene 2, as the five wives comment on the emptiness of Robert's tryst with April. The episodic structure of the play, punctuated by the repeated leitmotif, creates a protagonist who cannot change, cannot learn. He begins each episode with the same, undeveloped knowledge with which he began the previous episode, namely that marriage exists for the sake of company. Nothing that he does or experiences causes him to act or think differently; he never (until the finale) learns what the couples know, namely that marriage exists both for the sake of mere company and for the sake of genuine love.[10]

Even more marked than the unchanging nature of Robert's understanding of relationships is his constant ambivalence of desire, as if his existence outside of time and logic do not allow him to possess coherent desires. When Joanne offers Robert a cigarette, he explains that he never smoked. "Why?" Joanne asks. "I don't know. I meant to. Does that count?" replies Robert (108). That same indecisiveness appears throughout the play. For example, after his one-night stand with the flight attendant April (whom he mistakenly calls June), Robert begs her to stay with him instead of flying to Spain, as her job requires. Throughout the song "Barcelona," Robert tries to persuade her, and when she finally gives in, he sings in disappointment or even horror, "Oh God!" (100). Most pointedly, in the song "Someone is Waiting," when he dreams about his ideal mate, he describes this woman as "Cool as Sarah, Easy and loving as Susan —/ Jenny, / ... / Warm as Susan, / Frantic and touching as Amy —/ Joanne" (49). The perfect woman is a composite of his married friends, an aggregate of traits drawn from the women in his life. Not only does "Someone Is Waiting" provide an excellent example of the static nature of Robert's psychology, it also provides the exact model for what Robert himself is to the audience: a composite person, cobbled together in a discontinuous sequence of episodes. Since he does not develop in traditional, logical ways, we can only add up the characteristics we observe in him.

The idea of "adding up" is apposite when Robert finally does change in "Being Alive." Having just declared to Joanne that the reason for marriage is to have company, Robert accidentally — he claims he "didn't mean" it — rebuffs an advance by Joanne and her assertion that she will take care of him by asking, "But who will I take care of?" (111). Joanne marks the progress in character by stating, "I just heard a door open that's been stuck a long time," and, after a final repetition of the "Bobby Baby" motif to mark the imminent end of his static immaturity, Robert begins "Being Alive." During the first half of the song, Robert sings of his understanding of marriage as "Someone to hold you too close / Someone to hurt you too deep" (114).[11] Meanwhile, all the married friends interject encouraging remarks, the last two of which are significant for our purposes. Peter tells Robert, "Add 'em up, Bobby. Add 'em up" (115), and Amy says, "Blow out your candles, Robert, and make a wish. *Want* something, Robert! Want *something*" (116). Peter's instruction urges Robert to look back across the numerous, discontinuous episodes, and to "add up" the lessons that he can now glean from each, while Amy recalls the extra-temporal birthday parties and tells Robert that he now must step back into time and logic in order to form a real desire.[12] With that, Robert changes his mind — and his lyrics. He wishes, "Somebody hold me too close / Somebody hurt me too deep" (p. 116). His development is the resolution of his ambivalent desires, which we have expected through the entire play.

The play ends, though, not with Robert's declaration that he has finally come alive. Instead, we find a fourth repetition of the birthday party. This time, Robert does not come to the party. As Joanne observes, "may be the surprise is on us" (117). They all depart, leaving the cake behind (with candles burning!). After they are gone, Robert emerges from the shadows. He has been watching his friends one last time. He blows out the candles, presumably making a genuine wish, and the curtain falls. It is the still the same-but-different party. But this time the difference is that Robert himself has changed.

In *Pippin* (1972), by Roger O. Hirson and Stephen Schwartz, which first appeared on Broadway two years after *Company*, we again meet a protagonist with a problematic identity. Where *Company* opens with the birthday party in order to introduce the theme of ritualized and discontinuous time, *Pippin* accomplishes a similar effect with a metatheatrical song, "Magic to Do," and a metatheatrical narrator (Miller *Director's Guide* 193–201).[13] Our narrator, called only the Leading Player, tells us that we are about to witness an "anecdotic revue" (1). He further sings that the players will present "miracle plays." They have "parts to perform — hearts to warm," all of which amounts to splendid "magic" performed "just for you." The play will even include "a climax never before seen on a public stage" (3). We are therefore immediately prepared for a discontinuous narrative, a series of anecdotes in the style, perhaps, of a vaudevillian revue, whose discontinuity is foregrounded by metatheatrical devices.

To be sure, *Pippin*, unlike *Company*, has more of a through-going story, since the scenes certainly do at least happen one *after* another. It is constructed as a medieval quest, the object of Pippin's quest being a meaning for his own life. The quest begins as he graduates from university, when he promises his professors "not to waste my life in commonplace, ordinary pursuits,"[14] a promise that he knows he cannot fulfill merely with knowledge that can "be found in books" (5). Instead, he must journey to find "something completely fulfilling," a longing which he expresses in the song "Corner of the Sky." As Pippin finishes the song and exits to the ironic applause of the other Players, who are quickly becoming his antagonists, the Leading Player sings a brief reprise of "Magic to Do": "Journey — journey to a spot ex-/citing, mystic, and exotic / Journey — through our anecdotic revue." He reminds the audience that Pippin's quest for meaning is at the same time the audience's journey through *Pippin* and he reminds them that the structure of the following scenes, although they present a quest which ought to move like a rite of passage from questing start to liminal middle to fulfilling end, is likewise a series of anecdotes.

Each scene is a discreet attempt by Pippin to find fulfillment in one or another role in life. In scene two, he quickly finds that there is no use trying to live under the rules of his father, Charlemagne, who looks down on his education (despite nominal praise) and commands a life of leisure. Despite Charlemagne's protestations that an educated man is not a good soldier (16), Pippin in scene three tries to find fulfillment in war. That fails to satisfy him, and so in scene four he accepts the *carpe diem* advice of his grandmother Berthe and seeks the joys of sex. These leave him feeling "empty and vacant" and he still longs for "something worthwhile" (35). He finds a new chance for worth in political revolution. In scene five, he assassinates his father as he prays at Arles, only to discover that he has no political ability whatsoever. Fortunately, Charlemagne returns to life to keep the kingdom in order. Scene six is a moment of despair in which the Leading Player offers his encouragement. In scene seven, Pippin meets Catherine and her son Theo. He initially rejects them because he is too "extraordinary" for their ordinary life, but eventually, in the finale (scene eight), comes to believe that the ordinary life does hold fulfillment for him.

The metatheatrical play frequently interrupts the quest narrative, as the Leading Player repeatedly arrives to comment on the action, to lead Pippin from place to place and to address the audience directly. Also, we see Charlemagne remarking that his "part is to be portrayed by an actor of enormous power" (8), Charlemagne's resurrection, the presence of a microphone for Pippin's political revolution, and Berthe's sing-a-long—complete with a giant parchment so that the audience will know the lyrics. The metatheatricality culminates in that never before seen climax, when the Leading Player invites Pippin to achieve glory through self-immolation, so that he will "become a glorious synthesis of life and death" (76). When Pippin refuses his suicide, the Leading Player declares an end to the play. He and the other Players clear the stage of props and scenery, turn off all but a single work light, and strip Pippin, as well as Catherine and Theo, Pippin's adopted family, of their costumes. They order the orchestra to stop playing and leave the family alone on a dark stage. The metatheatricality, from the beginning to the end of the play, keeps the audience at a distance from the action, and keeps us aware that Pippin and the actor playing "Pippin" are two people inhabiting the same body. More importantly, it emphasizes the fact that in each of scenes two through seven Pippin seeks fulfillment in a different social role: son, warrior, lover, revolutionary and finally ordinary husband and father. Pippin changes which parts he performs, but he does not develop psychologically. His identity at any given time is the role he is performing, and it is not clear that there is anything more to him than the role. In the end, he chooses a role that makes him feel "trapped ... but happy" (83 [original ellipsis]). He is trapped not only inside Catherine's ordinary family, but trapped inside the role of husband and father. Even in this final moment, Pippin's development is not the creation of a coherent subjectivity, but the acceptance of his final social role. He accomplishes his quest when he comes to understand that his "something completely fulfilling" is life in a role, that only when one has a role to inhabit can one progress through life logically and coherently.[15]

To summarize briefly: The concept musicals *Company* and *Pippin* use discontinuous narrative in order to disrupt our normal expectations regarding character development. Techniques of discontinuity prevent the plays' protagonists from learning from their experiences as they experience them, and prevent any sense that one action or experience will cause another. They also prevent the audience from understanding the characters as psychologically and logically coherent people. Instead, their identities arise from an amalgamation of characteristics displayed in the discontinuous episodes. At least until the plays reach their climactic scenes, their identities are underdetermined in the sense that we cannot discern a coherent causation behind their actions.

If Robert and Pippin are underdetermined with respect to identity, characters in Greek Old Comedy are overdetermined; that is, they have too much identity. As mentioned at the beginning of this article, Greek presumptions regarding identity found coherence in a behavioral orientation toward success in life rather than in psychological subjectivity. A Greek audience could find development in a character from Homer's epic poems or from a tragedy by recognizing alterations in the character's orientation, alterations that come about as consequences of the narrative's events. In these genres, both narrative sequences and characterization are coherent in the sense that they follow discernible logics of causation. When a tragic character changes his orientation or has it changed by outside forces according to the tragedy's logical progression, the former orientation is abandoned in lieu of the latter because the two are incongruous. Old Comedy, in contrast, features discontinuous narrative techniques that subvert audiences' expectations regarding coherent characterization. As Michael Silk has written, Aristophanic narrative structure "is best seen as a sequence of relational states between one interest or party — often, but not always, one focal individual — and the world at large. The pattern involves a series of five states or stages: *A* dissatisfaction, *B* quest, *C* conflict, *D* victory, *E* celebration" (263). There is no necessary causal connection between each state, especially between conflict and victory. Because of Old Comedy's discontinuous narrative technique, characters tend to behave in one way in one scene and in another way in another scene, without any causal reason for each change.[16] Yet because the behaviors succeed one another illogically and thus because any behavioral pattern could — and often does — return without reason, the different, incongruous orientations coexist within a single character. The character is the aggregation of all these different behavioral orientations.[17]

The intruder-scenes that appear in most of Aristophanes' comedies provide a good example of the episodic nature of narrative structure and the overdetermined nature of characterization. For example, in Aristophanes' *Acharnians*, the Athenian farmer Dicaeopolis has concluded a private peace treaty with Sparta to bring an end to the Peloponnesian War, at least for himself, but no sooner has he established his peace than a series of interlopers arrive to beg a share in it. First comes a fellow farmer named Dercetes asking for a share of the peace because the Thebans have stolen his two cattle (ll. 1022–23). While we might expect Dicaeopolis to give generously of his truce to help a neighbor who has suffered like he has, he refuses.[18] On the other hand, a newlywed woman arrives and asks for a piece of the truce so that her new husband will not have to serve in the war. Dicaeopolis initially refuses to help this man escape the war. But, after the bride makes it clear that she is not so much interested in keeping her husband as in keeping her own opportunity for sex, Dicaeopolis gives her some of the truce. He wants to benefit her, rather than her draft-dodging husband, "because she is a woman and it's not right that she suffer from the war" (ll. 1058–68). One wartime victim, the helpless woman, wins Dicaeopolis's support, while another, the seemingly helpless farmer, is rejected out of hand. Dicaeopolis switches from one behavioral orientation to another as each episode occurs without any clearly logical development of character.[19]

Birds has many intruders, nine human interlopers who come seeking benefits from the newly founded city of Cloudcuckooland, four divine visitors who want to disrupt the city's creation, and the Titan Prometheus, the divine yet special friend of humans, who gives the hero Peisetaerus a strategy for outwitting the gods. Peisetaerus is gracious to some, tolerant toward others, dismissive of some, and brutal to others; there is rarely any apparent reason why some interlocutors find favor and others find fisticuffs. *Peace* also has intruders who attempt to disrupt the celebrations of the hero Trygaeus after he has, on a broader scale than Dicaeopolis, established an end to the Peloponnesian War. In *Wasps*, a few intruders enter to take to task Philocleon, the old man who has been saved from the corruption of city politics only to embark on a misguided life of debauchery. In all these plays, the intruders are inessential to the plot of the comedy, but serve as opportunities for the comic hero to deal with trouble and for the audience to enjoy the heroes' illogical behavior towards them. Inevitably, the hero triumphs over the interlopers, although his means are rarely consistent or consequential. Most often, the triumph is itself a piece of comic cleverness devised for the moment rather than a reasonable action. The episodic nature of these scenes allows the comic heroes, without cause or reason, to add new aspects to their identities insofar as they display new behaviors. The discontinuous changes may make the hero seem, as in the case of Dicaeopolis, now petulant and callous, now noble and generous, now carefree and hedonistic, but the good of the comedy is superior to the consistent characterization of the comic hero. The audience is given no means for discerning which behavior ought to be assigned priority as the real identity, and can only describe Dicaeopolis as petulant *and* callous *and* noble *and* generous *and* carefree *and* hedonistic. In a sense, he is like Pippin since he changes with each scene with no apparent logic to his alterations, but because of the Greek expectations regarding an identity based in behavior, Dicaeopolis's identity is not a cipher behind a series of role-based personae but the aggregation of the personae themselves.

The discontinuity of Aristophanic comedy makes possible even more complex manipulations of identity, such as the *Acharnians* episode in which Dicaeopolis defends himself to the chorus of Acharnians, who are angry because of Dicaeopolis's private peace. This long speech (ll. 497–556) is a rhetorical tour de force of overdetermined identity. Instead of the comic hero switching sequentially from one behavior to another across several episodes, as in the intruder-scenes, this speech features a character who changes illogically from one line to the next. Dicaeopolis makes his defense after visiting the house of Euripides, where he has borrowed from the trage-dian the costume of Telephus, a mythological king who (in a lost tragedy by Euripides) disguised himself as a beggar in order to infiltrate the Greek army. When Dicaeopolis begins his defense speech, then, he is disguised as a character from a Euripidean tragedy, namely a king who disguised himself as a beggar.[20] He alludes to his beggar's appearance (l. 498), even though the chorus and the audience would of course know very well who he is and would not be deceived by the disguise. He also directly addresses the audi-ence (l. 497) and asks their indulgence for discussing serious matters "while performing a comedy" (l. 499), since "comedy too knows what is just" (l. 500). He thus calls attention to the fact that he is an actor in a comic play. The greatest moment of illogicality comes when he uses the pronoun "I" to refer not to Dicaeopolis nor to Telephus, but to the playwright Aristophanes himself (ll. 501–503). The single individual onstage is Dicaeopolis *and* Tele-phus *and* the disguised beggar *and* the comic actor *and* Aristophanes. Each of the various *personae* that comprise this single individual has its own ori-entation toward success in life, and thus, in a sense, its own identity. As Dicaeopolis, the person wants to enjoy his peace. As Telephus, he will mea-sure success by his persuasive ability. As Aristophanes, he will be successful both by teaching the audience justice and by winning the comic festival. And so forth. But because of Old Comedy's ability to pack several incongruous behaviors into a single individual, each of these *personae* is only an aspect of this man's overdetermined identity.[21]

Just as the intruder-scenes caused us to understand Dicaeopolis as both callous and noble, so the defense speech on a more minute level causes us to understand him as the amalgamation of multiple *personae*. The comedy's character is, therefore, similar to the concept musicals' characters inasmuch as their discontinuous narratives require us to "add up" their characteristics, rather than to trace a consequentialist development, in order to form a com-plete understanding of who they are. They differ, however, because of the ways in which the genres, and their more consequentialist generic relatives, construct identity. The characters in the concept musicals, even when they change social roles, remain psychologically static from one episode to the next, and so the amalgamated identity contains no incongruity. Their behaviors change, but, because audiences, accustomed to the more traditional flow of Rodgers-and-Hammerstein–style musicals, expect character development to consist in psychological change, their identities do not alter with their behaviors, at least not until the final scene of each play, when change is in fact marked by a clear, psychologically significant decision. In contrast, the characters in Old Comedy are dynamic to the point of an amalgamated incoherence. Because Greek audiences, accustomed to the logical causation of tragedy and epic, expect character development to consist in reorientation of a character's behavior, they experience too much character development when they "add up" the different behaviors into a single identity. While the American musicals in the end satisfy audience expectation for development by allowing their protagonists to change, the Greek comedies never infringe on their protagonists' creative power to change by bringing them to a single, coherent behavioral orientation towards a single, coherent conception of success in life. Dicaeopolis and his fellow comic characters incessantly maintain their ability, as it were, to spin around and orient themselves in whatever direction is best at any moment.[22]

EAST CAROLINA UNIVERSITY

Notes

1. The episodic nature of Old Comedy is well recognized by modern scholars. Segal 132 calls the comedy of Aristophanes and his contemporaries "a kind of episodic vaudeville," in an attempt to suggest that their work did not reach the level of 'true' comedy. Silk 256–300 is more generous in his understanding of Aristophanes' discontinuities and their non–Aristotelian nature.

2. The term "concept musical" was coined by critic Martin Gottfried (qtd. at Huber 12). The central concept usually takes precedence over plot, often with the result that plots are episodic and non–Aristotelian. On the difficulty of defining the concept musical, see Banfield 147–48, and Miller "Concept Musical" 187–90.

3. I of course do not claim that this very brief description of the modern self is in any way comprehensive. Outside of the genre of musicals, audience expectations regarding character are likely to be very different from this mostly Romantic picture. One does not walk into a modernist or postmodernist play and expect to find this type of character. Musicals, though, have historically been a very conservative, rarely experimental genre.

4. This summary of the ancient Greek self is no more comprehensive than the picture of the modern self, and probably more controversial. For the argument that

Greek conceptions of identity do not inhere primarily in psychological descriptions, see Gill and Given.

5. Swain 316–17 criticizes the use of Cassie in *A Chorus Line* as the former star who is willing to take a job in the chorus precisely because Cassie reintroduces the frame's pretense into the otherwise demarcated internal episodes.

6. I cite the revised libretto published in 1996 (from two productions staged in 1995). The play was originally produced on Broadway in 1970; the revisions introduced in the 1995 versions do not affect my argument. I cite musicals by page number from their published libretti; I cite Greek plays by line number, and all translations are mine.

7. The exception is Act I, Scene 3 and Act II, Scene 3, the two scenes with Peter and Susan, which must be played in that order. In Act I, Peter announces to Robert their impending divorce. In Act II, the divorce has taken place, although Peter and Susan still live together.

8. Cf. Larry's remark: "We've gotten older every year and he seems to stay exactly the same" (p. 80).

9. The self-deception of the song is embedded in the dissonances of its accompaniment. See Banfield 166–67. The song was originally intended for the spot now occupied by "Being Alive," but was cut. It was reinserted into the play, at the end of Act I, in the 1995 revision. It was removed from the finale, says Sondheim (quoted in Banfield), because "we decided that ... that audience might not *get* the lie that Robert is telling himself." In the original conception of the show, then, Robert would not even have developed in the finale; the song "Being Alive" satisfies audience expectations for some development in Robert's character.

10. *Company* has the widely spread reputation of being anti-marriage, a stance which its authors have repeatedly denied. Audiences seem to be seduced by Robert's lack of development and his immature view of marriage because they assume that, since Robert's knowledge remains static for most of the play, his perspective for that entire time is the author's perspective. Besides the obvious fallacy of attributing a character's views to his creators, audiences and critics miss the fact that Robert does change in the end and more importantly miss the fact that Robert is himself short-sighted with regard to the couples' marriages through the entire play.

11. Orchestrator Jonathan Tunick calls attention to the parallel between Robert's immaturity in "Someone Is Waiting" and the first half of "Being Alive" by reusing the "Someone Is Waiting" melody in the orchestrations when Robert sings "Someone to crowd you with love" (Banfield 169–70).

12. Besides a reference to the birthday party scenes, Amy's remark also refers back to her own refusal of Robert's inappropriate marriage proposal. She explained to him that, in order to get married, "you have to want to marry *some*body, not just some*body*" (p. 68).

13. Although I did not have space to discuss metatheatrical devices in *Company*, they are present, primarily in the form of comment songs such as "The Little Things You Do Together" and "You Could Drive a Person Crazy." Metatheatricality is of course not limited to concept musicals. The recent *Urinetown*, for example, uses metatheatricality effectively to emphasize satire rather than narrative discontinuity.

14. He later repeats this same language at Catherine's house, when he complains that the farm life is not appropriate for one as "Extraordinary" as he (pp. 61–63).

Fastrada, Pippin's stepmother, uses the word ironically when she claims that she is "an ordinary housewife and mother" (p. 12). In the Finale, when Pippin initially hesitates to undergo his immolation and asks why the Leading Player himself does not attempt the glorious finale, the Player responds, "we're just ordinary, run-of-the-mill people" (76). The ultimate Finale, with Pippin's decision to remain with Catherine and the removal of all theatrical elements from his life, signals what philosopher Charles Taylor has called the "affirmation of ordinary life." (See Taylor.) He sees this affirmation as a rejection of (among other things) the military ethic represented in *Pippin* by Charlemagne, and argues that the affirmation of ordinary life is a key component in the modern self.

15. Mordden 109 suggests that Pippin, once he meets Catherine and Theo, "ultimately decides that there is no quest. There's merely life." He misses the fact that ordinary life is as much a performed role as any other.

16. This is not to say that Aristophanes' comedies completely lack coherence. Rather than coherence based in narration or characterization, the plays tend to find unity in thematic concerns, imagery and even musical structure. See, e.g., Parker's interesting comments on *Acharnians*' thematic and musical "subtle symmetry" (Parker *Songs* 123). One of this journal's referees makes the excellent point that the unity of Aristophanes' plays is "concept-driven" in the same manner as the concept musicals.

17. Silk reaches a different conclusion regarding the discontinuity of characterization in Aristophanes. He argues for a "kaleidoscopic impression" that demonstrates "a rich sense of human possibility, and the range of human possibility, not in the realist terms of a finite individual, but in some other, beyond the individual altogether" (245). Cf. his description of *Wasps*' Philocleon as seeming "to transcend the bounds of an individual" (255). Silk's sense of a "finite individual" is, I think, too limited. Similarly, I cannot accept arguments such as Fisher, which denies Dicaeopolis's claim that comedy can speak seriously because it cannot fathom multiple personae in a single individual. Just as present-day audiences are able to pick out Robert and Pippin as coherent individuals although they are underdetermined with respect to the causes of their identities, so I think an ancient Greek audience would have been able to pick out characters in Old Comedy as single, finite individuals. That is, comic characters do not stand in contradiction to characters in tragedy and epic; they merely take the techniques of characterization already present in these genres that are more organic (because more solidly grounded in logical causation) and extend the techniques to their extremes by dispensing with the logics that make character development coherent. Comic characters are finite and individual without being consequentialist or logically coherent. For more on this topic, see my forthcoming book, entitled *"Being Inside and Not Inside": Ethics and Identity in Greek Drama*, whose arguments are adumbrated in Given.

18. Evidence from inscriptions shows that there was a man named Dercetes alive in 425 B.C., and it is possible that Aristophanes was making a satirical charge against him; this might explain Dicaeopolis's refusal. (See MacDowell 159–60; Parker "Eupolis" 206.) The name may be, however, merely a coincidence. As our knowledge stands, Dicaeopolis seems merely capricious in this scene. Capriciousness seems to me a sufficient explanation for Dicaeopolis's behavior; to ask for a more rational basis for his decisions is to ask for a more psychologically coherent characterization than the play calls for.

19. Compton-Engle argues that Dicaeopolis does develop coherently during the play, from a rustic to an urban identity and from one who prefers a rural economy based on fair bartering to one who sets up shop in the urban agora and bilks his customers with deceitful barters. She suggests that after Dicaeopolis visits Euripides' house there is no reason to believe that he ever returns to his rural home and that after the parabasis he returns to the city itself (367–68). The former argument is probably incorrect, since Dicaeopolis presumably returns to the place where the chorus is angrily awaiting his defense speech, i.e., Dicaeopolis's own house. The latter argument is certainly incorrect, since Dicaeopolis's first line after the parabasis is "These here are the boundaries of my agora" (l. 719). He has brought boundary-stones out of his house and set them up to demarcate the space in which his private peace holds good; no such action would be necessary at the urban agora. Still, it is important to note that space in Aristophanes is as discontinuous as narrative and identity. It is easy in Old Comedy for Dicaeopolis to be in whatever space is right for the moment, whether it be his rural home or Euripides' urban house, just by walking across the stage. See Silk 272.

20. On the complex parody of Euripides' *Telephus* in *Acharnians*, see Dobrov 37–53; Rau 26–41; Slater 49–61. Elizabeth Scharffenberger's paper at the Comparative Drama Conference has also influenced my understanding of the *Telephus* parody.

21. Incongruities in comic characters' identities can even extend to contradictions. For example, the character Agathon in Aristophanes' *Thesmophoriazusae* is simultaneously both male and female.

22. I would like to thank the insightful referees for *Text & Presentation* and all those who commented so congenially on this paper at the Comparative Drama Conference. Their suggestions have greatly enriched this final version.

References Cited

Banfield, Stephen. *Sondheim's Broadway Musicals*. Ann Arbor: University of Michigan Press, 1993.

Bristow, Eugene K., and J. Kevin Butler. "*Company*, About Face! The Show That Revolutionized the American Musical." *American Music* 5 (1987): 241–54.

Compton-Engle, Gwendolyn. "From Country to City: The Persona of Dicaeopolis in Aristophanes' *Acharnians*." *Classical Journal* 94 (1999): 359–73.

Dobrov, Gregory W. *Figures of Play: Greek Drama and Metafictional Poetics*. Oxford: Oxford University Press, 2001.

Fisher, N. R. E. "Multiple Personalities and Dionysiac Festivals: Dicaeopolis in Aristophanes' *Acharnians*." *Greece and Rome* 40 (1993): 31–47.

Hirson, Roger O., and Stephen Schwartz. *Pippin*. New York: Drama Book Specialists, 1975.

Huber, Eugene R. "Stephen Sondheim and Harold Prince: Collaborative Contributions to the Development of the Modern Concept Musical, 1970–81." Ph.D. diss., New York University, 1990.

Gill, Christopher. *Personality in Greek Epic, Tragedy and Philosophy: The Self in Dialogue*. Oxford: Clarendon Press, 1996.

Given, John. "Intellectuals in Theory and on Stage: Euripides, Aristophanes, Protagoras." Ph.D. diss., University of Michigan, 2001.

MacDowell, Douglas M. "The Nature of Aristophanes' *Akharnians*." *Greece and Rome* 30 (1983): 143–62.

Miller, Scott. *From Assassins to West Side Story: The Director's Guide to Musical Theatre.* Portsmouth, N.H.: Heinemann, 1996.

_____. "*Assassins* and the Concept Musical." In *Stephen Sondheim: A Casebook,* ed. Joanne Gordon, 187–204. New York and London: Garland, 1997.

Mordden, Ethan. *One More Kiss: The Broadway Musical in the 1970s.* New York: Palgrave Macmillan, 2003.

Parker, L. P. E. "Eupolis or Dicaeopolis?" *Journal of Hellenic Studies* 111 (1991): 203–208.

_____. *The Songs of Aristophanes.* Oxford: Clarendon Press, 1997.

Rau, Peter. *Paratragodia: Untersuchung einer komischen Form des Aristophanes.* Münschen: C. H. Beck'sche, 1967.

Segal, Erich. "The *Phusis* of Comedy." *Harvard Studies in Classical Philology* 77 (1973): 129–36.

Silk, M. S. *Aristophanes and the Definition of Comedy.* Oxford: Oxford University Press, 2000.

Slater, Niall W. *Spectator Politics: Metatheatre and Performance in Aristophanes.* Philadelphia: University of Pennsylvania Press, 2002.

Sondheim, Stephen, and George Furth. *Company: A Musical Comedy.* New York: Theatre Communications Group, 1996.

Swain, Joseph P. *The Broadway Musical: A Critical and Musical Survey.* New York and Oxford: Oxford University Press, 1990.

Taylor, Charles. *Sources of the Self: The Making of Modern Identity.* Cambridge: Harvard University Press, 1989.

Views, Values and Worship
Religion and Social Class in the Plays of Romulus Linney

John Fleming

Abstract

The subject of religion runs as an undercurrent in the prolific career of American playwright Romulus Linney. Eschewing doctrinal debates, Linney uses the stress of religion to evoke primal states of emotion and to get characters to confront core aspects of their being, but notably the impact of religion tends to manifest itself differently depending on the character's social class. By looking at Holy Ghosts, Heathen Valley, Why the Lord Come to Sand Mountain, *and* Ambrosio, *one sees that Linney's lower-class characters tend to engage in non-mainstream or non-traditional religious practices and through their religion they find their identity, human fellowship, and temporal redemption. In contrast, Linney's upper-class characters, having a base level of identity and comfort, struggle with different issues and find their religion in conflict with their deeper nature and social commitments. In Linney's canon, religion both saves and damns, and often it is a matter of social class.*

Though never having a major commercial success, playwright Romulus Linney has earned critical acclaim from the theatre community, if not from the academic realm.[1] With over 30 plays to his credit, Linney has tackled a diversity of subjects, and within theatre circles Linney is known for his history plays, for his mastery of the one-act form, and for what Charles Paikert calls "a series of lyrical Gothic plays laced with primal themes of sex and religion set in a quasi-mythic Appalachia" (5). *Holy Ghosts* (1971), *Heathen Valley* (1987), and *Why the Lord Come to Sand Mountain* (1984) stand as the best examples of this genre and are three of Linney's most produced plays.[2]

Having been raised in the South, Linney is acutely aware of the central role that religion plays in Southern life and culture. Thus, it is not surprising that Linney's Appalachian-based plays often occur within a religious

134

context. When asked about the role of religion in his work, Linney commented: "I'm profoundly uninterested in religion itself ... but people under the stress of religion are brought to a pitch of human passion and emotion rather more quickly. There is almost nothing that makes people face themselves and all sorts of things more quickly than religious issues" (Wilmeth 198). In lieu of detailed theological debates, Linney uses religion to evoke primal states of emotion and to get characters to confront core aspects of their being, but notably the impact of religion tends to manifest itself differently depending on the character's social class.

While the religious practice of snake handling has struck some reviewers as "gruesome," "repulsive," and "revolting,"[3] it also provides the context for Linney's most produced play, the comedy-drama, *Holy Ghosts*. While Linney's southern plays are usually set in the past in the Appalachian Mountains, *Holy Ghosts* is a present-day story, set in an unnamed location in the rural south, probably somewhere in Tennessee. Socially and economically, the members of this sect of Pentecostal snake handlers live at the bottom of American life. Frank Rich aptly notes: "They have nothing but their religion, and their religion is a despised minority creed of the dispossessed"(17).

In *Holy Ghosts*, the negotiation between religion and social class involves both the textual aspect of the social-class status of the congregation as well as the meta-text of audience versus character subject position. The audience, presumably, is more middle class whereas the characters live on the fringes of society. Being an illegal, non-mainstream form of worship, snake handling is a ripe target for satire, condescension, trivialization, or some other form of representation that marks the snake handlers as objects of ridicule. In contrast to what might be expected, Linney compassionately portrays these marginalized figures as worthy of respect. In the *New Yorker*, Mimi Kramer writes: "Who would want to spend an evening with such characters? Who would care about them, except out of a sense of moral obligation?... But in the course of the evening your sympathies shift and you change your mind about whether or not [this sect] is a justifiable refuge from an imperfect world" (60).

At the outset, it is a legitimate question to ask why anyone would risk death by handling venomous snakes and/or by drinking strychnine? However, through the course of the play, the audience realizes that each character is some type of social outcast or has some type of spiritual or emotional cancer. A sampling of the congregation includes: a couple of gay truck drivers, a man dying of cancer, a woman dominated by her husband and everyone else in her life, a promiscuous woman who has worked her way through all the mainstream churches in town, and a man haunted by visions of his dead birddog. They come to this church because they feel they "have no place else to go" (*Holy Ghosts* 128). Rejected by mainstream society, they desperately seek human fellowship and individual recognition. As one character says, "What would we do, if we couldn't come to church?" (128). By society's standards they are failures and outcasts, but the church allows them to become the opposite of what they are in the world; they find support and tolerance within the sect, and the extremity and intensity of their worship mirrors the depths of their pain.

When Coleman, an outsider to the group, views this congregation he expresses the mainstream view that these people "are not all right in the head" (137); in contrast, one of the worshipers exclaims, "[W]hen we come in here, we felt the power! ... Because for the first time in our miserable lives, we knowed what a victory was!" (167). Likewise, the leader of the sect passionately defends their practices: "Lots of people say we're crazy, to need this worship this strong, this bad! But we do! That is our nature!" (170). For the rural poor of this sect, religion is not about damnation, but rather is about salvation, and it is a salvation rooted in the here and now. For those who have nothing, religion offers an avenue to momentary victory, to a sense of fulfillment. The methods are extreme, but they fulfill a need that has gone unmet and offer a confirmation of their existence. Emerging from the bottom of American social life, these characters desire an archetypal sense of "Home," and so they seek the refuge the church offers, a place where they will be accepted and not judged.

When the play moves in to the enactment of the snake handling ceremony, the vitality of their worship offers a glimpse of ecstasy rarely seen. Recounting his own viewing of snake handling ceremonies, Linney remarks: "I felt connected to rituals going back to ancient times. I felt like I was watching a Dionysian revel" (Papier). He adds: "Sure, [snake handling] is a primitive ritual, but it also must be an overwhelming religious experience. Even if you're losing everything, to win that one must be extraordinary" (Williams 15). Through the wild, ecstatic, spasmodic worship celebration the characters cathartically release all the sorrow and tension of their lives. Frank Rich comments: "The writhing fits of prayer, hymn singing, stomping, and sobbing might easily have degenerated into [a] lunatic side show.... Instead we find ourselves unexpectedly moved by the grace of lost souls who risk everything from ridicule to madness to death, in the blind hope that they might somehow yet be found" (17). The victory associated with snake handling offers momentary redemption as they achieve a sense of recognition and power that fulfills a spiritual quest while also giving them a sense of community and fellowship; this sect is their sanctuary from the everyday world and all its troubles.

Historically, the primary practitioners of snake handling have been rural, white people living on the lower rungs of the economic ladder.[4] Neither satirizing nor promoting snake handlers, Linney's play views them with compassion, understanding, and a measure of respect rarely accorded society's dispossessed. As he says: "The point of the play is the very unusual ways in which people find (to use a religious term) their personal salvation, (in the words of psychology) their adjustment to life, and (to use an aesthetic expression) their philosophy. [The play is about] what helps people stay alive when they're having trouble doing so" (Albright 16). In part, religion serves as a vehicle for the rural poor to persevere.

In *Heathen Valley*, winner of the American Theatre Critics Association Award for Best New American Play produced outside New York, the negotiation between religion and social class is more pronounced. Loosely based on historical events, *Heathen Valley* tells the story of the establishment and disintegration of an Episcopal mission in the mid–1800s in a remote region of the Appalachian Mountains in North Carolina.[5] The play also embodies the way in which social class affects religious belief, worship, and values. Bishop Ames, having heard about a valley that has "forgotten God," decides to establish a mission. His goal is to bring them "the Word of God" (9), to save their souls, and to create a spiritual home in the valley. Starns, a semiliterate drifter who grew up in the mountains, is appointed Deacon for this mission. Starns embraces the role because he sees the mission as an opportunity to improve the material lives of these impoverished people. While still expressing his belief that "Virgins don't have no babies" (7), Starns agrees to serve as deacon, proclaiming, "If you give them a decent life, then I will believe what you believe" (20). Starns's pragmatic compromise on religious issues embodies his social-class concern for first meeting fundamental material needs. At the same time it connotes to the historical dynamic of missions: missionaries have the economic safety-net of the church, and via the financial backing of the church they are empowered to engage in the *quid pro quo* of bartering material goods in exchange for the spiritual beliefs of the local inhabitants.

Since missionary activity is, in part, founded on negotiated terms, the playing out of the relationship relies on each side fulfilling its terms of the agreement. At the same time it potentially places two value systems at odds; in *Heathen Valley*, the Bishop's spiritual idealism ultimately clashes with Starns's pragmatism. As the Bishop travels through the middle and upper class portions of society raising money, Starns is left to run the mission. During this time Starns allows the inhabitants of Heathen Valley to live according to a combination of mountain mythology, superstition, and Christianity. While Starns compromises to achieve practical gains in their standard of living, the Bishop insists "a Christian cannot live in barbaric illusions" (37).

The contrasting value systems spur the second-act dialectic over the spiritual versus temporal role of the church in the world. Billy, an orphan turned missionary assistant, argues that the mission succeeds because "It's a farm that prospers, a school that teaches, a hospital that heals, and a church that doesn't presume. Isn't that enough?" (38). For the Bishop, it is not enough because "We must hunger! And Thirst! For God!" (39). As he becomes increasingly, rigidly ascetic, the Bishop rejects the communal function of the church. He even declares: "Human happiness is a temptation. It does not really exist. Human life, by itself, is nothing.... Worse than nothing. It is dirt. Where you will lie, when your soul stands at judgment" (40). For the Bishop, religion and the quest for God are primarily about the afterlife.

In his drive to impose his will, the Bishop insists that everyone associated with the mission wear cassocks. The Bishop declares: "This cassock teaches us humility. It makes us look the same before God. The way to salvation is to become no one, for God" (41). Starns rebuts: "Horseshit. The way to salvation is to be somebody, *for* somebody!" (41). Thus their opposing roads to salvation are the impersonal, lose-your-identity, spiritual approach versus the personal, gain-an-identity, service approach. While faith versus good works is a long-standing theological debate, in this case their theological differences might stem from a practical difference. The Bishop comes from a society that bases itself on position and prestige, and so from his view, salvation requires the reverse — humility and losing one's self. But the socially and economically downtrodden, the "Other," must first gain self-respect by finding an identity.

While the Bishop stresses tradition and praising God, Starns declares, "I don't *care* about no centuries of no church!! I care about this place right here and right now!" (41). With an almost Liberation Theology–like emphasis on viewing the world from the perspective of the poor, Starns's primary concern is in building a new social order. Sin and salvation are secondary to the praxis of brotherly love and providing basic human needs. But while Starns has built up the mission, he gives credit to the Bishop because the Bishop provided the financial resources for the mission's material successes. As missionary to the people, but also religious subject of the Bishop, Starns faces a conflict of loyalties. When Starns ultimately chooses obedience to the Bishop over helping someone who was injured while working on the Sabbath, the local people lose faith in the religion, and lose faith in Starns, because they "lowrate praying, when a body is cut and bleeding" (42). In this instance, Starns betrays his own nature as he violates his avowed values and principles; however, Starns's loyalty goes unrewarded as the Bishop betrays him by turning apostate.

When the Bishop tells Starns he is leaving the Episcopal Church in order "to save his own soul" (43), the final threads of the theological argument are laid out:

Starns: Maybe you love God, but you shore don't love us.
Bishop: It is God I serve.
Starns: You serve yourself is who you serve!...
Bishop: You can put man before God. I cannot!
Starns: I will put Cora and Harlan before God. They need me! God don't!
Bishop: God is not fellowship! God, Starns, is love!!
Starns: Oh, no, he ain't! Whatever God is, that he ain't! [43–44].

This exchange raises the recurring questions: In religion, should spiritual or temporal responsibility take precedence? At what point do love and duty towards God conflict with human fellowship? While Linney tends not to judge his characters, this play suggests that the Bishop is wrong for abandoning the mission. (With the Bishop gone, the Episcopal Church withdraws its financial support, and the valley sinks back to its barbaric ways.) Through Starns, the idea exists that perhaps one can best worship God through service to fellow human beings, and one suspects that the Bishop's turning to Catholicism shall bring him no closer to his goal than did any of the other religions he has tried. In Billy's eyes, he is the "Judas Bishop" (48) who betrayed and abandoned Starns. Linney himself refers to the historical incident as "a story of regeneration betrayed" (Arkatov).[6]

Overall, the Bishop's desire to create an Episcopal mission in an Appalachian valley is complicated by his failure to recognize the dynamics of social class and culture. The traditional notion of pride as one of the seven deadly sins is antithetical to a class of people who must first learn to have pride in themselves and their way of life. Starns's refrain line, "Poor folks has poor ways" (51), is a plea for understanding. It suggests that the simple folk have a different way of living life, so do not judge them, but rather try to understand and accept them for who they are.[7] While Starns is perpetually pragmatic, the Bishop is resolutely idealistic. Thus, the Bishop refuses to compromise with the locals' mix of material gains and religious faith; by acting on his religious conviction, the Bishop turns his back on those he came to save. In *Heathen Valley*, the different attitudes towards religion are, in part, rooted in social-class considerations.

The need to meld faith with a concomitant acceptance of different social standards is also a theme that runs through Linney's one-act play *Why the Lord Come to Sand Mountain*; in that play a rather bourgeois St. Peter would much rather spend time singing hymns with the prosperous middle class, whereas the Lord seeks out the poorest of the poor at the top of the mountain.

Discovering an unmarried couple with 14 children living in a broken-down shack, Peter never tries to understand them or their situation but rather rushes to judgment and blames their poor living conditions on their not being married, not going to church, and too much drinking. In contrast, the Lord forbids any further preaching or moralizing and instead accepts the mountain couple on their own terms. They break out the brandy and sit around telling tall-tales, "Smoky Mountain head benders," and religious parables told from a mountain perspective. When the couple starts to tell "Jesus Tales," they put Biblical stories such as Joseph and Mary into their own terms, giving the Biblical characters mountain characteristics. Stuck in his superficial ways, Peter only sees the surface while failing to grasp that their stories reflect their views of life. The Lord acknowledges this couple's need for understanding and acceptance by his appreciation and encouragement of their tales. Via their version of "Old Man Joseph and His Family," the Lord can see part of himself in them, and they in him. In contrast, like the Bishop in *Heathen Valley*, St. Peter is never able to drop the classicist bent of his religious views and accept the rural poor on their own terms.

Moving from the poor of Appalachia to a 16th-century Spanish monastery reveals a shift in the issues facing characters confronting religious views and values. *Ambrosio* (1992) is loosely based on Matthew Lewis's gothic novel *The Monk* (1797) as well as histories of the Inquisition. As a monk, Ambrosio has his material needs met and thus has the luxury of pondering abstract philosophical issues such as the nature and source of evil. Renowned for his sermons, Ambrosio, like Bishop Ames, must contend with the sin of pride. However, unlike the married Episcopal Bishop, Ambrosio's more challenging deadly sin is lust; his celibacy has repressed his sexual urges, but now they are expressed through his simultaneous love for both a young male novice as well as a young maiden. Notably, in the four Linney plays discussed here none of the rural poor ever consider sexuality in terms of sin, but those coming from the hierarchical church always do.

In Ambrosio's case, however, his sexual indiscretions with both the male novice and the young maiden are viewed not so much in moral terms as they are placed within the socio-political context of the dynamics of the Inquisition, a force used as much for wealth and power as for any religious concerns. In the play, a rational Inquisitor General differentiates between a priest who has love affairs and those who commit heresy, or as he says, "[I see] Vanity, lunacy, and lust, but not heresy" (32). However, since the Inquisition is part of a hierarchical church, it is also subject to politics and power struggles, and so the rational Inquisitor becomes victim to an ambitious priest who supplants the Inquisitor to become Inquisitor General himself. This new Inquisitor is bent on burning thousands of so-called heretics; however, the audience has already seen that his zeal is rooted in the confiscation of the wealth and property of those convicted as well as in his elimination of rivals. Due to their social position, institutional religions seem almost inevitably intertwined with wealth, power, and politics and any spiritual concerns must compete with, and can be compromised by, those forces.

As a significant social force, religion offers a means of exploring fundamental aspects of human behavior. While Linney is not particularly interested in specific theological questions or doctrinal differences, his plays suggest that religion often manifests itself differently across social classes. Admittedly the discussion here is partly skewed by the fact that Linney's characters that come from more well-to-do backgrounds are members of the clergy and are part of a hierarchical church.[8]

That said, in general Linney's lower-class characters are less mainstream in their religious practices and through their religion they gain a sense of identity and at least momentary redemption. Alternatively, they use religion as a source of communal fellowship among a group of people who will not judge them, but rather who will understand and accept them. In contrast, Linney's upper-class characters, having a base level of identity and comfort, struggle with different issues, tend to be more judgmental, and find their religion in conflict with their deeper nature and social standing.

While there are many nuances to the ways in which social class affects religious views, values, concerns, and functions, Linney's observations, for the most part, are in accord with the findings of sociologists. Barbara Hargrove notes that there is "a greater saliency of religion for personal identity and adjustment for lower-class persons" and that "in general, higher-status people need less reassurance from religious experience, since they receive more from other sources" (142). Likewise, Hargrove reports that studies have shown that by being members of a religious congregation, lower-class members of society receive the psychological benefits of comfort and hope. She writes, "Rejected by the outside world, they find their worth affirmed in the religious fellowship and the assurance of acceptance by a loving God at the end of this vale of tears" (145). In these plays where individuals face themselves via religious issues, Linney depicts a near-universal human desire for understanding, acceptance, self-identity, and human fellowship. In the process, he suggests that in a society where economic status is a barometer of success, those on the lower rungs of the economic ladder often turn to religion for a sense of self-worth and communal belonging denied them by mainstream society.

TEXAS STATE UNIVERSITY

Notes

1. My own scholarship aside, the academic writing on Linney is limited to one dissertation, one article, a couple of interviews, and an entry in *American Playwrights since 1945: A Guide to Scholarship, Criticism, and Performance*. In contrast, a sampling of Linney's recognition from the theatrical community includes: two Obie Awards (*Tennessee* and Sustained Achievement), two American Theatre Critics Association Awards for Best New American Play Produced Outside New York (*Heathen Valley* and *2*), six plays in the Best Short Plays series, the American Academy of Arts and Letters Award of Merit (1999), The Dramatists Guild of America Madge and Sidney Kingsley Award in Playwriting (2001), the Edward Albee Last Frontier Playwright Award (2003) and the William Inge Distinguished Achievement in the American Theater Award (2003). A much more detailed consideration of Linney's life and career will be available in my book *Romulus Linney: Maverick of the Theatre* (in progress).

2. The listed dates are for first production; publication dates are in the "references cited" section.

3. Takiff refers to snake handling as "a seemingly repulsive activity" and as a form of "gruesome worship," while George Burley refers to it as "revolting" subject matter.

4. Productions have successfully used multi-racial casting.

5. The central plot line is based on the founding and dissolution of an Episcopal mission in Valle Crucis, North Carolina, in the 1840s–1850s, but the surrounding details and characters are fictionalized. Linney's Bishop Ames is based on Levi Silliman Ives, the Episcopal Bishop of the North Carolina Diocese during the 1840s. Linney sticks fairly close to the historical Bishop for his characterization of Ames, particularly in regards to the theological issues with which the Bishop struggled. Linney took more dramatic liberty in his depiction of the Bishop's Deacon: William West Skiles in real life, William Starns in the play. All the valley inhabitants are entirely Linney's creation.

6. The phrase "regeneration betrayed" originally comes from an unnamed reviewer of Linney's 1962 novel version of *Heathen Valley*.

7. The idea is reminiscent of one of Brecht's themes in *The Threepenny Opera*: Do not judge morality until material needs are met.

8. Linney has acknowledged his own distrust of organized religion, an institution he associates more with corruption and hypocrisy than he does with genuine spiritual quests.

References Cited

Albright, William. "Religious fervor fascinates author of 'Holy Ghosts.'" *Houston Post*. (24 April 1983): F–16.

Arkatov, Janice. "How Linney Found a Play in His Novel." *Los Angeles Times*. (17 August 1989): VI–5.

Burley, George. "'Holy Ghosts' hilarious and revolting." *Everett Herald*. 3 Aug. 1979: n.p. [Linney's files.]

Hargrove, Barbara. *The Sociology of Religion*. Arlington Heights, Illinois: AHM Publishing, 1979.

Kramer, Mimi. "The Theatre: That Old Time Religion." *New Yorker*. (24 August 1987): 60–61.

Linney, Romulus. *Ambrosio*. In *Seventeen Short Plays*. Newbury, Vermont: Smith and Kraus, 1992.

_____. Heathen Valley. New York: Dramatists Play Service, 1988.

_____. *Holy Ghosts* (with *The Sorrows of Frederick*). New York: Harcourt Brace Jovanovich, 1976.

_____. *Why the Lord Come to Sand Mountain*. In *Sand Mountain*. New York: Dramatists Play Service, 1986.

Paikert, Charles. "A Playwright Who Fashions Then Into Now." *New York Times*. (3 Dec. 1989): III 5, 28.

Papier, Deborah. "A Dramatist's 'Pitch of Ecstasy.'" *Washington Star*. (5 October 1980): n.p. [Linney's files.]

Rich, Frank. "Theater: 'Holy Ghosts,' Salvation for the Lowly." *New York Times*. (12 August 1987): C–17.

Takiff, Jonathan. "On Stage." Source Unknown. [Linney's files. Article appeared in conjunction with the 1980 People's Light and Theatre Company (Malvern, Pennsylvania) production of *Holy Ghosts*.]

Wilmeth, Don B. "An Interview with Romulus Linney." *Speaking on Stage: Interviews with Contemporary American Playwrights*. Edited with an introduction by Philip C. Kolin and Colby H. Kullman. Tuscaloosa: University of Alabama Press, 1996: 193–204.

Williams, Christian. "Southern Discomfort." *Washington Post* (2 Oct. 1980): F–15.

Deviant Speech
Understanding Churchill's Use of
Feminine Linguistics in *Top Girls*
Melody Schneider

Abstract

*Though critics have condemned the overlapping dialogue in Caryl
Churchill's* Top Girls *as a sign of communication failure among the
characters, in linguistic terms, the dialogue actually reflects effective
communication patterns found within all-female groups in real life.
Women, in both the play and real world, rely upon simultaneous
speech to help them facilitate conversation with each other and to help
demonstrate support and active listenership. The characters further
reflect authentic female discourse in other ways which initially appear
to demonstrate poor communication. Not only do characters speak
upon separate topics at the same time, but also they narrate extended
personal stories, seemingly ignoring the stories just related by other
characters. Yet, women have a multi-layered style of topic development, so it is expected that women will speak upon separate sub-topics within a main theme. Moreover, women exchange personal
narratives in order to demonstrate shared understanding of experiences. Thus, the play's language reveals the depth of Churchill's
knowledge about all-female group linguistics.*

If men's speech is taken to the yardstick for comparison, then women's speech becomes secondary or
a deviation that has to be explained [Romaine 157].

Throughout the years, critics have consistently analyzed the plays of
Caryl Churchill from a feminist perspective. In these analyses, feminists have
been very careful to consider her works in terms that do not rely upon the
traditional presumptions of patriarchal society. However, at times these critics have been incapable of recognizing their own culturally influenced biases.
One notable case of such unrecognized masculine bias can be found in the
linguistic standards that have been applied by feminist critics to Churchill's

work *Top Girls*. The play contains an unusual production note in which Churchill explains that the members of her cast of all-female characters will regularly speak their dialogue while other characters are still talking. The predominant critical reaction to this stage device has been that this type of overlapping speech demonstrates the language breakdown of Churchill's "isolated," self-centered characters into a non-communicative "cacophony of accents" (Brown 127; Aston 39; Kritzer 140). Yet, this widespread perspective fails to take into account the linguistic situation that naturally occurs in real-world groups made up only of women. In real life, most effective communication in all-female groups is carried on in a manner quite similar to that of the first act of the play. If one considers actual feminine linguistic trends then, one can see that the overlapping dialogue in *Top Girls* is not demonstrative of the characters' inability to communicate or connect with each other, nor is it included merely to create a sort of chaos on stage. Instead, Churchill's inclusion of this unique dialogue pattern, along with other aspects of all-female group discourse, demonstrates how truly attuned she is not just to women's concerns, but to their language as well.

Before beginning a discussion of Churchill's socio-linguistics, one important caveat must be made. There is no such thing as "women's speech." Language itself is too indeterminate, and far too many exceptions occur in male/female speech patterns to label any one aspect of language as belonging to either sex (Romaine 184). However, linguists such as Jennifer Coates (whose influential work *Women, Men and Language* will be the basis of much of the present analysis) have studied the influence of gender on conversational styles and have noted clear differences between the speech of men and women as certain language features tend to be more predominant in one sex or the other.

One of the most notable patterns found in the language used by women — and in the language used by Churchill's characters — is the consistent occurrence of simultaneous speech. Simultaneous speech refers to speech acts in which more than one person talks at the same time, thus causing the speakers' dialogue to overlap. In many public realms (realms most often based on masculine behavior norms), simultaneous speech is viewed negatively, as though the speakers are competing for control of the discussion floor. Feminists analyzing Churchill's work have echoed this unfavorable sentiment in their overwhelmingly critical interpretations of Churchill's use of simultaneous speech. For example, Margarete Rubik, in her article "The Silencing of Women in Feminist British Drama," made the claim that the *Top Girls* characters fail "to speak in an authentic female voice," and that, "[as] is indicated by the use of overlapping dialogue and constant interruptions, the women of both the past and the present fail to communicate or to establish any common ground beyond a general world-weariness and sense of misery" (177, 181). Clearly, Rubik takes the overlapping dialogue in *Top Girls* as a sign that communication is not being effected among the characters, and she goes on to attribute this lack of communication, and thus lack of bonding, to the women's inability to escape the "male standards and values" which they have each internalized (177, 181). Rubik's article has merit in its notation that the characters in *Top Girls* have adopted and do reinforce male behavior patterns, especially Marlene and her coworkers who encourage women to behave as ruthlessly and aggressively as do men in the business world (Churchill 72). However, the overlapping dialogue is not representative of this internalization process, nor is it evidence of ineffective communication. Indeed, as one will soon see, the dialogue in Act One is as accurate an example of "authentic female" voices as one is able to find in the plays of modern theatre.

According to Jennifer Coates, women "tend to organize their talk cooperatively, while men tend to organize their talk competitively" (194). What this means is that while men are trained from youth to establish a hierarchy within all-male groups by obtaining control of conversation,[1] women are trained to facilitate discussion with each other, working "collaboratively to produce talk" (137, 188, 194). In groups of all women then, it is common for one speaker to make comments or ask questions while another person is speaking, to complete another speaker's sentences, to repeat or rephrase what another speaker has just said, or even to pursue a separate sub-topic of the major theme that is being discussed (138–139). So, while in all-male groups overlapping speech acts such as these would likely be viewed as an attempt to interrupt the speaker and gain control of the conversation, women use these speech patterns in addition to paralinguistic skills to show their "active listenership and support for each other" (138).

Applying the idea of collaborative talk to *Top Girls* then, one can see that though Churchill refers to the overlapping linguistic acts as interruptions (9), in context these speech acts function differently. The term "interruption" is misleading. It implies a violation "of the turn-taking rules of conversation" (Coates 109). In other words, the overlapping linguistic act is inappropriately timed in a conversation so that it is unwelcome or breaks the flow of thought. However, in *Top Girls* the overlapping speech acts do not cause malfunction in the conversations. Indeed, the characters' simultaneous speech serves a practical purpose, easily allowing for speakers to request clarification or to demonstrate support and interest. For example, in the following dialogue exchange relating Nijo's story of how she became a concubine, overlapping speech is used as a tool for clarification [the forward slashes mark the point of interruption]:

Nijo:	My thin gowns were badly ripped [by the Emperor]. But even that morning when he left / — he'd a green
Marlene:	Are you saying he raped you?
Nijo:	robe with a scarlet lining and very heavily embroidered trousers, I already felt different about him. It made me uneasy. No, of course not, Marlene, I belonged to him, it was what I was brought up for from a baby. I soon found I was sad if he stayed away. It was depressing day after day not knowing when he would come [Churchill 13].

Marlene's desire here to truly understand Nijo's story causes her to inter-ject a question right in the middle of one of Nijo's sentences. Marlene's inter-jection does not "interrupt" Nijo's flow of thought, however. Nor does Nijo ignore Marlene's comment. Instead, Nijo continues to tell her story until it reaches a natural pausing point, and then she responds to Marlene's ques-tion — a question that Nijo has obviously heard and processed correctly even though Marlene's speech has overlapped her own. Nijo's tale then continues on smoothly after the question and answer exchange. Indeed, one could argue that Marlene's short interjection is actually rather timely here, for it allows Nijo to be sure that her audience accurately understands the situa-tion she is trying to describe. As in real life, communication among these women has been properly effected not just in spite of simultaneous speech, but because of it.

In addition to using it for clarification purposes, characters in the first act of *Top Girls* use simultaneous speech to show support for each other and to establish a common ground with their fellow women. Nijo is especially skilled in this particular use of simultaneous speech as can be seen in her comments to Isabella shortly after their introduction. Within fourteen lines of dialogue, Nijo overlaps Isabella's speech three times, each time with a different connective or supportive purpose. First, as Isabella is in the mid-dle of explaining that she "studied the metaphysical poets and hymnology," Nijo breaks in with the statement, "Ah you like poetry. I come of a line of eight generations of poets" (Churchill 14). At first, this statement seems somewhat self-centered, as if Nijo wants to turn the conversation onto her. Yet upon consideration of Coates' findings that "women tend to acknowl-edge and build upon each other's utterances," one can see that Nijo's state-ment is designed to show Isabella that they have a common interest, some connection (136). Second, after Isabella claims that she is "more suited to manual work" than intellectual work, Nijo interposes the remark, "Oh but I'm sure you're very clever" (Churchill 14). Plainly, Nijo is complimenting Isabella here, thus creating an initial bond with her by supporting Isabella's positive self image. Finally, Nijo provides emotional support for Isabella through her third overlap of speech. As Isabella reveals to the group of women how grieved she was by her father's death, Nijo sympathizes by interjecting the comment, "Of course you were grieved" (15). Then Nijo goes on to discuss her own father's death, by which manner she demonstrates her empathy for Isabella's loss. Ultimately, within one short dialogue exchange, Nijo is able to use overlapping speech for three distinct, positive purposes: to make a connection with Isabella, to compliment Isabella, and to comfort Isabella. So, though Margarete Rubik, as mentioned before, believes that the "overlapping dialogue and constant interruptions" indicate that the characters are incapable of communicating or establishing "any common ground," it seems pretty clear that one way (perhaps the only way) in which the women do connect in this play is on the linguistic level (181).

Simultaneous speech is used in all-female discourse not only to signal that the "co-conversationalists" desire clarification of an issue or wish to demonstrate support of others, but also to signal that the speaker is being actively listened to by the rest of the group (Coates 138). In *Top Girls*, many of the examples of overlapping dialogue function in exactly this manner, as involved listenership. Through their use of minimal responses, paraphrases, and anticipatory statements, the characters reveal that they are carefully listening to each other. The term "minimal response" refers to short phrases or words such as "yeah" or "mhm" which are used to indicate "the listener's positive attention to the speaker" (109). One example of a minimal response found in Churchill's play occurs as Nijo is telling the group how she discovered that her father was dead:

> Nijo: My father was saying his prayers and he dozed off in the sun. So I touched his knee to rouse him. "I wonder what will happen," he said, and then he was dead before he finished the sentence. / If he'd
>
> Marlene: What a shock.
>
> Nijo: died saying his prayers he would have gone straight to heaven [Churchill 15].

Marlene's response to Nijo's story, "What a shock," is obviously not meant to interrupt the flow of conversation. Marlene is simply demonstrating her interest in the story by commenting upon it. Meanwhile Nijo — a person who definitely understands how simultaneous speech operates — is not disconcerted by Marlene's interjection. Instead, she accepts Marlene's statement without comment, and continues on with her story, reasonably assured that she has Marlene's attention.

Not much later in the text of *Top Girls*, one finds an example of paraphrasing used as a sign of active listenership. When Joan explains that she ran away from home as a child with a male friend, Nijo exclaims, "Ah, an elopement," even though Joan is still speaking (Churchill 19). No new information is presented by Nijo's statement, nor does anyone find it necessary to respond to Nijo. The statement simply paraphrases what Joan has already said about her own life. Yet, Nijo's comment is clearly a sign that she is making the effort to listen, for she reinterprets the situation in terms she can understand.

A third simultaneous speech act found in Churchill's play that demonstrates active listenership is the anticipatory statement. As previously mentioned, in real-world discourse, it is common for listeners to anticipate what the speaker is going to say and then complete the speaker's conversation for her (Romaine 158). Sometimes, what the listeners think the speaker is going to say differs from what the speaker actually wants to say. One such case can be seen in Nijo's interjected diagnosis of Isabella's problems before Isabella has completed her description of them:

> Isabella: I was sent ... on a cruise for my health and I felt even worse.... I shook all over, indefinable terror. And Australia seemed to me a hideous country, the acacias stank like drains. / I
> Nijo: You were homesick.
> Isabella: had a photograph taken for Hennie but I told her I wouldn't send it, my hair had fallen out... [Churchill 18].

Nijo's statement here is not just a minimal response or a paraphrase, for it communicates a fully developed conjecture on Nijo's part. Nijo believes that the theme of Isabella's discussion revolves around missing England, and therefore sums up Isabella's story by saying she was "homesick," which is what she expects Isabella to say next. Isabella, does eventually state that she "longed to go home," but first she continues discussing her physical condition, which is what she actually is focusing on in her conversation at this time (18). In truth, it is unimportant that Nijo's statement did not accurately predict what Isabella was going to say next, for without interrupting the discussion, her interjection did accomplish the task of showing Isabella that Nijo was actively listening to her. To attempt to predict where a conversation will next lead, one must have been listening carefully enough to know where the conversation has already been.

At this point, one should be able to see that Churchill's use of simultaneous speech in *Top Girls* does not indicate communication breakdown. Reflecting the patterns found in real-world female discourse, the characters use overlapping speech in order to clarify discussion points, to show support for other speakers, and to demonstrate active listening skills. Though critics perceive the overlap in speech as a sign that the women are relating to each other in a competitive manner, linguist Suzanne Romaine, drawing on the work of Deborah Tannen, argues that it is much more important to consider "how those whose talk is overlapped perceive the overlap" (Kritzer 139–140; Romaine 158). And since it is clear that the characters do not react negatively to other people speaking at the same time (i.e. becoming angry, losing their line of thought, or pointing out interruptions), then it can be assumed that the female characters are "comfortable speaking collaboratively" (Romaine 160).

A second major critique leveled at the women in *Top Girls* is that they are "terrible egotists"; they are "self-centeredly caught up in their own individual narratives," and function within their own linguistic worlds (Brown 127; Aston 39). One can see how a critic may get this impression. In addition to speaking at the same time as other characters, the women also speak upon, what appear to be, unrelated or wholly personal topics. For example, Isabella says at one point, "Well I always traveled as a lady and I repudiated strongly any suggestion in the press that I was other than feminine" (Churchill 19). Marlene's response to this statement is, "I don't wear trousers in the office. / I could but I don't" (19). At first, Marlene's mention of her office seems unrelated to Isabella's story about traveling and the press. Yet, upon considering the subtext of these statements, one can see that they are both sub-topics within the main theme of retaining femininity through clothing. This discussion pattern of women speaking on separate sub-topics of one main theme is common in real female discourse. According to Coates, in all-female group discourse "topics are developed slowly and accretively, with participants building on each other's contributions" (138). What this means is that women tend to focus on one general topic for an extended period of time, and that during this time, members of the group will offer thoughts and interpretations of their own which help to advance the discussion. Moreover, women resort to overlapping speech once again "when two or more speakers pursue a theme simultaneously; this does not threaten comprehension, but on the contrary permits a more multi-layered development of topics" (139). Therefore, women speaking upon separate topics at the same time is not necessarily a sign that the speakers are self-centered or "isolated" from each other (Aston 39; Brown 127). Instead, within the context of all-female discussions, it is expected that members of the group will contribute to the topic in their own unique way, showing their interest and support for the speaker by relating how the main topic has affected their own lives (as Nijo did when she empathized with Isabella by telling the story of her father's death).

Indeed, one may argue that a main topic cannot be identified until several speakers have offered their input. In the play, as is often true in real life, no one person states what should be the first topic of discussion. In Act One, the first topic ends up being about family matters. Yet, one can only note with certainty that this is the general topic until Nijo has already discussed her father, her lover, and her upbringing and Isabella has discussed her sister, her father and even the horses she considers to be part of her family. The same indefinite focus is also evident in the next two topics in the text, religion (sin, penance, and nothingness) and men (taking on masculine roles, relationships with men, and dead lovers). For the characters in the play, the sub-topics make up the discussion. So, though the characters' multi-layered style of topic development may seem disconcerting at first, one can see that, as is true of their simultaneous speech, the women are just working collaboratively to create conversation.

Even if a critic does accept multiple sub-topics, however, she may still argue, as Elaine Aston does, that the characters' language shows they are self-centered, for throughout Act One characters launch into extended stories about their personal lives, seemingly ignoring the stories others have just told (39). Yet, this fact, too, can be explained linguistically. All-female group conversations are often "therapeutic" in nature (Coates 190). This means that when women get together to talk, they often see "conversation as an opportunity to discuss problems, share experience and offer reassurance and support" (190). As a result, the topics chosen for discussion tend to be rather personal, with women sharing "a great deal of information about themselves and [talking] about their feelings and their relationships" (188). One can see in the play that personal topics do get focused on most, for, as mentioned before, family, religion and men (lovers) are the first three topics of Act One. A very important aspect of this therapeutic female discourse is that often one speaker will disclose very private information about herself, and in a show of understanding, another speaker will "respond with a matching self-disclosure" (191). If the returned self-disclosure is long enough, the exchange may lead to story-chaining. According to Romaine, story chaining is the process in which, "the telling of a story suggests a story to another member [of the group] who then tells a story" (166). These stories are not used "as an attempt to top the previous narrator's story," as often would be true in groups of all-men (166). Rather, women show empathy by demonstrating through story-chaining that they have shared similar experiences and feelings (166). Story-chaining occurs all throughout Act One, but probably the most interesting example occurs right at the end of the act — the point at which many critics seem to feel that all communication has broken down, especially since the characters are drunk and Joan is speaking in Latin. After Griselda has finished her story about losing and regaining her children, Marlene asks her, "Weren't you angry?" (Churchill 37). From this point on, each character tells a story of her own which in some way reflects the anger and depression Griselda must have internalized throughout her situation. Isabella starts by telling a short story about how frustrated and ill she became trying to live as her sister did in "depressing circumstances" (37). Nijo follows up with a story of how sad she was about not being allowed to attend the Emperor's funeral and how angry she was at him for letting other men hit her. Finally Gret speaks, and she tells of her trip through Hell and how "mad" she was at the "bastards" whose evil caused her children to die (40). Even Joan's drunken, Latin ramblings can be seen as a reflection of her anger, for one of the last coherent things she says is, "I can't forgive anything" (37).

Clearly, story-chaining is being actively used at this point in Churchill's play, for each story functions as a sub-topic within the larger theme of anger or depression. The therapeutic nature of women's discourse is, thus, maintained through such story-chaining because it has allowed the speakers to feel more comfortable about their self-disclosures by having at least one other person respond on the same intimate level. So, once again, what appears to be a competitive linguistic situation turns out to be a cooperative one, for the women of the play are operating within the same collaborative, supportive systems as do women in real life.

A final significant factor that must be taken into account in any linguistic situation is the group dynamics. Group dynamics are affected by a variety of issues such as the setting, the reason that the group is meeting, the social status or roles of each member in the group, and group size. In her play, Caryl Churchill demonstrates a clear understanding of the impact of these dynamics. The setting for Act One of *Top Girls* is a restaurant, a setting chosen by Marlene so that the women can gather to celebrate her promotion. It is logical that in a restaurant the waitress will interrupt the conversation at times and food will be discussed at some point. Certain critics, however, have found the setting to be unsuitable for the deeply personal topics of discussion. One such critic, Lisa Merrill, states:

> In addition to the amusing juxtaposition of incongruous characters, the mundane restaurant setting with its constant interruptions of ordering, serving, and consuming food and drink, renders all conversation trivial... [The] interplay between serious topics and mention of food, coupled with simultaneous speech by several [characters], leads to absurd resonances [83].

Despite Merrill's recurring mention of food, one must recognize that her true focus in the above statement is her doubt that such a "mundane" yet busy, public speech environment would be likely to foster private discussions. Yet, though the characters are in a public place and in a diverse group, they remain within a setting of all women. Even the waitress is female.

Therefore, since the women have an opportunity to join in all-female group discourse, they allow themselves to discuss topics which may not be considered appropriate in mixed gender settings. Furthermore, neither the theme nor the "therapeutic" nature of their discussions is lost when the waitress interrupts to take orders. For example, one of the most heated discussions in Act One — a discussion in which the characters almost argue about religion — takes place at exactly the same time that the characters are ordering their dinners (Churchill 15–16). Merrill believes that continuing this discussion while other characters are calling out orders of "soup" or "potatoes" "leads to absurd resonances" (83). Yet, in consideration of the setting and the characters' interest in the discussion, it seems realistic that the women would order food and then quickly turn back to the main discussion. One may then question why Churchill felt she had to set Act One in a restaurant at all. Churchill herself explained her motive for using this setting: "I suppose I set them around a dinner table because it's a place where you can celebrate and I wanted it to be a festive scene where they were celebrating what they'd done as well as talking about the hard times" (Goodman and Burk 238). Churchill's statement here is intriguing, for it demonstrates not only her understanding that a restaurant is a logical place to gather for a party, but also her recognition that one can discuss "hard times" in a festive setting without the conversation leading to absurdity. So, even though Churchill chooses a public setting for the meeting and she allows certain interruptions to occur, the interruptions are short in duration, and the women still are able to maintain an intimate level of discourse within their all-female environment.

The issue of setting in this play becomes most fascinating, however, when one realizes that very few overlaps of speech occur in the scenes which take place in Marlene's employment agency. It is to these scenes which most feminist critics point when they want to demonstrate how Marlene and her coworkers have taken on masculine behavioral roles as a result of their internalization of "male standards and values" (Rubik 177). Marlene and her coworkers, Win and Nell, do indeed espouse traditional patriarchal values in their work environment, a setting which historically has been male dominated. For example, Marlene encourages one applicant to hide her engagement so potential employers will not think that the applicant is a short-term hire, and later Nell tells another applicant that a female salesperson should not be "nice" or consider the needs and feelings of the buyer (Churchill 43, 72). However, at the same time that the characters' behavior becomes noticeably more masculine, the characters' language begins to depend far less upon the usage of simultaneous speech.

Critic Sharon Ammen summarizes the effect of this linguistic change well, stating, "[i]nterestingly, it is in the rest of the play, during which over-laps are used only sparingly, that characters more effectively silence each other" (91). The silencing of other characters — true communication break-down — can be seen most plainly in the interview scenes. Not only do Mar-lene and her coworkers repeatedly ignore the concerns of their interviewees, but also it is within this setting that the play's most definite example of an interruption takes place, as Win cuts off an applicant mid-sentence by say-ing, "You shouldn't talk too much at an interview" (Churchill 64). Win's statement is clearly designed to prevent the applicant from speaking further, and thus the statement fits most neatly into Coates' definition of an "inter-ruption," in that it is a "violation of the current speaker's right to complete their turn" (192). So though the simultaneous speech in the first scene ini-tially appears to reflect the characters' inability to communicate, really it is not until the characters enter the more specifically "masculine" setting of a workplace and stop speaking collaboratively, that they lose their ability to communicate smoothly. Thus, simultaneous speech is not, as many critics have claimed, an identifiable result of the characters' adoption of masculine behavior.

Clearly, Churchill's setting affects the characters' behavior and the group dynamics in her play. Yet, group dynamics can also be affected by the social status or roles of each member in a group. Many critics who analyze Chur-chill's *Top Girls* focus on the socio-economic backgrounds of each group member in Act One. Considering the socialist leanings in Churchill's plays, this seems a logical issue to consider. However, critics such as Amelia Howe Kritzer have correlated social class with differing linguistic styles too directly, claiming that the characters' varied class backgrounds have prevented them from communicating with each other (144):

> The titled Isabella and aristocratic Nijo ... dominate the conversation, fre-quently interrupting and overlapping others.... Gret, the uneducated peas-ant ... speaks very little. The two contemporary women present show an even greater contrast: Marlene directs the progress of the dinner, while the waitress serving the party does not speak at all [144].

It is true that social class can affect how much a person talks in a situ-ation. Yet, it is not necessarily true that those in lower social classes will be the ones to talk less (Coates 135). The amount people talk depends upon a number of factors such as their cultures' linguistic standards, their comfort within a given situation, their knowledge of the topic being discussed, and, of course, their gender (Romaine 159, 169; Coates 134). Thus, one cannot simply equate the reason Isabella and Nijo speak more with the fact that they are from the upper class. Indeed, if one looks closely at Isabella and Nijo's "dominating" language, one can see that they help facilitate conversation and they are concerned that others participate. As is common in real life groups of women, "the active members [of the group] are concerned to draw out more reticent speakers" (Coates 137). Therefore, throughout Nijo and Isabella's dialogue, one finds many questions, some very specifically designed to get the "more reticent speakers" involved. For example, Isabella asks Gret's opinion on books, and when she receives no response, she immediately follows up with a question about pets: "Did you have any horses, Gret?" (Churchill 14). Finally, Gret answers with one word, "Pig" (14). But though the response was short, Isabella has achieved the task of making sure Gret is included in the conversation. So though certain characters appear to dominate the conversation, in many ways they are ensuring that conversation continues.

Using questions to ensure participation is a common tactic in real life female discourse. In group situations, women use questions "as part of a general strategy for conversational maintenance," seeing "them as facilitating the flow of conversation" (Coates 189). Those who function in the role of host within a group are especially likely to ask a variety of questions (121). In the first act of the play, Marlene is the host of the party. Therefore, she operates as the main facilitator of conversation, the term "facilitator" here referring to "those responsible for ensuring that interaction proceeds smoothly" (12). In her capacity as facilitator, Marlene asks many personal questions, introduces new topics, and even prevents a potential argument about religion (Churchill 16). Considering Marlene in terms of being the one "responsible for ensuring" smooth interaction then, one is not surprised that she "directs the progress of dinner" (Coates 121; Kritzer 144). Nor is one truly surprised that the waitress "does not speak at all" (Kritzer 144). Marlene speaks more because she is more centrally significant to the party, not just because she is of a higher social class than the waitress.

Obviously, the linguistic patterns in any situation are affected by many factors in addition to social class. As in real life, the setting and speakers' roles in Churchill's play impact how the women talk and relate to one another. However, one of the most important factors within group dynamics, group size, still needs to be considered in connection to Churchill's play. Though a common critique of the characters in Act One is that they carry on separate conversations, the size of the group actually demands that this happen. With each person that is added to a group, the number of available linguistic relationships is increased exponentially, and "[by] the time six people join one conversation, fifteen different relationships connect them, so the group usually divides at this point" (Macionis 183). In Churchill's play, the group in the first act is made up of exactly six women. So, as is expected in a group this size, the conversation breaks in two. One may imagine that having two separate conversations running simultaneously would create chaos on stage. However, Churchill makes sure that none of her characters overlap important information with their own speech, and she designates who each character should be addressing in any given situation. For instance, when Nijo is discussing her lover at the same time Joan is discussing John the Scot, the stage directions make it clear that Nijo is to speak "to Isabella" and Joan is to speak "to Marlene" (Churchill 21). In this manner, Churchill is able to keep her audience on track with what is going on in the play, and, meanwhile, she is able to demonstrate her awareness of the linguistic realities which affect large group dynamics.

By now, one can see that Caryl Churchill is knowledgeable not only about the impact of group dynamics on language, but also about the linguistic patterns found within all-female discourse. Though her use of simultaneous speech and separate discussion topics has caused a lot of negative criticism to be directed at the women in her play, each surprising use of dialogue can be explained in real-life linguistic terms. In both the play and in reality, simultaneous speech is used to show support and active interest in a conversation, women use sub-topics to develop one main theme, and group dynamics affect conversations in complex ways. Ultimately, though critics may focus on how Churchill's characters in *Top Girls* take on masculine roles and attitudes in their lives, one must recognize that some part of their femininity, and their ability to relate, is retained through their collaborative speech. Ideally, future criticism of the *Top Girls* characters will begin to demonstrate a true understanding of feminine linguistics, and will stop conveying the idea that the "women's speech... [is] a deviation that has to be explained" (Romaine 157).

WESTERN MICHIGAN UNIVERSITY

Notes

1. Coates bases her argument that men tend to have a more competitive conversational style than do women upon her own work and upon the studies of other linguists such as Marjorie Harness Goodwin, Elizabeth Aries, and Victoria DeFrancisco. Goodwin's studies (1980; 1988; 1990) of children playing in single-sex groups recorded boys using many more direct commands with their friends than girls used (Coates 124). Aries' work (1976) with all-male discussion groups suggested that men are concerned about establishing hierarchical relations in a group, ultimately leaving participants in either dominant or submissive positions (137). And DeFrancisco's study (1991) of married couples showed that men are responsible for significantly more turn-taking violations (such as delayed responses or interruptions) in cross-sex communication than are women (114).

References Cited

Ammen, Sharon. "Feminist Vision and Audience Response: Tracing the Absent Utopia in Caryl Churchill's *Top Girls*." *Utopian Studies* 7.1 (1996): 86–102.

Aston, Elaine. *Caryl Churchill.* Plymouth: Northcote House, 1997.

Brown, Janet. "Caryl Churchill's *Top Girls* Catches the Next Wave." *Caryl Churchill: A Casebook.* Ed. Phyllis R. Randall, 117–130. New York: Garland, 1988.

Churchill, Caryl. *Top Girls.* New York: Samuel French, 1982.

Coates, Jennifer. *Women, Men and Language.* 2nd ed. London: Longman, 1993.

Goodman, Lizbeth, and Juli Thompson Burk. "Contemporary Women's Theatre: *Top Girls*." *Literature and Gender.* Ed. Lizbeth Goodman, 229–251. London: The Open University, 1996.

Kritzer, Amelia Howe. *The Plays of Caryl Churchill.* Houndmills: Macmillan, 1994.

Macionis, John J. *Sociology.* 4th ed. Englewood Cliffs, NJ: Prentice Hall, 1993.

Merrill, Lisa. "Monsters and Heroines: Caryl Churchill's Women." *Caryl Churchill: A Casebook.* Ed. Phyllis R. Randall, 71–89. New York: Garland, 1988.

Romaine, Suzanne. *Communicating Gender.* Mahwah, NJ: Lawrence Erlbaum Associates, 1999.

Rubik, Margarete. "The Silencing of Women in Feminist British Drama." *Semantics of Silences in Linguistics and Literature.* Eds. Gudrun M. Grabher and Ulrike Jessner, 177–190. Heidelburg: Universitatsverlag C. Winter, 1996.

Adrienne Kennedy's Deadly Parts

Pictures, Portraits, and Plays

Johanna Frank

Abstract

This essay responds to a symptom of identity politics gone awry: biographical criticism locates Adrienne Kennedy and her life experiences (as expressed in her non-dramatic texts or by critics' personal encounters with her) as referents to authenticate her plays. The critical practice of employing Kennedy's supposed "autobiographical" texts People Who Led to My Plays *(1987) and* Deadly Triplets: A Theatre Journal *(1990) as concordances to her plays is a misled practice because it undermines the politics of Kennedy's plays that disrupt the body and embodied identity. While the concepts of "experience" and "calculated intellect" are not mutually exclusive, this essay argues that Kennedy's non-dramatic texts establish a model to read her plays. They posit the performance of identity as the process of storytelling and represent history and memory as the incomplete layers of presence.*

> Now, in the Photograph, what I posit is not only
> the absence of the object, it is also, by one and the
> same movement, on equal terms, the fact that this
> object has indeed existed and that it has been there
> where I see it.[1]
>
> — Roland Barthes

> Duchess: We are tied to him unless, of course,
> he should die.
> Victoria: But he is dead.
> Duchess: And he keeps returning.[2]
>
> — Adrienne Kennedy

In *People Who Led to My Plays* (1987), the last entry in the section titled Junior High 1943–1946, under the heading *"My mother and my face,"* Adrienne Kennedy writes, "My face as an adult will always seem to be lacking because it is not my mother's face" (51). As one of hundreds of textual reflections intermixed with photographs and a variety of other visual iconography in a publication that readers and critics take as her autobiography, this quote seems quite innocuous. It speaks of the self in relation to the family and site of origin, and describes an interior perception of an exterior self in the terms of portraiture and representation. Yet this quote like all the other entries in *People Who Led to My Plays* is more than a mere declarative or descriptive sentence: it speaks of a relationship of absence and presence, desire and loss, distance and intimacy; all terms in juxtaposition of one another depending on perspective. The heading reads "My mother and my face," not my mother's and my face; possession belongs to the speaker, and her perspective reveals a comparison of another's whole to the speaker's part.

This relationship is quite different from that revealed in the entry itself, in which Kennedy employs the possessive to designate "my face" and "my mother's face." The entry states, "My face as an adult will always seem to be lacking because it is not my mother's face." Whereas the heading compares a part of the speaker to the entire subjectivity of the speaker's mother — a comparison on equal terms of two unequal entities — the entry itself reveals how two seemingly equal parts — two faces — are in fact not equal due to temporal and spatial differences. Temporality is key: the speaker as an adult reflects on her face in the continuous present in relation to her younger self's perspective of her mother's face, which was present in the past. Temporality prohibits the speaker's possession of her mother's face as her own and hence, prohibits the speaker possessing and/or becoming the mother. Simultaneously, temporality enables the speaker in the present to reflect on a past perception of an anticipated future that connects her to the mother figure whose face stands in for both the literal and symbolic self. The daughter's face resembles and is similar to the mother's face, but is not and never will be the speaker's child perception of the mother or the mother's face.

So, why this attention to a close reading of one entry in Kennedy's supposed autobiography? *People Who Led to My Plays* reveals few specifics about Kennedy and her life. In the entry I examine above we never get the child, the adult, or the mother who, within the boundaries of the genre, should be the subjects of the autobiography. Instead, all that Kennedy posits is the relationship between the present and the past, the present and a past present, and a past and an anticipated future. The entry is less a commentary on the self, the mother, or their embodied identity as it is about the multiple temporal and spatial layers of memory, history, and existence that overlap but never quite connect.

Maybe because the structure of *People Who Led to My Plays* follows a chronological time line of twenty-five years of Kennedy's life — beginning with elementary school in 1936 and ending with her return from Africa in 1961— it is taken most commonly as her autobiography. It employs verbal portraiture reminiscent of Gertrude Stein's text-based portraits, and inter-mixes if not juxtaposes that non-fiction text with photographs and draw-ings of personal, popular, and cultural images from the twenty-five year period under discussion. It is a scrapbook of people, figures, images, and objects of influence. As the speaker states in her opening remarks, the text is a response to the questions, "Who influenced you to write in such a non-linear way? Who are your favorite playwrights?" (3). Yet what unfolds is not an answer as much as a series of reflections — in the form of an annotated list — that detail and enact the ephemeral and never complete status of the self.

In this twenty-five-year span, the speaker details memories, snippets of information, and flashbacks about the people (including literary, historical, artistic and musical figures) and objects that shaped her in the first quarter of her life. More often than not the entries are quite long, and express anec-dotes directly or tangentially related to the listed item. Through fragments we receive reflections on the self, family, popular culture, and the environ-ment — sources that have offered (if not model) inspiration, courage, beauty, and pain. In addition to the written text, the speaker incorporates personal pictures and portraits along with headshots of famous celebrities, icons, bib-lical and historical drawings and portraitures, movie scenes, and newspaper clippings. Often listed entries are repeated in a given chronological section (or across various sections), but contain different, or slightly varied explana-tions and/or detailed descriptions. Repetition is never exact (in this regard, again, Kennedy's entries follow a model similar to what Gertrude Stein called insistence and resemblance). Sometimes the pictures accompany the textual anecdotes but do not necessarily have direct relationships with the texts.

Kennedy has suggested that only autobiography interests her, and for this reason many critics have turned to *People Who Led to My Plays* to serve as a roadmap or concordance for her plays. In fact, in much of the criticism of Kennedy's work, her words expressed in this and other "autobiographical" materials are employed to make sense of her creative production or provide a framework or basis for understanding her plays' respective plot and char-acter motivation.[3] Reading an author's life to illuminate his or her texts is most certainly not an uncommon critical practice in literary and theatre stud-ies. And why not? I, too, am drawn to an image from her life: a young woman, sitting in a room in a foreign country, late at night, isolated, alone, piecing together paragraphs from drafts of her manuscript that will become the play *Funnyhouse of a Negro*. The image romanticizes the author's task at hand: amidst a displaced sense of location, she brings together seemingly disparate voices and establishes a structure for an otherwise unstructured set of paragraphs. The memories of objects, people, and locations — from a multiplicity of spaces — exist on the singular plane I perceive as Kennedy's desk. As such, my imaginary scene enacts what Kennedy narrative achieves: multivalent and temporal worlds existing simultaneously.

While this romanticized reading relies on biographical information about Kennedy's years in Africa, there is a difference between employing that information to assess how an author may have constructed a text and perceiving the author's life experiences and events as explanations of or absolute referents for the contents of her texts. In *The Other American Drama,* for example, Marc Robinson conflates the playwright with her protagonist or else conflates the playwright with the project of the play (as a form of self and personal exorcism). He proposes that the quest for a deeper understanding of the self becomes Kennedy's quest, and she must dispose of her oppressive feminine self (one of the multiple and fragmented identities of a black woman in a racially divided, over-determined white patriarchal Western society) in order to achieve her full capacity and capability as a successful writer. Consider the following:

> Kennedy killed off Sarah, and in a sense killed off the self she knew up to 1963. From now on, she wouldn't have to worry about losing herself in the no-man's-land of marriage or motherhood, Cleveland or the Congo, the unsatisfying identities of "black writer" or "woman writer" or, worse, no writer at all [132].

Robinson thus argues that Kennedy's protagonists, who fail to unite the elements of their identities into subjects, reveal and embody the fragmented psychic landscape that Kennedy herself shares. Drawing on her autobiography, Robinson contends that "It was on one of those first trips that she realized London was capable of unlocking something in her that had lain low at home ... she could sense that 'just beyond that darkness was a completed person, a completed writer, a completed life.... The city held a key to my psyche'" (138). Robinson directly applies Kennedy's comments from her autobiography to read *Funnyhouse of a Negro* not as a metaphor for the black woman playwright, but as a therapeutic if not psychoanalytic explanation of one individual: Kennedy. Robinson asserts that Kennedy created a character with whom she could identify and work out her own "feelings about her race" as well as the "attractions and curses of European culture and African history" in order to show the "pain of rootlessness" and the sense of isolation she felt (132).

In Herbert Blau's essay on the work of Sam Shepard and of Kennedy, Blau presents an anecdote of a time he approached Kennedy to write a play for the Repertory Theatre of Lincoln Center and she was different than he expected. In his essay, this anecdote functions as support for his argument that there is no possible way Kennedy's work can be aligned with the aggressive nationalism of the Black Arts movement. Blau recounts that when he encountered Kennedy her "demeanor was deceptive" because she "reminded" him of "nothing so much as a kindergarten teacher, girlish and shy, awed by such attention" (531). His comments suggest that he assumed Kennedy would be something other than what he experienced, and that he felt betrayed by the expectations — while his own — set up by Kennedy's literature. He then asserts in his essay that it is only when he turns to information about Kennedy's childhood (information that he finds in her autobiography *after* his encounter at Lincoln Center) that he makes sense of his experience of the playwright. But more importantly, he suggests, his encounter with Kennedy and his reading of *People Who Led to My Plays* disrupts his previous reading of her dramatic work that represents a violent environment full of the realities of prejudice and racism.

To reconcile these perceptions of Kennedy and her work, Blau contends that Kennedy's demeanor as well as his acquired knowledge of her "bourgeois" and "unexplosive" prayer-like childhood environment are, for him, "out of place in the emergence of Black Power" that "erupted" in a "ruthlessly aggressive style" (531). As such, Blau justifies his reading of Kennedy's plays as well as of her: he concludes that she was never at home "in the world of black jive," and locates her work as outside of the "militant and existential blacks" of the activist sixties (531). The subtext of Blau's essay is that violence is something that one, particularly a woman playwright, should not and cannot enact; that violence is neither necessarily an inherent quality in middle class women nor a quality that they, in good nature, act upon.

The common thread among all such criticism is the contrast between the figure of Kennedy and the imagery in her plays. In what seems like a symptom of identity politics, the figure of Kennedy in this manner reduces identity to corporeality as a means to authenticate her texts and fill the absence they produce. She becomes the referent onto which critics latch so as to replace or explain the absence produced in her plays. Yet by aligning the events and experiences of Kennedy's personal life with those imagined in her plays, such scholarship not only distracts from a more critical engagement with the plays, but also, in its focus on Kennedy's life, reveals the trap of identity politics as well as a certain subtext: an anxiety surrounding the plays' expression of the emotional and physical violence of power and the ways in which such violence directly and indirectly contains, penetrates, and shapes the individual in every day life.

Such biographical criticism runs the risk of substituting an imagined history as the key to meaning. But even more so, what is available in such criticism is sociology: it illustrates political lessons caused by the positionality of the character whose art is an excrescence of experience rather than calculated intellect. In other words, it treads very dangerously on the ground of positing African American women playwrights as creating art as an outgrowth of experience rather than as an exercise of intellect. And it is that ground that I critique. Of course, it's not my intention to suggest that all scholars claim that Kennedy's plays are solely autobiographical or that autobiography is off limits as a genre useful to critical practice. Moreover, it is not my goal to set-up critical straw-men; however, because the maneuver of perceiving autobiography as "an indispensable guide to her plays," as Philip Kolin has stated, is taken to an extreme in the case of the criticism of Kennedy and her work, I run the risk of doing just that (303).

Relying on Kennedy as the referent outside of the purview of the imaginative and dramatic world locates her embodied identity as the referent from which to understand the plot, symbolism, and/or character motivation in her plays. I find this critical maneuver problematic — the maneuver of claiming the body of the playwright as the ground where socio-political determinants take hold and/or are realized — because it undermines Kennedy's politics that lay precisely in the way her dramatic and non-dramatic texts disrupt the body and embodied identity. I want to reopen conversations on the limitations of autobiography as a concordance to creative production and ask, what are the consequences of positing art as an outgrowth of experience rather than as an exercise of intellect? How do we read the blurry line between the two?

Deadly Reading: Kennedy's Non-dramatic Texts

I began this essay with an analysis of an entry from *People Who Led to My Plays*, a quote that is a bit of an allegory for Kennedy's work, and quite possibly, an outlet to the critical problem I describe above. But I want to turn my attention to Kennedy's lesser-known "autobiographical" text, *Deadly Triplets: A Theatre Mystery and Journal* (1990), to consider how the status or labeling of these publications as autobiographies is misleading to the respective works as well as Kennedy's plays. Most importantly, I will suggest this non-dramatic text *models* a strategy for reading and/or viewing Kennedy's plays rather than provides a concordance to her plays.

Deadly Triplets links the imaginative and the pseudo-documentary into three distinctly separate sections: short-story fiction, photograph montage documentation, and non-fiction portraiture. Officially, according to the table of contents, the text is divided into two sections; however, I perceive the inclusion of the section of photographs as an additional section since it is divided from the others by a heading page. For the sake of clarification, though, as I will note, the photographical section appears second, between the two other sections. The first section, titled "A Theatre Mystery: Deadly Triplets," is a fictional account — in the form of an interior monologue — that follows the character of Suzanne Alexander, an American living in London for three years. In this narrative we learn she partakes in the mysteries surrounding the disappearance of her adoptive mother, finding her adoptive sister, adapting a set of texts by John Lennon into a play, and locating an actor friend and his estranged brother.

The third section of *Deadly Triplets*, titled "A Theatre Journal," is a text that most resembles *People Who Led to My Plays*. This section lists and details various celebrities and members of the theatre and literary circles the speaker encountered while in London. In contrast to *People Who Led to My Plays*, in which the unnamed speaker's perspective is from that of an unnamed present moment reflecting on the past, the speaker in *Deadly Triplets* is a visiting faculty member at UC–Berkeley who, in the present, reflects upon a past time she spent in London. She lists each figure she meets, from Edward Albee to John Lennon to James Baldwin, and provides a paragraph description of each encounter.

These entries in the last section, as the preface declares, reflect Kennedy's real experiences in London, England. The preface, then, clearly sets up the expectations of genre: autobiography. Yet, the combination of a fictional story (that incorporates semi-autobiographical references) and the non-fictional list of an unnamed speaker's personal encounters, pull together, juxtapose, and challenge the genre status of each section. This is underscored further by the inclusion in *Deadly Triplets* of the middle section of the text: photographs of people and documents from Kennedy-the-playwright's "real" experiences during her three-year stay in London. Entitled "London," these several pages, which physically separate "A Theatre Mystery," the first section of the text, and "A Theatre Journal," the third section, contain images of reproduced photographs and documents of Kennedy's experience in Europe and the productions of her dramatic works. Pictures of Kennedy, her two sons, the flats where they lived in London (each dated from 1967 to 1969), flyers from the productions of *Sun* (1969) and *Cities in Bezique* (1969), a still photo from the production of *Funnyhouse of a Negro* at the Petit Odéon in Paris (1968), and the front jacket of *The Lennon Play* (1968) all reference both Kennedy-the-writer's experiences as well as the work she produced during the three years she actually lived in London with her sons Adam and Joe. The photos include captions that label and identify each as such.

As pictures, these documents seem very *present,* particularly in their location in the middle of the book *Deadly Triplets.* One might argue that the photographs offer the image of the body of the author as that which verifies and validates the rest of the book. However, I contend that these pictures play with readers' assumptions about genre; that the genre sets up the photographs as "real" and as providing access to some truth of the rest of the book. I base this claim — that Kennedy consciously manipulates audience expectations of the autobiographical and the visual — on the fact that neither "A Theatre Journal" nor "London Sketches," the first and third sections of the text, mention by name Adrienne, Adam, or Joe Kennedy or refer to any of the places, locales, play and production documents that appear in the photographs and the captions beneath them. In this second section, though, the real-life Kennedy and her sons are the referents to which the images refer. To borrow Roland Barthes' phrase, they are "the *necessarily* real thing[s] which [have] been placed before the lens, without which there would be no photograph" (76). However, the photographs do not refer beyond the pages of this middle section. In other words, these photographs are not supplements to the other two sections of the text or vice versa, but comprise the second and only the second of the three sections.

This distinction is important because the photograph section is central to how Kennedy employs this text to develop and express absence and loss. Rather than link the first and third section of *Deadly Triplets,* the photographs call attention to the fragmentation of self and challenge the notion of an authentic self and/or "I" at the core of the text. Similar to the descriptions and photographs in *People Who Led to My Plays,* the photographs in *Deadly Triplets* offer the signifiers of the people and objects for which we have no signifiers. The photographs only point to the absence of individuals (or, as both Susan Sontag and Roland Barthes have called it, the "Death" of the person photographed). One can never access the person or event depicted in the image; the photograph never sums up the person or event in its totality. Whether or not the photographs correspond with components of the preceding and subsequent prose is irrelevant. The photographs provide no more or less access to the truth of an experience, time, or space than the other two sections of the text. To echo Barthes' assertion in the quote I employ as an epigraph, the photograph posits "not only the absence of the object, it is also, by one and the same movement, on equal terms, the fact that this object has indeed existed and that it has been there where I see it" (115). Kennedy and her sons — Adam and Joe — are simultaneously present and absent from the text.

Moreover, in marking the division between the interior monologue and narrative portraits (the first and third sections of the text) the images of

"London" disrupt the continuity of the "autobiography." They do not confirm or modify the fictionalized story of the preceding pages, and they do not verify the speaker's presence in England during which she met the people detailed on the subsequent pages. The photographs present a temporal real that is both real and not real, which suggests that rather than validate the written texts, the photographs emphasize the ephemeral quality of any autobiography or self-representation as well as their inability to function as expressions of reality outside the narrative of the text. Constituting the second of three sections of the text, "London" insures that the "triplets" of the title — the three segments of the text — remain deadly: they each resemble yet contradict one another. Like the adult speaker in *People Who Led to My Plays* who perceives her face as lacking because it is not her mother's face, the three overlapping yet distinct segments of *Deadly Triplets* ultimately produce absence rather than presence; the various layers of time and place call into question the stability of any single moment, event or object — not to mention authorship — in constituting a coherent self.

Reading Deadly: Kennedy's Drama

Deadly Triplets' content and structure provide a model to read Kennedy's plays: they produce absence first by relying upon and then manipulating expectations of presence. All of Kennedy's plays, to a certain degree, involve multiple bodies, personae, and voices that interact across different planes of time and space. The self is either split into many characters that exist in multiple planes of time and location (scattering identity across bodies), or one actor embodies multiple characters that merge, morph or transform from one to the other (projecting multiple identities onto one body). Such multiplicity makes bodies appear as hyper-present, which makes them seem to be the sites that tie, relate, and connect various memories, times, spaces, and locations. Yet her dramatic oeuvre is very much about the failure to locate embodied identity as the source of authority or authenticity of experience and hence, the multiple sites of presence fail to materialize or compensate for the fragmentation in her plays. Ultimately, the absent figure or event, which more often than not either is suspended off-stage or repressed in the psyche, is that which prevents the individual from tying, relating or connecting memory, space and place as a means to access truth.

Moreover, corporeal presence always remains ephemeral. The father in *Funnyhouse of a Negro*; Clara in *The Owl Answers* and *A Movie Star Has to Star in Black and White*; Mark Essex in *An Evening with Dead Essex*; and David Alexander in *She Talks to Beethoven, The Film Club* (A Monologue by

Suzanne Alexander) and *Dramatic Circle* each remain absent figures who never "return" corporeally, but exist within the drama as endless deferrals that inhibit the protagonist(s) from acquiring a coherent sense of self. In the later plays, *The Alexander Plays, Letter to My Students on My Sixty-first Birthday* by Suzanne Alexander, *Motherhood 2000*, and *Sleep Deprivation Chamber*, a traumatic event of the past, which "returns" through memories, dreams, hallucinations, and voices, functions as that which the protagonists strive to reclaim but never can.[4] Throughout Kennedy's oeuvre the figure or event remains a component that has died (or is removed from one's access for one reason or another) and keeps returning (in one form or another) to haunt characters across multiple layers and junctures of time and space. As the Duchess and Victoria claim in *Funnyhouse of a Negro*, the relationship between absence and presence is not a matter of contradiction as it is an accepted state of existence: "Duchess: We are tied to him unless, of course, he should die./Victoria: But he is dead./Duchess: And he keeps returning" (3–4). Materializing what is absent and finding closure — alleviating the pain of loss — remain impossibilities.

Kennedy's early plays are excellent examples to examine the production of absence; however, for the purposes of this paper I will limit my discussion to a very brief consideration of *She Talks to Beethoven*, the first of *The Alexander Plays* (1992), a compilation of four separate but interrelated plays that involve a storyteller/writer who tries to come to an understanding about herself by looking to her past. Each of these plays posit a traumatic event as that which "returns" through memory, dreams, hallucinations, and voices as the protagonists strive to access truth about an event. They all engage the protagonist Suzanne Alexander, who is a character that frequently appears in Kennedy's oeuvre. While each Suzanne Alexander is a version of a previous Suzanne Alexander in that each shares common identity and personality traits, each is not necessarily the same character across plays. Throughout the compilation Suzanne Alexander maintains all or some of the following characteristics: she is a black writer who lives in Accra, Ghana, London, or the United States, has an academic husband who becomes involved with African politics, teaches playwriting at various U.S. universities, and has family in Washington, D.C. and/or Cleveland.

She Talks to Beethoven involves three characters: Suzanne Alexander, a writer, Ludwig van Beethoven, the composer, and David Alexander, Suzanne's missing husband. Set in a room in a house in Accra, Ghana, in 1961, *She Talks to Beethoven* follows Suzanne's thoughts during the time she is bedridden, recovering from an unknown surgery, writing a play about Beethoven, reading diaries about Beethoven, listening to news and voices on the radio (as well as those outside her window), and waiting for information about her husband who has been missing for an unmentioned duration of time. The present is intermixed with simultaneous encounters with the past: Suzanne hears former radio recordings of herself and her husband reading the poetry of Frantz Fanon, reads diary entries written by contemporaries of Beethoven, and enacts her imagined encounters with Beethoven shortly before he dies.

This is a play about the quest for truths, and that search exists simultaneously on two layered planes: the present and the past. The larger frame of the play is a search for the truth about David Alexander and his disappearance in a post-revolution nation (the sounds of African music are constantly heard from Suzanne's window and the "voice" of Africa fills the space of her apartment via the radio). Yet the secondary story seems to dominate the stage action: a search for the truth about Beethoven's *Fidelio* as a research topic that will inform Suzanne's play about the great composer. In searching for the truth about Beethoven, Suzanne looks beyond diaries and to the original source, Beethoven himself. She thinks that if she returns to the origin, she can access unmediated information about the man and his work. She dives into learning about Beethoven, ultimately, because facing the situation regarding her husband's possible return is too emotionally painful (not to mention she's powerless in her current, bedridden, post-surgery state to take any measures to find him). Yet it is in her research of and interaction with Beethoven that Suzanne finds evidence for her husband's existence: a message that David leaves in Beethoven's conversation books encourages Suzanne to keep writing. And it is during her encounters with Beethoven that she hears over the radio information about her husband's abduction and possible return.

She Talks to Beethoven engages several distinct sections that co-exist over multiple temporal and spatial planes. And it is only in the collapse of those planes, the layering of one over the other and the weaving of each together, that Suzanne accesses the truth of her quest: she learns of not only the events surrounding the opening production of Beethoven's *Fidelio* as well as Beethoven's subsequent death, but also her husband's kidnapping and the status of his well-being. Suzanne cannot access this information within individual planes. For example, she does not acquire the return of her husband in and through speaking with Beethoven; however, she serendipitously learns of David's status by accessing both her own and David's written texts, her voice for her new play, and David's letters placed in Beethoven's conversation books. These text-based documents represent the mind, ideas, and identity of David — the referent that is not present — that transcend time even as his is physically absent from Suzanne's immediate world. We never find out what happened to David during his abduction; instead, we are presented with versions of him: his informal writing to Suzanne, his poetry and lectures on the radio, and his channeling through Beethoven that, in their multiplicity of presence, merge the body of the husband with the body of the text. The truth of his existence during the time he is missing as well as his own corporeal presence, are endlessly deferred.

Kennedy employs a similar move in *The Film Club* (A Monologue by Suzanne Alexander), *The Dramatic Circle*, and *The Ohio State Murders*, the remaining three plays in *The Alexander Plays*. In fact, as an entire set, *The Alexander Plays* represents a multiple perspective text (each play is a segment that offers a different perspective — across time and place — of a series of experiences). *The Film Club* is an interior monologue delivered in the present by Suzanne Alexander and involves her reflections on events in 1961 when she lived in London with her sister-in-law Alice Alexander, and waited to hear news about David Alexander, their husband and brother respectively, who was missing in West Africa for fifteen months. *The Dramatic Circle* depicts a similar set of events but is told from Alice's perspective. She is the narrator who speaks in an undesignated present (but her present occurs chronologically before Suzanne's present narration in *The Film Club*) about events that happened in London in the year 1961. *The Ohio State Murders*, the fourth play of *The Alexander Plays*, is a text that also frames the past with the present and seeks to explain and understand a traumatic event. Ultimately, though, it is a story about memory and the search for truth. It posits storytelling as one method for the search for truth of origin, but implies that the story itself will never lead one to the site of origin. The process of storytelling, not the story itself, is the only truth one might ever grasp.

All four plays work together and against one another in a similar fashion as the three segments in *Deadly Triplets*. Like Kennedy's non-dramatic texts, the gap between the present and the past is marked by memories that are insufficient because they cannot capture the exact experience — the truth — of what transpired during a set period of time in the past. Of course, memories are never simple. They never completely identify an experience. Instead, they continually defer it. Each play's reflections into the past reveal how events infiltrate the present and how memories are insufficient to provide either access or closure to one's experiences. Through memory, the past and the present coexist in multiplicity. The sense of loss produced in such plays resides in the fact that Kennedy's protagonists fail to recognize that it is not the content of their stories, but the acts of speaking them — layering the present day with the past that is enacted in the memories and flashbacks — that offers redemption. As a storyteller, the protagonist seems to be a referent for the past and for the possible future, but she is not a referent as much as the container for stories, pasts, and futures. The storyteller becomes the vehicle through which she and we as spectators gain access to the past, but also are ultimately denied such access. The body of the text, the text of the body, the text of the playwright-as-author, and the writing self are never complete; they remain suspended elsewhere. All that Kennedy presents is a search — as a process in the layering — for a unified subject that never exists.

CORNELL UNIVERSITY

Notes

1. *Camera Lucida* (New York: Hill and Wang, 1981) 115.
2. All subsequent references to *Funnyhouse of a Negro* are from *Adrienne Kennedy in One Act* (Minneapolis: University of Minnesota Press, 1988) 3–4.
3. For the purposes of this paper I limit my discussion to the work of three critics. For a more exhaustive analysis see "Seeking the 'I': Absence and the Plays of Adrienne Kennedy" in my dissertation *Beyond Visibility: Feminism, Performance, and the Dramatic Text* (Indiana University, 2003). Female and Kennedy-specific life experiences are held up as explanations of or anomalies to the anger and violence in her plays. In this manner, the turn to biographical criticism is a return to the body and its experiences of its environment, and limits any analysis of her creative work to through the lens of personal experience and/or or perceives a given character as an "avatar" of the playwright.
4. These plays are collected in *The Adrienne Kennedy Reader* by Werner Sollors (Minneapolis: University of Minnesota Press, 2001).

References Cited

Barthes, Roland. "The Rhetoric of the Image." *Image/Music/Text*. Trans. Stephen Heath. New York: Hill and Want, 1977. 32–51.
_____. *Camera Lucida*. New York: Farrar, Straus and Giroux, 1977.
Blau, Herbert. "The American Dream in American Gothic: The Plays of Sam Shepard and Adrienne Kennedy." *Modern Drama* 27:4 (1984): 520–39.
Frank, Johanna. *Beyond Visibility: Feminism, Performance, and the Dramatic Text*. Ph.D. diss., Indiana University, 2003.
Kennedy, Adrienne. *Adrienne Kennedy in One Act*. Minneapolis: University of Minnesota Press, 1988.
_____. *People Who Led to My Plays*. New York: Knopf, 1987.
_____. *Deadly Triplets: A Theatre Mystery and Journal*. Minneapolis: University of Minnesota Press, 1990.
_____. *The Alexander Plays*. Minneapolis: University of Minnesota Press, 1992.
Kolin, Philip C. "Orpheus Ascending: Music, Race, and Gender in Adrienne Kennedy's *She Talks to Beethoven*." *African American Review* 28:2 (1994): 293–304.

Robinson, Marc. *The Other American Drama*. Cambridge: Cambridge University Press, 1994.

Sollors, Werner. *The Adrienne Kennedy Reader*. Minneapolis: University of Minnesota Press, 2001.

Sontag, Susan. *On Photography*. New York: Farrar, Straus and Giroux, 1977.

Faces of Contemporary Turkish-German Kabarett[1]

Erol Boran

Abstract

In its early phase, Turkish-German Kabarett focused exclusively on issues of identity and integration. Both the Kabarett Knobi-Bonbon *(1985–1997) and the* Bodenkosmetikerinnen *(1991–1999) presented clichéd images of Turks with the intention of deconstructing them and of counteracting instances of social discrimination. In the latter half of the nineties, the scene underwent major transformations. This was primarily due to a new generation of performer, like Serdar Somuncu, Django Asül and Kaya Yanar; in addition, German society itself had changed over the years. In consequence, Turkish-German Kabarett has made a distinctive move to leave the ethnic corner to become an integral part of an extended German art scene. Less than twenty years after the first projects were launched, the heirs of the* Kabarett Knobi-Bonbon *have reached a point at the crossroads, i.e., a point where Turkish-German Kabarett (and Turkish-German art in general) has to question its methods and subject matters and has to rethink its future directions.*

> Laughter is much more dangerous than a political manifesto, than complaining and whining, or throwing a tantrum on stage.
>
> Şinasi Dikmen[2]

Despite a certain presence in the media, Turkish-German artists still do not figure prominently within the German cultural scene, neither as producers nor as subjects. In addition, they are all too often restricted to portraying and representing stereotypical characters and cliché-ridden roles. The main reason for this misrepresentation, as well as for the many cases of outright lack of representation, dates back to the nineteen sixties and seventies: When the Turkish *Gastarbeiter* (guest workers) arrived in Germany, they were expected to simply do their jobs and to return home afterwards. Turks were invited as laborers — most Germans were neither prepared nor willing to deal with their need for and ability of cultural and artistic expression.[3]

But, in fact, a wide range of people with different educational backgrounds reflecting social stratifications already present in Turkey migrated to Germany, among them intellectuals and artists. While there were some early artistic endeavors and even a certain amount of German support, on the whole, circumstances in Germany were adverse for Turkish artists. Turks as factory workers, vegetable vendors, tailors or cleaning women — these images became fixed clichés in the German mind that hardly left any space for Turks as artists, intellectuals or politicians. Furthermore, there was neither an infrastructure nor an audience available to them. On their way to success, the artists among the first generation immigrants had to overcome prejudices and fight against stereotypes — and, additionally, in order to be heard their struggle had to take place entirely in a foreign language.

The German Kabarett tradition dates back to the beginning of the twentieth century.[4] A rich and varied metropolitan Kabarett scene oscillating between literary Kabarett and varieté-shows evolved and flourished especially in the Weimar era. With the Nazis' accession to power, Kabarett suffered severe censorship and prosecution; in 1944, the last stage was closed down. After World War Two, German Kabarett made a new beginning. Primarily employing elements of satire (such as irony, sarcasm and hyperbole), the new form of political-satirical Kabarett dealt critically with political events, German society and its members, at the same time intending to engage its audience. In the sixties, a young, critical generation triggered a political radicalization of the Kabarett stage. Countering the spirit of the student movement, the seventies, in turn, witnessed a continuous rise of popular nonsense shows. This juxtaposition of high-brow critical Kabarett and less demanding nonsense shows provides the backdrop for early Turkish-German Kabarett endeavors. Due to restrictive governments in their home country, Turkish migrants did not have a native Kabarett tradition they could draw upon. The only significant stage, the *Dedekuşu* (ostrich), was opened in the late sixties. Satire and other indirect forms of social criticism, however, have a long history in Turkish literature and performance arts, e.g., in the Karagöz Shadow Theatre.

Turks had been flocking to Germany since 1961, the year of the labor contract between the two countries.[5] But even some twenty years down the road, Turkish migrant workers were still social outsiders without a political voice. Their adverse social situation and their particular living conditions initially lent themselves less to nonsense shows than to critical-satirical forms of Kabarett. Consequently, the early phase of Turkish-German Kabarett, represented here by the *Kabarett Knobi-Bonbon* and the *Bodenkosmetikerinnen*,

dealt entirely with sociopolitical topics. The second half of the nineties witnessed a variety of new Kabarett projects, most notably Muhsin Omurca's
caricature Kabarett and Serdar Somuncu's dramatized Hitler-readings.
Another new form was Ethno Comedy, represented mainly by Django Asül
and Kaya Yanar, both second generation Turks who were born and raised in
Germany. As this phenomenon continues to be influential to the present
day, I will touch upon it towards the end of this article; the main concern
of my presentation, however, lies with political-satirical forms of Kabarett,
as the majority of the Turkish-German Kabarettists continues to be indebted
to this tradition and rejects means of entertainment that are void of a political message.[6]

In the satires he started writing in the late seventies, Şinasi Dikmen
effectively set the parameters for later Kabarett projects. His narratives represent a departure from the so-called *Betroffenheitsliteratur* (Literature of
Affliction): During the seventies and early eighties, the literature by Turkish authors in Germany mainly dealt with themes such as homesickness and
cultural displacement, often employing a lamenting tone.[7] What distinguishes
Dikmen's texts from this body of works is a spirit of humor and witty counter-
attack: "You will not find a single text of mine written in a whining tone.
To make fun of [people or situations] means to be still eager to fight. Once
you start lamenting, you have already given up and accepted your fate" (Dikmen, personal interview). Thematically, Dikmen's satires pick up issues of
Turkish-German everyday life, focusing on matters of integration, identity
and discrimination.[8] With cutting irony, the author attacks instances of prejudice and discrimination with which Turks find themselves confronted in
Germany. Reproducing cultural clichés and polarizations, he exaggerates
them in a way as to render them transparent, thereby allowing a twisted
view behind the scenes. By using this technique, Dikmen effectively debunks
normative roles and stereotypes and exposes mechanisms of social exclusion.

The short narrative "Wer ist ein Türke?" (Who Is a Turk?), for instance,
recounts how the narrator, a Turk lacking typical 'Turkish' markers such as
a black moustache, is denied his Turkish identity on grounds of his reading
a leading German weekly. The following short conversation takes place
between an older German lady and the Turk:

> "You cannot possibly be a Turk."—"Why not?"—"Just because."—"I am a
> Turk. Do you want me to show you my passport?"—"You don't need to,
> because you aren't Turkish."—"How can you be so sure?"—"Firstly, well,
> hmm, firstly, I don't know, but, hmm … you're certainly not a Turk."—"Why
> not?"—"Because, hmm, because—how shall I put this?—hmm, because
> you're reading *Die Zeit*" ["Der andere Türke" 10].

This refusal to accept the narrator's Turkish identity represents a discriminating gesture on part of the German who arrogantly enforces an image of Turkishness informed by ignorance and prejudice; as such it is beyond the reach of any rational argument. And, in fact, there is also an identity crisis involved on the part of the narrator, which is expressed in an interior monologue: "Am I a Turk, or am I not a Turk? If I am not a Turk, what then is it I am? And what if I am a Turk after all?... Could it be that I am a *getürkter Türke?*" (8). Employing the derogatory German coinage *getürkt* ("Turked," meaning "faked"), the narrator articulates a problem that he supposedly shares with many of his fellow Turks living in Germany: Constantly confronted with superficial and cliché-ridden concepts of Turkishness (e.g., the assumption that Turks do not read German intellectual journals), Turks ultimately surrender to them: The labels gradually sink in and become prescriptive to the Turks' own way of regarding themselves. On the one hand, Dikmen's short narrative points at the constructedness of any such labeling; on the other hand, it highlights the difficulties of creating a cultural identity in an area of conflicting notions between outside-perception and self-determination.

The years between the publication of Dikmen's two volumes of satires in 1983 and 1985 mark his turn towards Kabarett. Through Kabarett, Dikmen hoped to reach a greater audience with his texts; in addition, he felt the need to prove to Germans what migrants were "capable of doing" if they really set their mind to it.[9] Dikmen's turn to Kabarett coincided with the founding of several other Turkish-German theatre groups, most notably the *Tiyatrom* in Berlin and the *Arkada Theater* Cologne. All of these ventures articulated the need of artistic self-expression among the Turkish migrants; the theatre projects were designed to infuse new themes into the German culture scene and to increase the visibility of the Turkish minority. For too long, Turks in Germany had been voiceless objects of description — now they demanded to be subjects in their own rights, they insisted to be heard and seen.

In 1985, together with the caricaturist Muhsin Omurca and supported by the German theatre director Ralf Milde, Dikmen founded the *Kabarett Knobi-Bonbon* (short: the *Knobis*), Germany's first ethnic Kabarett. The German audience was stunned; they had never before encountered anything like it. Milde describes the beginnings of the *Knobis* as follows:

> At first, the fact alone that a Turk entered the theatre stage and spoke in broken German created a sensation. People said: 'Great how the Turk utters a sentence!' You absolutely have to move beyond this stage as fast as possible. People have to say: 'This has class! It really challenges me!' And with *Knobi-Bonbon* that truly happened. They earned the respect of their audience

because they became amazingly good at what they were doing [Personal Interview].

Dikmen and Omurca complemented each other perfectly, not only artistically but also visually: the more experienced Dikmen with his short and stocky exterior; and Omurca as the slender and energetic youngster. The *Knobis'* debut program of 1985 already featured the two characters that, over the years, were to become their trademarks: the traditional Turkish street sweeper Ahmet (Omurca) and the hyper-integrated know-it-all Şinasi (Dikmen).[10] The themes the *Knobis* dealt with in this and in the following four programs were for the most part similar to the ones Dikmen had addressed in his satires, with an even stronger focus on issues of political and cultural integration. In Germany, integration had long been equated with assimilation. This particular German definition of integration lent itself perfectly to satirical representations on stage. In fact, to this day, Turkish-German Kabarett takes its cues and subject matters mainly from the tension created by the German misconception of integration.

In *Vorsicht, frisch integriert!* (Caution, Recently Integrated!), the overly integrated and overly naïve Şinasi (whose name gradually mutates into Schimanski, the name of a popular German TV-hero) attempts to convert the street cleaner Ahmet to become a good German. He perpetuates stereotypes and discriminations: "Turks like you, who are not yet integrated, spoil everything. You guys don't speak proper German and you behave like savages, rude and insulting" (Dikmen, *Der andere Türke* 86). The suitcase he carries with him turns out to be a veritable integration kit: "With this integration suitcase," he explains, "I travel through Germany and integrate anything I can lay my hands on" (94). Ahmet, the more intelligent and critical-minded of the two characters, finally turns the situation upside-down. Step by step he lures Şinasi back into acknowledging the repressed Turkish sides of his character. In the course of this 're-integration' process, the tragic aspects of Şinasi's attempt to pass as a German are revealed: Although he had embraced German values and notions of integration unconditionally, he had at

Dikmen, Milde and Omurca (caricature by Omurca, mid–1980s).

no point been accepted as a member of German society. Ironically, toward the end of the play, it is Şinasi who receives an official government letter stating that his residence permit has expired and that he has to leave Germany immediately.

At the end of the program, the actors, without transition, start reflecting about the performance and their audience:

Ahmet: We are finished with them, and yet they remain seated.
Şinasi: (to audience) What do you think you're doing? You can't sit here forever!
Ahmet: Don't you realize that we don't need you any longer?
Şinasi: You've got to do something. After all, you were the one who got them here.
Ahmet: I asked for spectators, but humans came [100–101].

Particularly with the last words — a slightly altered quote by Max Frisch: "We called workers, but humans came" (comp. Kraus 122) — the grand reversal of the program takes place: The audience is metaphorically turned into *Gastarbeiter.* In the end, the two actors revoke the audience's residence permit and send them on their way.

Over the years, the *Kabarett Knobi-Bonbon* achieved a tremendous popularity. In 1987, Dikmen and Omurca were awarded the German Kabarett Prize, they filled Kabarett houses throughout Germany, and the Goethe Institute even invited them to put on German shows in Turkey (where they performed their program in German). Their presence in the German cultural scene, as well as the explosive content of their performances, inspired and encouraged other Turkish artists to follow in their foot steps. One of them was the all-female Kabarett group *Die Bodenkosmetikerinnen* which Nursel Köse founded in 1992. Asked for the reason why she chose Kabarett as a mode of expression, she explained:

> In this country, you hardly have a chance to be heard. Either you are a politician or you pursue an artistic career. And Kabarett actually goes one step further: Here, you can say a lot without getting anyone angry at you. You can use Kabarett as a means to state certain truths in an utterly exaggerated fashion that will make people laugh while, at the same time, they take your message home with them [Personal Interview].

The ensemble, whose name ("floor cosmeticians") is a euphemism for "cleaning women," consisted of five (at times, up to eight) women, including a German. Köse describes the project as follows: "We were first of all women, then foreign women, and finally Turkish women. In us, all clichés were compact. We presented scenes based on our own life experiences and made fun of them and of ourselves" (personal interview). At times more upfront than the *Knobis*, the *Bodenkosmetikerinnen* thematically focused on the discrimination against foreigners in general and against (foreign) women in particular, playfully deconstructing clichés and thwarting cultural expectations. One of the recurring images of their shows is the character of the cleaning woman, serving as leitmotif to their programs that addresses wide-spread stereotypes regarding Turkish women. In addition, it also added to the highly visual character of their performances.

The scene "Gravierende Probleme" (Severe Problems), which is part of the debut program *Weggekehrt* (Swept Away, 1992), recounts a conversation between a German therapist and her Turkish cleaning woman. When the German finds out that her cleaning woman gets beaten by her Turkish husband, she feels called upon to treat her as a patient. It has to be emphasized that the Turkish woman at no time asks for help; rather, it is forced upon her by the German analyst. The analyst's attempt to assist her is well-meant, yet she offers her advice from a perspective of cultural superiority, reducing the Turkish woman to the clichéd role of the victim. Ultimately, however, the Turkish character assumes control of the situation, and scene closes with a complete reversal of traditional cultural roles (strong Western woman versus victimized Oriental woman): It is the Turkish cleaning woman who, like a mother, rocks the crying German therapist in her arms — a powerful counter-image to "the great father of psychology" Sigmund Freud whose presence dominated the first half of the scene.

In the second half of the 1990s, the first phase of Turkish-German Kabarett came to an end. For over a decade, the critical-political tradition of German post-war Kabarett had set the parameters of Turkish-German Kabarett. When its two founding fathers Dikmen and Omurca, finally split ways in 1997 and embarked on impressive solo careers, Turkish-German Kabarett entered a new phase with more experimental and innovative projects. Two years later, in 1999, the *Bodenkosmetikerinnen* terminated their project as well. This was partly due to the surging comedy wave that threatened to drown political Kabarett. Köse explains: "We were determined to remain faithful to our themes. We didn't want to go down that road" (personal interview).

Among the diverse Turkish-German Kabarettists of the 2000s, Dikmen could be classified as the traditionalist. Even after the breakup of the *Knobis*, he remained true to his subject matters and the legacy of political-critical Kabarett. Dikmen immediately realized his old dream of opening up his own Kabarett stage. In March 1997, one week before the last performance of the *Knobis*, the *Kabarett Änderungsschneiderei* (short *KÄS*) opened its doors in Frankfurt am Main. The name literally translates to "alteration tailor" and refers to a long tradition (as well as the cliché) of Turkish tailors in Germany. Dikmen's particular twist is that he applies the term to language: "In Germany, the tailor's profession is a Turkish domain. The Turks sew, mend, shorten or lengthen the German, so to speak. Accordingly, in a tailor Kabarett, the German language is mended and changed" (qtd. in Paul).

In his first of to date five solo programs, *Kleider machen Deutsche* (1997), Dikmen utilizes the image of the Turkish tailor both in the title and on stage. The title is Dikmen's own variation of the German proverb *Kleider machen Leute* (clothes make people), replacing "people" with "Germans." The message is clear: Only by dressing like Germans (i.e., by assimilating, both visually and intellectually) are Turks recognized as citizens and humans. Needless to say, the program adds a satirical twist to the story: It is the Turkish tailor, Dikmen's alter ego on stage, who is in charge of altering the German clothes. However, Dikmen does not propose to revolutionize — or even just change — German Kabarett. Similar to his earlier stage character, but more successfully, Dikmen strives to be part of the established Kabarett scene. Although he acknowledges his Turkish origins, it is his expressed intent to present professional German Kabarett, albeit with Turkish themes. Communication is absolutely crucial for Dikmen: "Me, up on the stage, the audience down there — but we understand each other," he says, adding with a twinkle in his eye: "And while they are laughing, I sneak in my message, my personal take on things" (personal interview).

The initial risks of founding his own stage were high, but after a slow beginning, Dikmen's reputation as a solo performer kept spreading and, before long, he played to sold-out houses. In the fall of 2002, Dikmen was able to move into a bigger theatre space of his own design, and in October 2003, he was awarded the Culture Prize of Frankfurt's SPD party. The party chairman paid tribute to Dikmen declaring that, through his artistry, he had greatly contributed to turning Frankfurt into Germany's "capital city of humor" (Remlein). Dikmen has, without a doubt, become an integral and quite prominent part of the German culture scene.

Unlike Dikmen, Omurca considers himself an artistic nomad and never intended to settle down. Omurca had been a caricaturist before his migration; he continued drawing in Germany throughout the *Knobi*-years and, over time, won international acclaim. However, it was only with his solo debut *Tagebuch eines Skinheads in Istanbul* (Diary of a Skinhead in Istanbul, 1998) that he combined his two fields of artistic expertise to create a novel form of Kabarett, the cartoon Kabarett. He describes the fusion of these two art forms as a logical progression: "It is the same with satirical texts and caricatures: You have to find the punch line. ... A cartoon strip or a caricature story is nothing but a drawn scene, a drafted script" (personal interview).

The inclusion of visual images to Omurca's program serves multiple purposes: The caricatures replace a partner, provide a visual background, facilitate a dialogue with the audience and add additional layers of meaning to the performance. Caricatures are also reflected upon within the play: On waking from a nightmare in which he saw himself reduced to a drawing glued to a wall, the Turkish interpreter Simulti Ali exclaims: "I'm flat. Two-dimensional only. Just the etching of a Turk. A sheet of Turk" (Omurca, *Tagebuch*). The Turk as a "flat character," an erasable sketch lacking depth and agency, reduced to its outside representation, an artificial construct of German society — Omurca succeeds here in creating a powerful image of cultural suppression.

While certain correspondences to the *Knobi-Bonbon*–times are apparent, *The Diary of a Skinhead*, a satirical unmasking of xenophobic tendencies in German society presented with approximately 35 images projected on a big screen, comprises a departure in more than just a formal respect. No longer focusing on issues of identity and integration, Omurca's play recounts the story of a German skinhead Hansi who is sentenced to four weeks of "re-education therapy" in Istanbul for setting fire to a Turkish apartment house. The narrative is rendered in the form of a slide show which Hansi, who enters the stage saluting Hitler, presents to a group of right-wing radicals — a provocative move that implicitly turns the German audience into Hansi's accomplices and fellow *Neonazis*. Not surprisingly, the absurd re-education therapy results in a complete failure: Not only does Hansi's xenophobia remain uncured, but, in addition, his companion, the psychotherapist Botho Kraus, progressively loses his hair and converts into a skinhead.[11] In conclusion, Hansi ironically suggests a joint excursion to Turkey at the expense of the German tax payer, thus hinting at the futility and absurdity of such endeavors.

Satirical programs about right wing radicals are by no means commonplace in German Kabarett. Not surprisingly, Omurca's daring performances alarmed and annoyed right-wing extremists throughout Germany, and especially in the East. Omurca relates the story of how the police had to escort him to the stage during a 1998 performance in Saalfeld, a stronghold of German neonazis. But although his play centers on the character of a skinhead, the scope of Omurca's criticism is not restricted to the fascist scene alone. At one point, Simulti Ali admits that clearly discernible radicals are not his main concern: "What about the others?" he asks the audience. "How am I to recognize the other skinheads who still have hair on their heads?" (*Tagebuch*). Thus, in addition to forms of radicalism, the program also comments on latent instances of discrimination and xenophobia (e.g., in bureaucratic practices and social institutions).

Like Dikmen, Omurca has succeeded in establishing himself as a solo performer of renown. For *Skinhead*, he was awarded the German *Kabarett Sonderpreis* in 1998, and he has since released another two successful solo programs. As a performer, Omurca does not feel called upon to adapt to German mainstream Kabarett. For instance, unlike his former partner, he refuses to "cleanse" his stage language of its Turkish traits: Sporadic grammatical mistakes and mispronunciations are part of his show; he regards them as "a special coloring of the German language" (personal interview). A perfect example of Omurca's biculturally-informed performances is his own Turkified (or "Turked") version of the German national anthem, an idea he had already come up with in his *Knobi-Bonbon* times and which has now become both his signature tune and one the highlights of his shows. Omurca's version of the anthem emphasizes the idea of "sameness with differences," refuting (German) notions of integration based on cultural assimilation; at the same time, it acknowledges a shared history of Germans and Turks that, all too often, goes unrecognized.

Unlike the artists mentioned so far, Serdar Somuncu grew up in Germany; and it was in Germany that he studied theatre and became an acclaimed actor and director. However, despite his distinctly German artistic background, Somuncu's name and his appearance mark him as non–German. When he set out to perform dramatized readings of Hitler's *Mein Kampf* in 1996, the fact that a "Turk" had adopted this topic created an outright sensation. A major German newspaper (the *taz*) even named Somuncu "man of the year." Not all reactions were equally positive: Many critics expressed skepticism about Somuncu's choice of subject matter; others were worried that his (the Turk's) intention might be to criticize them (the Germans) and their problematic past from a position of moral superiority. And, of course, right-wing extremists were furious. Throughout his eight years of performing Hitler and Goebbels, Somuncu received countless threats. The reading in Potsdam on January 30, 2001 (the anniversary of Hitler's appointment as German chancellor), for instance, had to take place under strong police protection and Somuncu himself had to wear a bulletproof jacket (comp. Schicketanz).

Like Omurca, Somuncu believes in a shared history of Germans and non–Germans living in Germany. On the one hand, he regards fascism as "a global issue" (qtd. in Scheper), on the other hand, he declares Germany's particular Nazi past as a matter of concern to all people living in Germany. He feels responsible for participating in the revision of German history:

> Although we Turks do not have a grandfather who was a member of the NSDAP, even though we do not have a relative with a brown [i.e., national

socialist] past, it is nonetheless our responsibility to share in the critical revision of the German theme. We cannot insist on a common present and future without also claiming possession of the process of coming to terms with the German past [Somuncu 173].

Somuncu's performances represent a daring and provocative entry into new thematic realms on the part of a "Turkish" actor — or rather, one that the German public perceives as Turkish. This venture, more than others, raises questions concerning the ethnic and cultural belonging of German artists of Turkish heritage. Somuncu himself seems unwilling to discuss this issue. He simply mentions "the advantages of a dual existence" and concludes: "To know a lot means to be able to do a lot. ... In life, as well as in art, each new perspective enriches the comprehension of the observer" (Somuncu 102).

As an additional form of contemporary German Kabarett, comedy has to be mentioned. The rise of these apolitical shows was facilitated by the spread of US-forms of entertainment and coincided with the emerging *Spaßkultur* ("culture of fun"), a new phenomenon in German society. Mainly propagated through private TV, these comedy proliferated throughout the 1990s and soon became a serious competition, if not a threat, to political-critical Kabarett (compare the *Bodenkosmetikerinnen*). Within recent years, two artists of Turkish origin, in particular, gained immense popularity: Django Asül and Kaya Yanar. The various projects of these and other artists have given rise to the term "ethno-comedy": comedy that is presented by minority artists and/or deals with questions of ethnicity.[12]

In 2001, Yanar started hosting his own TV comedy show *Was guckst du?!* and, practically overnight, he became one of the most prominent and successful comedians in Germany: The German weekly *Die Zeit* dedicated a long article to "the new star of ethno-comedy" (Kaiser). Unlike Asül, who started out as a more serious cabaretist, Yanar, from the very beginning, refused to become politically involved on stage. "It is not about foreigner discourses; it is all about finally envisioning comedy and foreigners together, without ending up with political cabaret."[13] While recognizing that any Turkish-Arabic performer inevitably also bears a political implication, he dislikes political cabaret's tendency to lecture and moralize (comp. Thomann). Nevertheless, Yanar's performances cannot be dismissed as trivial nonsense shows. He chooses his subject matters with care, and his stage characters are equally carefully designed. As a critic notes: "Kaya's show is all about precision, nuances in gesture and language: With him, Turk does not equal Turk [i.e., not all Turks are alike]" (Kaiser). Yanar himself comments: "There is a vital difference in the presentation of clichés in sketches: Either you use them and then make fun of them in order to dissolve them, or you use them to ridicule the people they describe" (qtd. in Loh/Güngör 169). This attitude has made him popular with Germans and non–Germans alike.

While many political cabaretists dismiss ethno-comedy as a trivial form of entertainment lacking a social message, it can nevertheless be regarded as one of various departures from what had by the mid–1990s become "conventional" Turkish-German Kabarett. The year 1997 in particular (the breakup of the *Knobis*) marks the beginning of a new stage of what, parallel to Ethno Comedy, might be called Ethno Kabarett. The various projects of the performers presented in this chapter comprise a new diversity of forms and subject matters announcing the advent of the new millennium.

Early Turkish-German Kabarett had focused exclusively on issues of identity and integration. Both the *Kabarett Knobi-Bonbon* and the *Bodenkosmetikerinnen* presented clichéd images of Turks with the intention of deconstructing them and of counteracting instances of social discrimination. Their programs were designed both to inform and to instruct the German public. In the latter half of the nineties, Turkish-German Kabarett underwent major transformations. This was primarily due to a new generation of performers entering the Kabarett stage. Somuncu, Asül and Yanar, who were born and or raised in Germany, naturally have a different relationship with and attitude toward German society. In addition, German society itself had changed over the years. The *Knobis* launched their stage career in 1985, at a time when a conservative German government passed laws to encourage "guest workers" to return to their home countries. The *Bodenkosmetikerinnen*, in turn, started performing in the wake of racist attacks following German reunification. While the political, social and economical discrimination of "foreigners" (or people of partly non–German background) continues to present challenges to present-day German society, the election of a liberal government in 1998 also indicates an atmosphere of increased cultural open-mindedness at the turn of the millennium.

These changes have left their mark on Turkish-German Kabarett. As some of the latter projects described here demonstrate, Turkish-German Kabarett has made a distinctive move to leave the ethnic corner to become an integral part of an extended German art scene. Less than twenty years after the first projects were launched, the heirs of the *Kabarett Knobi-Bonbon* have reached a point at the crossroads, i.e., a point where Turkish-German Kabarett (and Turkish-German art in general) has to question its methods and subject matters and has to rethink its future directions: As Turks have settled and become an integral part of a many-cultured German society, traditional methods of portraying them as "foreigners" have to be reconsidered — as does, in fact, the very question of what it means to be an artist of Turkish origin in Germany.

In this respect, the title of Dikmen's latest program is very suggestive: *Quo vadis, Türke?* (Where are you going, Turk?, 2002). Where, indeed, is the Turk going, and where is he taking his Kabarett? On stage, Dikmen appears to have moved beyond presenting cultural displacement; issues of identity and integration no longer are the focal points of his performances. "I am both Turkish and German," Dikmen states in a recent interview, adding: "So I am neither German nor Turkish. I am an individual and, over time, I have come to like my individual[ity]" (personal interview). Omurca, as well, has clearly moved beyond binary oppositions: In *Kanakmän—Tags Deutscher, nachts Türke* (German by Day, Turk at Night, 2000) he plays with notions of dual citizenship and creates a comic Turkish superhero. "We used to say," he remarks, "that we neither belong to Turkey nor to Germany; now we say that we belong both to Germany and to Turkey. ... Now the Germans are having an identity crisis" (personal interview). Omurca's comment highlights a general German predicament: In a society whose major cities consist of up to thirty-five percent non–Germans, what can be considered German "mainstream" culture these days? But even more importantly, the remark exemplifies the grown self-confidence of Turkish-German artists.

In March 2004, the *Bodenkosmetikerinnen*, now reduced to the duo Nursel Köse and Serpil Ari, celebrated their come-back with the program *Arabesk—Selbst erfüllende Prophezeiungen* (Self Fulfilling Prophecies). Excerpts from the advertising materials read as follows: "We are German Turkish women — in us dwells the powers of two cultures and two languages. ... Where ever we turn, we have a new perspective on society. ... We re-composed the symphony of integration ... This is a duet that has to be performed with equal rights if its melody is to caress our ear." German politicians may still be quarreling over outdated concepts of identity and integration, but, as this and other projects indicate, German artists of Turkish origin have moved beyond the times of identity crises (but *not* beyond the topic of identity!). Perhaps Omurca's statement that it is now the Germans who are having an identity crisis precisely hits the mark. And as Kabarett thrives on instances of crises, it is unlikely that it will not run out of material anytime soon.

"Kanakmän" (caricature by Omurca, around 2000).

THE OHIO STATE UNIVERSITY

Notes

1. By using the spelling "Kabarett" throughout this article, I distinguish between the specifically German form of (political-satirical) Kabarett and other types of cabaret (e.g., featuring dance).

2. The quote is taken from a personal interview I performed with Dikmen. The translations of all personal interviews and all German text quotations are my own.

3. Deniz Göktürk makes this point in respect to migrant film in her article "Migration und Kino — Subnationale Mitleidskultur oder transnationale Rollenspiele?" (Chiellino, "Literatur" 329–347).

4. For the following short account, compare Volker Kühn and Budzinski/Hippen.

5. For a concise introduction to the Turkish labor movement to Germany, see Terkessidis, *Migranten*.

6. So far, hardly any literature has been published on Turkish-German Kabarett (and on Turkish-German Theatre in general). Exceptions are Pazarkaya's article and Terkessidis' "Kabarett und Satire deutsch-türkischer Autoren" in Chiellino, "Literatur" 294–301.

7. For Literature of Affliction, compare Arens 34–54.

8. Compare Tantow, who calls the texts "integration satires" (in Dikmen, "Der andere Türke" 103–109).

9. Interview with Dikmen in Chiellino, "Reise" 111–125: 123–4.

10. In these characters, influences of the Turkish Shadow Theatre tradition are very apparent.

11. A satirical allusion to the playwright Botho Strauß and his problematic representation of Turks, e.g., in *Groß und klein* (1978).

12. This is my own working definition of the term, which, to my knowledge, has never coherently been defined. It has to be mentioned though that the term has also been applied to comedy shows by German performers.

13. Yanar on the website to his TV-show <http: //www. sat1. de/wasgucks tdu/>.

References Cited

Arens, Hiltrud. "*Kulturelle Hybridität*" in der deutschen Minoritätenliteratur der achtziger Jahre. Tübingen: Stauffenberg-Verlag, 2000.

Budzinski, Klaus, and Reinhard Hippen, eds. *Metzler Kabarett Lexikon*. Stuttgart: Metzler, 1996.

Chiellino, Carmine, ed. *Die Reise hält an. Ausländische Künstler in der Bundesrepublik*. München: Beck, 1988.

_____, ed. *Interkulturelle Literatur in Deutschland*. Stuttgart: Metzler, 2000.

Dikmen, Şinasi. *Der andere Türke*. Berlin: EXpress Edition, 1985.

_____. Personal Interview. Berlin, 6 Dec. 2002.

Kaiser, Andrea. "Noch'n Türkenwitz. Vor Kaya Yanar, dem neuen Star der Ethno-Comedy, ist keine Randgruppe sicher." *Die Zeit* 15 Feb. 2001: 36.

Köse, Nursel. *Weggekehrt.* Unpublished Manuscript, 1992.

_____. Personal Interview. Berlin, 19 Jan. 2003.

Krauss, Hannes, ed. *Vom Nullpunkt zur Wende. Deutschsprachige Literatur 1945–1990.* Essen: Klartext, 1994.

Kühn, Volker. *Die zehnte Muse—111 Jahre Kabarett.* Köln: vgs, 1993.

Loh, Hannes, and Murat Güngör. *Fear of a Kanak Planet— HipHop zwischen Weltkultur und Nazi-Rap.* Höfen: Hannibal, 2002.

Milde, Ralf. Personal Interview. Ulm, 19 Feb. 2003.

Omurca, Muhsin. *Tagebuch eines Skinheads in Istanbul.* Unpublished Manuscript, 1998.

_____. Personal Interview. Berlin, 17 Jan. 2003.

Paul, Peter. "Wo die deutsche Sprache genäht und geflickt werden kann. Gespräch mit Şinasi Dikmen (ehemals 'Knobi-Bonbon'), dem Gründer des Kabaretts." *Frankfurter Rundschau,* 3 Sept. 1997: 24.

Pazarkaya Yüksel. "Zwei Länder im Herzen." *Zeit Punkte* 2/1999: 76–81.

Remlein, Thomas. "Der Türke mit dem bayerischen Humor." *Frankfurter Neue Presse* 18 Oct. 2002: 18.

Scheper, Alexandra. "Hitler minus Macht ist eine Komödie: Der Türke Serdar Somuncu und seine Lesungen aus Hitlers *Mein Kampf.*" *Süddeutsche Zeitung* 27 Nov. 1996: 15.

Schicketanz, Sabine. "Kritische Lesungen: 'Danke an die Polizei'. Die 'Nationale Bewegung' konnte Lesung nicht verhindern." *Der Tagesspiegel* 1 Jan. 2001: 20.

Somuncu, Serdar. *Nachlass eines Massenmörders. Auf Lesereise mit Mein Kampf.* Bergisch Gladbach: Verlagsgruppe Lübbe, 2002.

Terkessidis, Mark. *Migranten.* Hamburg: Rotbuch, 2000.

Thomann, Jörg. "Vor dem müssen wir keine Angst haben. Heilsame Komik: Was 'Ethno-Comedy' sich in Zeiten des Krieges leisten kann." *Frankfurter Allgemeine,* 12 Oct. 2001: 60.

Oedipus in New York
Greek Tragedy and Edward Albee's
The Goat, or, Who Is Sylvia?

Thomas M. Falkner

Abstract

In the published version of The Goat, or, Who is Sylvia?, *Edward Albee adds the subtitle:* Notes toward a definition of tragedy. *The play can be regarded as an exercise in applied theory that offers a "definition" that consistently references Greek tragedy, beginning with its title, which alludes to tragedy as "goat-song," and the hybris of its protagonist, which confounds the distinctions between human and animal and recalls the kinds of transgressions that epitomize Greek tragedy, in particular* Oedipus the King. *The play largely employs the tragic form that Aristotle recommends and consistently quotes materials from Greek tragedy, including Martin's relationship with "Sylvia," which has a strong Dionysiac dimension. The protagonist is best regarded as a failed hero or anti-hero, yet one who displays a kind of virtue in his struggle against conventional measures of morality. Despite the absurdity of its premises and abundant humor,* The Goat *constitutes perhaps the most classically tragic play Albee has written.*

Like Mark Twain on reports of his death, concerns about the waning of Edward Albee's theatrical career have proved, to say the least, greatly exaggerated. *The Goat, or, Who is Sylvia?*, which won the 2002 Tony Award for Best Play, succeeded in being both popular and provocative for its shocking subject matter.[1] Martin Gray, successful architect, loving husband and father, and respected professional, is involved in a prolonged sexual relationship — as Martin insists, in love — with a goat. Martin has concealed the situation from family and friends and apparently made some effort to change his behavior. But in the first act of the play, he reveals himself, twice: first playfully to his wife Stevie, who in clever repartee enjoys the joke; then more seriously to his friend Ross, who has come to their home to film a television interview recognizing Martin for his latest accomplishments. In the following two acts, which take place the next day, the family responds to a letter from Ross in which he reports that Martin is having "an affair with a certain Sylvia who, I am mortified to tell you, is a goat." In act II, a classic Albee *agon*, Stevie and Martin "discuss" the situation; she exits with the threat "You have brought me down, and, Christ!, I'll bring you down with me!" In act III, Billy (who is gay) and his father (who disapproves) try to reestablish their relationship, and the two embrace desperately, just as Ross reappears, in what Albee indicates is "a deep sobbing, sexual kiss." In the horrific finale, Stevie enters disheveled, dragging behind her the slain and bloody carcass of "the goat."

Like most of the playwright's work, from *The Zoo Story* to the recent *The Play About the Baby*, *The Goat* is unconventional and deeply disturbing, but it also represents a different approach from what audiences have come to expect. Albee more often sends us home questioning the relationship between speech and truth, illusion and reality, as he collapses the differences between them. *The Goat*, on the other hand, does not question whether Martin has done what he claims but leaves us struggling to understand why.[2] How can Martin have done this, and what is the meaning of his bestiality? How should his family respond and how are we, the audience, to react? In this paper I want to approach these questions by looking at the play in relation to genre — indeed, in the published version the playwright fairly invites us to do so with a parenthetical subtitle: *Notes toward a definition of tragedy.* I want to suggest that in these "notes," which can be regarded as an exercise in applied theory, Albee offers a definition of tragedy that refers us repeatedly to Greek tragedy,[3] suggesting what he regards as essential features of the genre and yielding perhaps the most classically tragic play Albee has written.[4]

Albee anchors his approach in the title, which links the play to Dionysus and the mythical origins of the genre. The word tragedy or *tragôidia*, of course, means "goat-song" and *tragôidoi* (the chorus) "goat-singers," with *trag-* from the root for "goat" and *-edy* related to our "ode." According to ancient sources, *tragôidia* took its name from the fact that either (a) the winner among the competing tragedians received a goat as prize, or (b) a goat was sacrificed as part of the festival of Dionysus, or (c) tragedy derived from the satyr play, with its chorus of goat-footed satyrs. Although these traditions are of questionable value (Else 1965.9–31, Burkert 1966), the name of the genre clearly references the animal that is sacred to Dionysus, the god and patron of tragedy. The goat is also one of the familiar forms the god can assume, a point to which we will return. Albee features "the goat" at the center of the play as a potent and conspicuous symbol of the genre. And he writes a script that plays against some of the most basic myths, themes and conventions of Greek tragedy, as these are evidenced in the texts, in particular *Oedipus the King*, and in the most widely regarded study of tragedy, Aristotle's *Poetics*.[5]

The Goat reaffirms the Greek view that tragedy is fundamentally about transgression (*hybris*) and the violation of boundaries that define the human and locate it between the realm of the gods (above) and that of the beasts (below).[6] Greek tragedy describes men who in their actions or ambitions disregard their proper place in the moral universe, whether by appropriating divine prerogatives or sinking to sub-human levels of behavior, and the suffering this brings in its train. Greek tragedy focuses on behavior that is violent or sexual in nature and whose transgressive force is often increased by being located within the nexus of family relationships. *The Goat*, with its powerful meld of the violent, the sexual, and the domestic, literally confounds the distinctions between human and animal, recalling myths that epitomize the genre: Atreus' cooking and serving the sons of Thyestes; Agamemnon's sacrifice of his daughter Iphigeneia ("on the altar like a goat," according to Aeschylus)[7]; Ajax's slaughter of cattle and sheep that in his madness he has taken for Greeks; Agave's display of the head of her son, whom she has hunted and still perceives as a lion.[8] In this regard, Albee models *The Goat* most of all against *Oedipus the King*, whose protagonist's incest, albeit unwitting, violates a taboo that distinguishes human society from the animals. Indeed, in an age in which the idea of incest may no longer have, in popular or theatrical terms, the "shock value" it did in Sophocles' Greece or even Freud's Vienna, Albee looks to bestiality for an equivalent to the horrors at the center of *Oedipus*. As if to make sure that we make the connection, Albee includes in act III materials that are quasi-incestuous and further evidence of Martin's alleged perversity: in Martin and Billy's passionate embrace, and in Martin's detailed account of a friend who once became sexually (though involuntarily) aroused while holding his infant child on his lap.

If Martin's transgressive movement is "downward" toward the animal, one can describe that of "the goat" as upward toward the human — the play asks *who*, not what, is Sylvia. When Ross is first told about Martin's affair with "Sylvia," he assumes falsely on her species until he comes to realize that she is, in fact and truly, a goat. And while Martin harbors no illusions that she is other than a goat, he regards her throughout as a person, his beloved, and refers to her only with the bucolic name he has given her. In a parody of Shakespeare, Stevie thinks to ask why:

> Stevie: ...Why do you call her Sylvia, by the way? Did she have a tag or something?

> Or, was it more: Who is Sylvia,
> Fair is she
> That all our goats commend her...
> Martin: No, it just seemed right. Very good, by the way [63].

But the pastoral song in *Two Gentlemen of Verona* (IV, 2) reads "Who is Sylvia, what is she?," and it is significant that Martin does not correct Stevie on this, even as he compliments her on the allusion. Throughout the play Martin refuses, over her objections, to refer to Sylvia as an "it" rather than a "she," and over the bloody carcass he mourns: "What did she ever *do*? I ask you, what did she ever *do*?" He notes repeatedly that he was undone by "those eyes of hers"—"THEM eyes!" (80), Stevie fires back, as if to drive the bestiality from her living room into the backwoods where it belongs. Indeed, the most powerful recognition (*anagnôrisis*) in the play is less that brought about by Ross's letter than Stevie's realization that Martin is truly in love with Sylvia. Stevie sees Martin's sex with the goat as monstrous, but he refuses to yield.

> Stevie: ...You take advantage of this ... creature!? You ... *rape* this ... ani-
> mal and convince yourself that it has to do with *love*!?
> Martin: (*Helpless*) I love her ... and she loves me, and ... [87].

Stevie responds with "a huge animal sound," overturning a bookcase in her rage. It is the very human love that Martin gives to Sylvia that transforms her into a mistress and a rival and Stevie into a tragic heroine capable of bloody revenge. Only at the end of the play does she change her pronouns: "I found her. I killed her," she says, because "She loved you ... you say. As much as I do" (110). The play's finale recalls the *ekkyklêma* scene of the *Agamemnon*, where a gore-spattered Clytemnestra revels over the corpses of Cassandra and her husband.[9] From another perspective, Stevie's slaughter of Sylvia shows just how far Martin has brought her down: like Sophocles' Ajax, who sits in disgrace amid the carnage of the cattle and sheep he has tortured; like Euripides' Hecuba, whose brutal vengeance on Polymestor so dehumanizes her that she is literally metamorphosed into a bitch.

The categorical confusion of the human and the animal has a counterpart in the confounding of the audience's response, evidenced in the play's abundant humor and the audience's frequent if sometimes uncomfortable laughter. There is no question, of course, that tragedy can accommodate comic elements, and Greek tragedy is replete with humorous passages and scenes of comic relief.[10] In *The Goat*, however, the tragic and comic dimensions are parallel and simultaneous, as the audience responds to a situation that is at once terrifying and absurd.[11] In another context, the results might simply be farcical. For instance, the scene in which Ross slowly pries the truth out of Martin has a tragic model in the nurse's interrogation of Phaedra in Euripides' *Hippolytus*: like the nurse, Ross hits pay dirt when Martin admits he is in love and he gets him to name his beloved.[12] But the scene also provokes laughter, as Ross takes lascivious delight in what he imagines as a roll in the hay with a farmer's-daughter type, and when Martin resolves the confusion by showing Ross a wallet photo he keeps of Sylvia. In act I as a whole, the humor is not limited to particular moments of dialogue but grows out of the larger incongruity between what the audience knows and Stevie and Ross know. Indeed, the play's subject matter and the considerable advance publicity it enjoyed virtually ensured that the audience would come to the play "knowing the story" at least in outline, much as the audience at *Oedipus* enjoys multiple levels of irony by its epistemological superiority.

The whole of act II likewise offers occasions for humor at every turn: grotesque ironies, bitter invective, sarcastic abuse, and trademark Albee-esque word play and semantic confusion. The sequence in which Martin describes his sessions with a support group for zoophiliacs (which Stevie dubs "goat-fuckers anonymous," 66) is in any other context simply and hysterically funny, with its stories of men and women involved with dogs, geese, and piglets; and Ross's ill-timed entrance in act III otherwise comes straight out of sit-com. But again it is the absurdity of the overall premises of the play that provides the license for laughter (and in a way that would hardly have been the case had Martin's secret involved, for instance, rape or pedophilia). Albee offers us a kind of satyr play in reverse: where the Greek satyr play relocates heroic characters to a sylvan setting of goats and goat-men that subverts their tragic standing, *The Goat* brings Sylvia, figuratively and literally, into Albee's domestic combat zone, yielding a tragedy with a strong "tragi-" comic dimension (pun fully intended).[13] While the humor of the play and the absurdity of its premises are at odds with the seriousness of the situation, they do not cancel its reality or mitigate the suffering it causes the family. The conclusion of the play is relentlessly and terrifyingly tragic, as if Albee were insisting on a tragic catharsis and the play's tragic character, even as he eschews the more singular focus of Greek tragedy.

The tragic character of *The Goat* is also pronounced in its ethical dimension, which Albee has organized around concepts familiar from Aristotle's *Poetics* and the paradigmatic *Oedipus*: a plot that arouses pity and fear by moving from prosperity to unhappiness; a reversal (*peripeteia*) accompanied by recognition (*anagnôrisis*); and a protagonist whom the audience might recognize as someone undeserving of his misfortune, who (apart from the behavior in question) is neither wholly good nor wholly bad but "like us"—*peri ton homoion* (*Poetics* 1453a4–6). Martin is cast as a contemporary Oedipus, whose shameful secret is brought to light and who brings his household to destruction. His prosperity provides the play's *mis-en-scène*. Just turned fifty, he has achieved all he might have hoped for; the living room, with its expensive books, overstuffed furniture and African *objets d'art*, exudes affluence though not extravagance. He has received an international prize for his work and been awarded a lucrative contract to design something called "the city of the future." He is a likeable person, with intelligence, personality and looks, and he and Stevie are happy in their marriage: their sexual compatibility is emphasized, and until the episode in question neither has been unfaithful to the other. Notwithstanding his criticism of Billy's gayness, the family is a scene of domestic happiness, free from the kind of resentments and power struggles we expect in Albee's families.

Yet Albee confounds Martin's ethical standing with behavior that is repulsive and incomprehensible: as Stevie puts it to Billy, "He's a decent, liberal, right-thinking, talented, famous, gentle man (*hard*) who right now would appear to be fucking a goat." But Martin's view of his own behavior and his experience is sharply at odds with that of others. He knows that the world disapproves of bestiality — that is why he joined a group for those who want to be "cured" of it — but he finds the notion problematic: "when I realized something was wrong. I mean when I realized people would *think* something was wrong, that what I was doing wasn't..." (65). He rejects the name of "monster" but admits that he is "deeply troubled, greatly divided." The symptoms of his distress are clear. Stevie teases him for his absent-mindedness, which so frustrates Ross that he cancels the interview. During the sound check, Martin likens himself to the haunted Orestes:

> Ross: I hear a kind of ... rushing sound, like a ... wooooosh!, or ... wings, or something.
> Martin: It's probably the Eumenides.
> Ross: More like the dishwasher. There; it stopped.
> Martin: Then it probably wasn't the Eumenides; they don't stop.
> Ross: (*Agreeing*) They go right on.
> Martin: Right [22].

Here the confounding of the tragic and comic — is it the Furies or the kitchen appliances?— reflects the confusion of the protagonist and is the segue to his disclosure to Ross. Martin's confession is not accidental — like Phaedra again, he needs to be coaxed into confessing. But he is also driven to open up, he says, "Because I needed to tell *somebody*, somebody with his head on straight enough to hear it." Cornered by Ross at the end, he will allow, unconvincingly, that his behavior is sick and compulsive, even wrong, even as he protests that he "could have worked it out" (106–7).

For Stevie there is no confusion. Martin's behavior is beyond the pale, and he fails in his attempt to bring her to a more sympathetic understanding. Bestiality cannot be fitted into the world she knows, and the life they have lived has come to an end: "did you ever think you'd come back from your splendid life, walk into your living room and find you had no life left?" (61). She understands that in the course of a marriage almost anything can happen, but she also sees that "Something can happen that's outside the rules, that doesn't relate to The Way the Game Is Played" (59).

> The fucking of animals! No, that's one thing you haven't thought about, one thing you've overlooked as a byway on the road of life, as the old soap has it. "Well, I wonder when he'll start cruising livestock. I must ask Mother whether Dad did it and how she handled it" [60].

Martin has screwed up, as Stevie puts it, "because you've broken something and it can't be fixed!" (88). Her rage turns the room, its artwork and furniture, into a shambles. She is dumbfounded by Martin's insistence that he loves her *and* the goat, by the realization that he can go from sex with the goat to sex with her:

> That you can do these two things ... and not understand how it ... SHATTERS THE GLASS!!?? How it cannot be dealt with—how stop and forgiveness have nothing to do with it? and how I am destroyed? [89].

Stevie's tragic language describes a world that is broken and a reality that cannot be accommodated. Yet her focus is entirely on the consequences of what Martin has done to her life and the family's happiness. She has little interest in—indeed, will hardly allow Martin to speak of—his experience or his suffering.

Stevie speaks of "the rules" and "the game" from the world of convention, but it would be unfair to dismiss her perspective as bourgeois. This is a fairer description of Ross, in whom Albee locates the platitudes of what-the-world-will-think. Martin's oldest friend, he offers no sympathy and makes no attempt to help him, and Martin rightly regards his letter as a breach of their friendship. When he intrudes on Martin and Billy's desperate embrace, he can only react: "You're sicker than I thought" (103). Ross provides a kind of "choral" voice that offers an external perspective and a narrow practical wisdom but without compassion or understanding: he even allows that it all comes down to "what we can get away with" (108). Ironically, Martin finds his most sympathetic response in Billy, whose filial affection and struggle with his own emerging sexuality opens an emotional space where the two can meet; although he is baffled by his father's behavior, and angry at his hypocrisy in criticizing his homosexuality, his vulnerability enables the two to find a share in each other's suffering.

Martin resists Stevie's anger and the humiliation Ross would inflict and speaks instead of the need to *understand*— he uses the word repeatedly. And as ostensibly vile as his behavior has been, his tragic potential is enhanced by his willingness to consider "what it *means*" (108)—with the "it" implied in the question, "who *is* Sylvia?," which is asked as much of the audience as of him. Why *has* Martin done this— or perhaps rather, why has this happened to him? To this question Albee offers only partial answers. Martin's and Billy's embrace, like Martin's story of the father aroused by his child, shows that a spontaneous sexual response can be generated by an unlikely and inappropriate source, though this is different from Martin's sustained relationship with Sylvia. In this respect, the play recalls Greek ideas of the irrational and paradoxical nature of erotic experience: of Eros as a daemon that seizes the lover even against his will and drives him to submit himself to his beloved. The Greek view of the power of Eros, so powerfully portrayed in the illicit desire that Aphrodite visits on Phaedra in *Hippolytus*, is relevant here for two of its features: the abasement and humiliation that the lover willingly undergoes in hope of possessing his beloved, regardless of his age or class or privilege; and the sudden and unpredictable nature of the onslaught of Eros, who strikes the lover from without and robs him of his senses. As a god, Eros is frequently imagined as concealed within or beneath the object of one's desire, and it is especially through the *eyes* of the beloved that Eros captures the lover and enters his soul— reflected in Martin's frequent references to the power of "those eyes" of Sylvia.

If one answer to the question "who is Sylvia?" is "Love" or "Eros," another is "Dionysus." Martin's experience is not only sexual and erotic but also metaphysical and spiritual. Although he is not a religious man, his words depict his initial encounter with "Sylvia" as a meeting with the divine: "And there was a connection there— a communication — that, well ... an epiphany, I guess comes closest, and I knew what was going to happen" (82). The exceptional nature of Martin's experience and the collapse of the moral, cultural, and physical boundaries it involves, hearkens to the Dionysiac ecstasies of Euripides' *Bacchae*, to an encounter with the elemental forces of nature, sexuality, and the human personality. The goat is a powerful symbol of the god, one of his familiar manifestations, and Albee looks to Dionysus to suggest a construction of Martin's experience as a primal encounter with divinity: irrational and incomprehensible, oblivious to social convention, transcending good and evil. Martin struggles to express the profound otherness of his experience the first time he saw Sylvia, and when Stevie interrupts repeatedly, he erupts in anger. It is significant that the word "tragic" appears here alone in the play, twice.

Martin: (*Angry; didactic*) I will *finish* this! You *asked* for it, and you're going to *get* it! So ... shut your tragic mouth! (STEVIE *does a sharp intake of breath, puts her fingers over her mouth*) All right. Listen to me. It was as if an alien came out of whatever it was, and it ... took me with it, and it was ... an ecstasy and a purity, and a ... love of a ... (*dogmatic*) un-i-mag-in-able kind, and it relates to nothing whatever, to nothing that can be *related* to! Don't you see? Don't you see the ... don't you see the "thing" that happened to me? What nobody understands? Why I can't feel what I'm supposed to!? Because it relates to nothing? It can't have happened! It did, but it *can't* have! (STEVIE *shakes her head*) What are you doing?

Stevie: (*Removes fingers*) Being tragic. I bet a psychiatrist would love all this [81].

Stevie, perhaps understandably, will not allow the reading that Martin attempts to offer of his experience — her reference to a psychiatrist means only to shield her and belittle him. Martin's later description of his experience — "Why can't anyone understand this ... that I am *alone* ... all ... *alone!*" (109) — describes not only the unique nature of his encounter but also his sense of tragic isolation. Indeed, his inability to persuade anyone that his experience is not merely deviant calls to mind the Sophoclean tragic hero in particular, whose refusal to compromise serves only to isolate. To the end, Martin is unwilling to deny his love for Sylvia, even as he acknowledges its devastating consequences on all of them. His final words in the play, a triple "I'm sorry," are less an apology than a recognition of its awful consequences.

Nor does Albee explain why this should have happened to Martin, any more than why Oedipus should have met his singular destiny, although he does identify his protagonist as unusual in several respects. Martin betrays an obsessive attention to language and expression: to questions of grammar and syntax, forms of linguistic statement and misunderstanding, context and allusion. For Martin and Stevie such verbal play is a kind of parlor game (in the opening scene they play with the plural of "ranunculus"), but there is nothing so serious as to escape this gamesmanship. When Ross first establishes "This is Sylvia ... who you're fucking" (45), Martin thinks to correct him: "Whom." When Billy struggles with his father and Martin faults him for his language, Billy calls him a "Semanticist" (94) and Martin compliments him for his vocabulary. So too, even as he and Stevie hone in on the full and awful truth:

Stevie: Yes! More! Finish it! Vomit it all up! Puke it out all over me. I'll never be less ready. So ... *do it*! DO IT! I've laid it all out for you; I'm naked on the table; take all your knives! Cut me! Scar me forever!

Martin: (*Thinks a moment*) Before or after I vomit on you? (*Gently; hands up to appease*) Sorry; sorry.
Stevie: (*A shaking voice*) Women in deep woe often mix their metaphors.
Martin: Yes; yes.
Stevie: Get on with it! (*Afterthought*) Very good, by the way.
Martin: (*Rue*) Thanks [77–78].

This kind of linguistic play is vintage Albee, something that Martin and Stevie share with other of Albee's smart and difficult couples. Yet for Martin language also serves as a kind of wall, a barrier between him and the world.[14] Such discourse keeps him at a remove from others, from what ought to be immediate, perhaps from his own experience. His language, like his secular and rational approach to life, is a part of his deep loneliness and makes him, like the isolated and autocratic Pentheus in the *Bacchae*, a candidate for an encounter with the Dionysiac.

Martin's desire to take seriously the meaning of his own experience and his refusal to dismiss himself as merely sick or deviant, are at least potentially ennobling features of his character, and here again Oedipus provides the paradigm by which he is to be understood and evaluated: Sophocles' hero is defined above all by an uncompromising drive to discover the truth of the regicide and his own birth, whatever the cost to him and the disgrace it might bring. At the same time, given the nature of Martin's situation and the social world in which it is set, he is better regarded as anti-heroic than heroic, and the characteristics Martin displays put him in the company of other of Albee's anti-heroes who display honesty and determination. Set in a world that wants to see things in black-and-white, Martin (whose surname, we should remember, is "Gray") is in comparison bold and even courageous. In a recent essay, Robert Siegel identifies the positive value of the modern tragic anti-hero as "greatness in failure," a phrase he borrows from Jasper: "though he [the anti-hero] may not get to the whole truth or leave the world a better place, his attempt is always illuminating and his defeat is exhilarating because of the vitality that he brings to the battle." Martin does not arrive at the truth of his situation or his experience, whatever that may be, but he does possess the will to attempt it and has some success in exposing the shallowness and hypocrisy of the world around him.

In *The Goat*, Albee offers a "definition" of tragedy that references Greek tragedy at every turn: the god, the experience he brings, the form he assumes. He employs the tragic form that Aristotle recommends and consistently quotes or alludes to materials from the Greek tragic corpus. And his protagonist, by virtue of his sexual secret and the catastrophic consequences of its revelation, is an Oedipus for our time. But Albee also gives us in Martin an anti-hero whose behavior is shocking and grotesque, yet who displays a kind of virtue in opposing the predictable responses of family and friends and the inadequate conventional measures of morality. The final product is a curious medley of the ancient and modern, serious and absurd, tragic and anti-tragic. These ambiguities persist to the very end of the play. When Stevie enters with the remains of Sylvia, she not only proves herself a vengeful tragic heroine but also demonstrates, by sacrifice of a goat, the living tradition of Greek tragedy and the enduring power of the genre it represents.

McDaniel College

Notes

1. *The Goat* won the 2002 Best Play awards for the Tony, New York Drama Critics' Circle Award, the Drama Desk Award, and Outer Critics Circle Awards. It opened at the Golden Theater on March 10, 2002, for what was to be a three-month run, with Bill Pullman and Mercedes Ruehl in the roles of Martin and Stevie, respectively. A second run with Bill Irwin and Sally Field in the lead roles closed on December 15. This essay has benefited from the original production and that at the Goodman Theatre in Chicago.

2. Several reviews have questioned whether the relationship with Sylvia (like Albee's imaginary child) should be taken at face value, as there are no witnesses to the bestiality. But Albee includes bits of external "evidence" (comments on the smell of goat, the wallet photo, the goat itself) to disabuse us of that suspicion; Stevie satisfies herself as to the factuality of the situation at 58–59.

3. Albee's use of Greek tragedy is also discussed, for instance, in Amacher 1969 and in Dukore 1964.

4. Albee flags these generic concerns at the beginning of act II, when to Billy's cry "Oh, Dad!" Martin responds "Poor Dad?," punning on Arthur Kopit's *Oh Dad, Poor Dad, Mamma's Hung You in the Closet and I'm Feelin' So Sad* (1959), whose subtitle was *A Pseudoclassical Tragifarce in a Bastard French Tradition.*

5. The Greek, Sophoclean, and Oedipal associations of the play were not lost on critics and reviewers: Hedy Weiss (Chicago Sun Times) called it "the ultimate in Greek drama"; Martin Ball (The Australian) spoke of the play's "Sophoclean wrath and fury"; Don Shewey (*The Advocate*) called Martin "a contemporary version of Oedipus."

6. On the three-tiered Greek view of the universe, consult in general the work of J.-P. Vernant, especially "Between the Beasts and the Gods" in Vernant 1990.

7. *Agamemnon* 233.

8. Although the perpetrator is a god, one may also consider the hybris of Zeus in *Prometheus Bound*, which transforms Io into a hybrid of maiden and cow.

9. The Greek ambiance of the scene was underscored in the New York production by the set design of John Arnone, which located the entrances (stage left to the interior of home, stage right to outside) at a higher elevation and up a small

flight of stairs from the living room, forming a kind of *theologeion*, so that Stevie's entrance becomes a virtual *ex machina*.

10. See, for instance, "Euripidean Comedy" in Knox 1979 and Taplin 1996.

11. Indeed, the best parallel is to be found in *Bacchae* in the scene of Pentheus' cross-dressing by Dionysus, as the audience responds to both the humor of the king-in-drag and the horror of his participation in his own preparation as sacrificial victim.

12. It is significant that the motif of "the letter" that Ross sends to Stevie also has its dramatic origins in the incriminating letter Phaedra writes in *Hippolytus*.

13. However, the play falls short of the philosophical premises of modern tragicomedy, which Foster 2004 well describes as "comic characters, denied the dignity of meaning something, at odds with an indifferent universe that allows no chances at all" (199).

14. In this regard, Martin's persistent use of qualifiers is telling, as when he prepares to describe formally the encounter with Sylvia:

Martin: (*Sighs*) All right. As I said to Ross…
Stevie: (*Broad parody*) "As I said to Ross…" NO! Not "As I said to Ross." To *me*! As you say to *me*!
Martin: (*Annoyed*) In any event…
Stevie: Not "in any event!" No! *This* event!
Martin: (*Won't let it go*) As I said to Ross…
Stevie: (*Impatient acquiescence*) Very well; as you said to Ross [63–64].

References Cited

Albee, Edward. *The Goat, or, Who is Sylvia? (Notes toward a definition of tragedy)*. Woodstock and New York: Overlook Press, 2003.

Amacher, Richard E. *Edward Albee*. New York: Twayne, 1969 (rev. 1982).

Burkert, Walter. "Greek Tragedy and Sacrificial Ritual." *Greek, Roman and Byzantine Studies* 7 (1966): 87–121.

Dukore, Bernard F. "A Warp in Albee's Woolf." *Southern Speech Communication Journal* 30 (1964): 261–68; reprinted in *Critical Essays on Edward Albee*, Philip C. Kolin and J. Madison Davis, eds., Boston: Hall, 1986.

Else, Gerald F. *The Origin and Early Form of Greek Tragedy*. New York: Norton, 1972 (orig. 1965).

Foster, Verna A. *The Name and Nature of Tragicomedy*. Hants, UK: Ashgate, 2004.

Knox, Bernard. *Word and Action. Essays on the Ancient Theater*. Baltimore: Johns Hopkins, 1972.

Siegel, Robert. "Tragedy and Anti-tragedy: The Modern Antihero and the Postmodern Non-Hero" (unpublished manuscript).

Taplin, Oliver. "Comedy and the Tragic," in *Tragedy and the Tragic*, M.S. Silk, ed., Oxford: Oxford University Press, 1996.

Vernant, Jean-Pierre. *Myth and Society in Ancient Greece*, tr. Janet Lloyd (1990) New York: Zone Books, 1990.

From the Prophetic Performer to the Scribal Performer

William Doan and Terry Giles

Abstract

Evidence suggests that the oral pronouncements of the Hebrew prophets were performances. Yet these performances are not presented to us unmediated. They were preserved and codified in texts by a scribal tradition that sought to take control over both the lives and the messages of the prophets. In essence, both the prophet and scribe were responsible for the creation of the prophetic literature in much the same way actors and playwrights have shared in the creation of many theatrical traditions. In the case of the prophet and scribe, the scribe, as creator and presenter of prophetic texts takes control over both the mode of presentation and the content. The prophet's power, though given to him by the Lord, could only be enacted by the prophet himself until the scribe appropriated the character of the prophet.

Introduction

There is ample evidence in the Hebrew Bible to conclude that some of the oral pronouncements of Hebrew prophets were performances. Therefore, it is reasonable to suggest that performance criticism can help us understand the dynamics of the prophetic presentations still embedded in the prophetic literature. Yet, those performances are not presented to us unmediated. Rather, those preserved performances became codified in a text and became subject to a second set of dynamics in addition to those social forces operative at the time of the prophetic performance. The prophet and scribe together were responsible for the creation of the prophetic literature. In what follows, we examine the relationship of the prophet to the scribe and ask questions concerning the social power struggle between the two, using the prophetic book of Amos as our test case.

To foreground this investigation, we offer the following graphic image which establishes a visual representation of the prophetic performance as an enacted event, one that functions as theatre according to the following definitions: *theatre occurs when another or others, isolated in time and space, present themselves to another or others; drama occurs when another or others, isolated in time and space, present themselves in imagined acts to another or others.*[1] The graph also visualizes the central problem: there was a prophetic tradition tied to the actual lives of the prophets that ended in a scribal, or written tradition that no longer had the presence of the prophet as the primary medium of the presentation. As the graph demonstrates, Amos the Shepherd becomes Amos the Prophet as a result of being called by God. His power comes from that fact. When he performs as prophet, he is able to bring God before his spectators. The scribe, in order to create the drama of Amos, has to appropriate Amos the Prophet, both in his writing and reading of the text, if he is to achieve the power of the prophet.

The Prophet and the Scribe

One of the tenets of conventional wisdom concerning the formation of the prophetic literature of the Hebrew Bible is that the literature was created from preserved traditions about the prophet kept alive by disciples of the prophet. Presumably, the prophet, through his own charisma, the status of his social position or the attractiveness of his message, was able to gather around himself a "school" or group of disciples that became committed to preserving the message and social vision of the prophet long after the prophet himself was forced to put aside his prophetic mantle.[2] With this social dynamic in mind, it has been assumed that the transformation from prophetic utterance to prophetic literature was smooth and quite peaceful as the disciples honored their master by preserving traditions and sayings attributed to the prophet. The disciples sought to be faithful to their prophetic master, even if the literature they created did require that the original material be reworked and altered here and there in order to make it compatible to the new social and political context in which the disciples lived. Conventional wisdom said that, in the prophetic literature, the disciples sought to "re-present" their master in the centuries following the prophet. In terms of social power, the process was thought to be a relatively uneventful transformation of power from the charisma of the prophet to the pen of the scribe.

Recently, however, there have been those who have questioned this conventional wisdom. Philip Davies has made his doubts quite clear. He states:

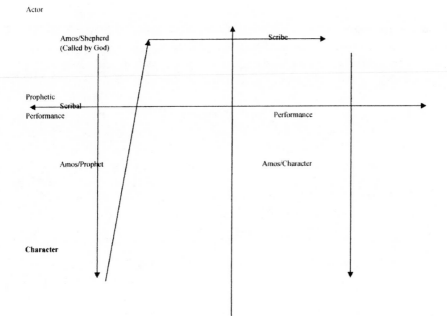

The view that the prophets had disciples who preserved and updated the sayings of their masters has never been supported by anthropological or literary evidence; it merely supplies a convenient mechanism whereby these edited compositions can be traced back to an individual prophet.[3]

Davies notes that if indeed the prophetic literature, particularly that of the twelve minor prophets, was intended to honor the prophetic master it is strange that the literature contains so few references to the "historical context, the life and the deeds..." of the prophets that were being honored (117). Leaving aside Jonah, of the twelve, only the books of Amos, Haggai and perhaps Hosea have any narratives about the prophet. Amos and Hosea are presented as contemporaries but never find mention in one another's books. Even the superscriptions in which the honored prophet is mentioned, and from which the book now derives its name, may be "guesswork" (118).

Guesswork or not is hard to prove. But, we do agree that the relationship between the prophet and a presumptive "school" is still unclear. The identity, role and function of the "disciples of the prophets" deserves further investigation and Performance Criticism provides anthropological tools by which to pursue the inquiry. A performance analysis of the prophetic event and literature suggests that the relationship between the two is analogous to the relationship between a performer and a script. The prophet is a performer who exercises social power through the immediacy of the performance. The message and delivery come together in the person of the prophet. A skillful performance by the prophet effectively holds sway over the audience by impacting upon the audience the correctness of the prophet's point of view. In the moment of performance, the prophet is not only a messenger but is the personification of the message. The message has power because the prophet has power.[4]

But this melting together of message and messenger is fleeting. It has no staying power because the prophet — the messenger — is transitory. Permanence can be achieved only through replication, only through a script that, when read, allows others to approximate the role of the messenger. Permanence can be achieved only by usurping the role of the prophet. And this is where a tension results. Rather than a smooth transition from prophet to literature, it is much more likely that the evolution from prophetic performer to prophetic literature was characterized by a struggle for power. The prophetic scribe (or perhaps better, the prophetic playwright) is dependent upon the prophetic performer for his inspiration and derives his credibility from an attachment to the prophetic performer but, nonetheless, is bent on replacing the prophetic performer. His intent is to script the prophetic performance and in so doing to control the prophetic performance. The writer of the script can only exist as a replacement to the prophetic performer and cannot afford an encore performance by the prophet. Therefore a future outbreak of the prophetic spirit is met with the darkest of warnings (Zechariah 13:1–6).

(1) On that day a fountain shall be opened for the house of David and the inhabitants of Jerusalem, to cleanse them from sin and impurity. (2) On that day, says the LORD of hosts, I will cut off the names of the idols from the land, so that they shall be remembered no more; and also I will remove from the land the prophets and the unclean spirit. (3) And if any prophets appear again, their fathers and their mothers who bore them will say to them, "You shall not live, for you speak lies in the name of the LORD"; and their fathers and their mothers who bore them shall pierce them through when they

prophesy. (4) On that day the prophets will be ashamed, every one, of their visions when they prophesy; they will not put on a hairy mantle in order to deceive, (5) but each of them will say, "I am no prophet, I am a tiller of the soil; for the land has been my possession since my youth." (6) And if any-one asks them, "What are these wounds on your chest?" the answer will be "The wounds I received in the house of my friends" [New Revised Standard Version].

The prophet, on the other hand, just like any performer, is resistant to the imposition of limitations that a script represents. In the performance, the performer reserves for himself the ownership of the message. The prophetic performer admonishes his audience to "Hear the Word of the LORD" and rarely to read it.

Orality in Text

There are already recognized parallels to the transformation that we are suggesting here. Although not within the context of a performance, others have commented upon the power struggle that persists in the transition from an oral tradition to a written one. James Crenshaw has put together a cogent argument for the transformation of an oral transmission to a written one within the educational traditions of Ancient Israel that may be analogous to a prophetic performance dynamic.[5] He contends that the transformation of an oral tradition to a written text is a significant event, one that converged several lines of social power. Crenshaw writes,

> Sparsely populated villages had little need for literate persons, and the scribal guild zealously guarded its monopoly on writing. In such an oral culture, written words (icons) *shimmered with the power of the sacred*, and religious figures used popular awe to their own advantage [italics ours].[6]

But the act of committing the performance to writing invokes a new social power. Crenshaw describes this transformation by quoting a Yoruba proverb, "The white man who created writing also created the eraser" (43). The master of the written medium is also master of the tradition commit-ted to writing. And control of that tradition may not have been surrendered willingly or happily.[7] The dynamic of power and control over the written medium is altogether different than the dynamic at work in an oral medium for, as Crenshaw again observes, "a written text can not choose its readers" while, a speaker can choose to whom he speaks (43). Once put into writ-ing, the tradition is subject to the manipulation of the literate and the rest of the oral population must now rely upon the literate as the intermediary guardian and dispenser of the power of the tradition.

At this point, a fascinating characteristic of the way in which the prophets are depicted in the Hebrew Bible should be mentioned. With rare exception, the prophets have no closure. Unlike the Biblical portrayal of kings or other significant community figures, who died and slept with the fathers, or who are given some other statement of finality, there is no such conclusion to the lives of most of the prophets. They don't die, ride off into the sunset (excepting Elijah) or live happily ever after. They are open ended. Even those whose ends are recorded are presented in a way that prevents closure. Moses is secreted off by God and, although mourned by the community, his burial spot is known only to God. Yet, Mosaic prophecy does not end and becomes a hope for the community (Deuteronomy 18:18–20). Likewise, the previously mentioned Elijah may make a dramatic exit in the fiery chariot, but his mantle falls to Elisha who continues in the Elijah tradition (2 Kings 2:19–24). And it is this same Elijah whose return is expected (Malachi 4:5).

The point to be made is this; the prophets find no conclusion because the scribes writing the prophetic literature will not allow them to conclude. The scribes create prophetic *characters* out of the prophets themselves (prophetic actors). And, it is the character that continues long after the actor has left the scene. Yet, even though the scribes create and preserve the character of the prophet, the scribes are not interested in the resumption of prophecy itself. Prophecy reaches a conclusion (the Zechariah 13:4–6 passage) even if the prophetic character continues. It is the difference between character and actor that resides at the crux of the struggle for power and control between the prophet and the scribe.

Presentational vs. Literary

The conflict between prophet and scribe is expressed in the fundamental conflict between the literary and the presentational mind. That conflict has to do with control and point of view. If we are to understand the relationship between performed and non-performed literature, we must recognize that there is a fundamental antagonism between literature and show. Though they did not cast the distinction in these terms, both Plato and Aristotle made a sharp distinction between the poet speaking in his own voice and speaking through the characters. Plato saw it as fundamental. For him, the poet speaking through others was creating a lie, providing a pale imitation of an imitation. In his own voice, at least, the poet kept close to the truth.

Aristotle did not hold the same moral position regarding the distinction, but he did recognize it as an aesthetic matter and sought to describe the peculiar features of the dramatic mode. The effect has been to mute the critical conflict between the literary and the presentational mind.[8]

As stated above, that basic conflict between the literary and the presentational is a conflict over control and point of view. We must remember that material meant to be shown (presented) is not necessarily connected by style or theme, "but by the idea of common presentation" (Beckerman, *TP*, 89). In the history of presentation, we find the full range of performances; some that went on for days, to performances that lasted under an hour. For example, a presentation of the medieval Wakefield Cycle plays probably began around 4:30 a.m., ending at sunset, with potentially thirty-two plays being presented on wagons moving from station to station throughout town. Each of the plays constitutes an "act," but only the whole constitutes the show. And though the cycle plays are thematically linked, the variety of modes of presentation, in terms of spoken vernacular, use of comedy, farce, and specific skill was a loose connection of choices determined by the local guild responsible for each individual act. The ultimate power was (and remains) in the hands of the performer who controlled the spectator's relationship to the act, not only by what was performed, but by *how* it was performed. With the presentational mind, the performer uses his own identity to create his own relationship to the spectator; a relationship he controls by having control over both the "what" and "how" of his performance.

If we follow Plato's line of reasoning, the poet speaking in his own voice maintains his own point of view. He shapes his emotion or thought in the lyric and his narrative in the epic to express a consistency of outlook, a consistency over which he can exert control if he wishes. The result is that a literary work, in its very being, tends toward coherence. But when the poet allows his characters to speak in their own voices, he has to attain an objectivity or effect a disappearance so that the characters seem to be autonomous creatures. Moreover, conceived as a show, that independence is magnified by the fact that the roles of the characters are assumed by actual human beings, performers with their own identities. To this, one must add the fact that the process of creating sustained attention in performance is very difficult. The same meter or the same subject continued at moderate length seems interminable. The need for variety makes itself felt. Consequently, the autonomy of the performing elements, together with the constant change required to hold an audience's attention, undermines many of the values so dear to the writer. "Only a writer who is knowledgeable, cunning, and imaginative can devise a subterranean control over work that is intended for show" (Beckerman, *TP*, 91).

From a literary perspective, the performative mind has an inherent resistance to the unitary point of view (Beckerman, *TP*, 91). The performative mind is keenly aware that it must juggle the twin demands of variety and intensification in order to move the work forward and to keep spectators engaged. Unity is derived more from performative structures such as voice modulation, gesture, proximity to spectators, pauses, rhythms of movement etc., than from the narrative of a text. Certainly, these are aspects not susceptible to literary criticism. In the case of the scribes, who were creating text that still had to be spoken and performed for the majority of their audience, we suggest that it was the performative mind and imagination of the prophet they sought to capture. The prophet (in the act of performing as prophet) was the medium through which God appeared. It is the scribe, both as writer and speaker of the text, who engages in a kind of impersonation that brings us to the point of theatrical analysis. From a phenomenological perspective, the question becomes, "What kind of being would choose impersonation as a means of securing any advantage?"[9]

> Surely theatre's origins and purposes are not exhausted in the idea that man wants to imitate the world, as it is or as it should be, or to make the crops do his bidding, or to honor the gods, or simply to entertain his fellow man, if by that we mean offering fictions about his social and private life. If the impersonation has the power to do these things, then the power itself must be prior to and independent of them.... It remains beneath all purposes an assertion of a certain power to create, to bring forth [States, 2].

This is precisely the power the prophets themselves had; the power to *bring forth* the presence of God. In discussing a phenomenological approach to understanding the theatre, States references both Heidegger and Hegel as a way of reaching beyond the Aristotelian problem of mimesis and imitation.[10] Both these references are useful here as they address the question of why a being would choose impersonation as a means for securing advantage, but also the seriousness of the imaginary, or illusory world of the object created: in our case, the prophetic drama.

> [The sculpture] is not a portrait whose purpose is to make it easier to realize how the god looks; rather, it is a work that lets the god himself be present and thus *is* the god himself. The same holds for the linguistic work. In tragedy nothing is staged or displayed theatrically, but the battle of the new gods against the old is being fought. The linguistic work, originating in the speech of the people, does not refer to this battle; it transforms the people's saying so that now every living word fights the battle and puts up for decision what is holy and what unholy, what great and what small, what brave and what cowardly, what lofty and what flighty, what master and what slave.[11]

In the prophetic tradition, it is the prophet through whom God Himself is present. In the scribal tradition, it is the scribe who, as actor, *creates* the character of the prophet in order for God Himself to be present. The prophet brought the truth of God onto the stage, whether it was on a threshing floor, standing on a wall, or amidst a crowd gathered in the street. "It is the truth of the god that arrives on the stage and not the stage that refers to a real god beyond it, existing in some unavailable form" (States, 3). As States notes, Hegel's explanation of this phenomenon is that "[The gods] are made, invented, but are not fictitious. They certainly come forth out of the human imagination in contrast to what actually exists, but they do this as *essential* forms, and this product of the mind is at the same time recognized as being what is essential."[12]

What Heidegger and Hegel are both talking about is a principle of presence, which is different from a referential principle as the basis of art. The prophet *himself* was the presence through which God appeared to the people of Israel. This was more than a linguistic moment; it was a moment of full sensory engagement for both the prophet and the spectators. The scribe, both as writer and speaker of the prophetic text cannot create that moment. He must impersonate the prophet, by creating the prophetic character, in order to create the illusion of the prophetic experience. In this sense he creates the prophetic drama. He impersonates the prophet in order to bring forth the presence of the prophet, which will bring forth the presence of God. Though the scribe writes, "Thus says the LORD," his words are meant to be spoken and heard; the prophet is brought forth so that God can be made present. In doing so, the scribe has appropriated the prophet's power to create. The scribe is simultaneously the creator and the actor of the text. The prophet is now a character, portrayed by the scribal actor. The drama no longer belongs to the prophet — it is now under control of the scribe.

The transition from performer to playwright as the primary power figure in establishing the tradition of tragedy is as much the study of a socio-cultural shift of power as an aesthetic one. As Beckerman points out about ancient Greece, the modes of presentation arise from the social balance between individual and community,

> ...with the individual endowed with an appearance that heightens his superhuman qualities. Whatever passions or circumstances these schemes signify, the schemes themselves embody forces other than the fictive or mimetic. What we find among the Greeks is similar to what we find at the initial stages of any dramatic tradition and what we are finding in the developments of the twentieth century... Whether the form that did arise came about purely because of socio-religious influence or was partly the result of esthetic play, may be impossible to ever discover. But whatever its genesis, an act-scheme [mode of presentation] embodies in its structure a resolution or impulses stemming from deep social causes. As presentation, these act-schemes not

only provide a form for displaying these varied impulses but also serve as a means of transcending the limits that contain them.[13]

Conclusion

The scribe, as both creator and presenter of prophetic texts, takes control over both the scheme, or mode of presentation, and the content. The prophet's power, though given to him by the Lord, could only be enacted by the prophet himself until the scribe appropriated the character of the prophet. In reality, scribes had the governing structures of prophetic performance before them for a long period of time, providing them with a range of language, gesture and activity to which they could bring shape and form. However, to do this, the scribe had to wrest the performative away from the prophet and put in on the page.

MIAMI UNIVERSITY OF OHIO, Bill Doan
GANNON UNIVERSITY, Terry Giles

Notes

1. Bernard Beckerman, *Dynamics of Drama: Theory and Method of Analysis* (New York: Drama Book Specialists, 1979). Beckerman establishes and explores these definitions in chapter one of this book.

2. William R. Harper, *A Critical and Exegetical Commentary on Hosea and Amos* (Edinburgh: T. and T. Clark, 1905), Wolff, *Joel and Amos* (Philadelphia: Fortress, 1973), James Luther Mays, *Amos* (Philadelphia: Westminster Press, 1969), Jorg Jeremias, *The Book of Amos*, translated by Douglas Scott (Louisville: Westminster John Knox, 1998).

3. Philip Davies, *Scribes and Schools: The Canonization of the Hebrew Scriptures* (Louisville: Westminster, John Knox, 1998) 118.

4. Julius Wellhausen spoke eloquently to this when he wrote, "It belongs to the notion of prophecy, of true revelation, that Jehovah, overlooking all media of ordinances and institutions, communicates Himself to the *individual*, the called one, in whom that mysterious and irreducible rapport in which the deity stands with man clothes itself with energy. Apart from the prophet, *in abstracto*, there is no revelation; it lives in his divine-human ego." *Prolegomena to the History of Israel* (Edinburgh: A. & C. Black, 1885) 398.

5. James Crenshaw, *Education in Ancient Israel* (New York: Doubleday, 1998).

6. James Crenshaw, "Transmitting Prophecy Across Generations," *Writings and Speech in Israelite and Ancient Near Eastern Prophecy* edited Ehud Ben Zvi and Michael Floyd (Atlanta: Society of Biblical Literature, 2000) 41.

7. I am reminded of a professor colleague who characterizes computers as sim-

ply "fancy typewriters." In his disparagement of electronic communication he is actually expressing frustration concerning his loss of control over information as a result of his lack of ability in navigating the new and, for him, unfamiliar medium.

8. Bernard Beckerman, *Theatrical Presentation: Performer, Audience, and Act* Ed. Gloria Brim Beckerman and William Coco. (New York: Routledge, 1990) 91.

9. Bert O. States. *Great Reckonings in Little Rooms: On the Phenomenology of Theatre.* (Berkley: University of California Press) 1985, 2. States asks this question as a different question than the usual historical inquiry into the origins of theatre. It has particular value here since the scribes were engaged in both an impersonation of and a re-creation of the prophets.

10. As States argues in the introduction of *Great Reckonings*, "The longstanding problem of mimetic theory is that it is obliged to define art in terms of what it is not, to seek a source of artistic representation in the subject matter of art, and to point to a place where it can be found, if only in a set of abstract ideas or truths, or in some field of essences or archetypes." *Action*, however, refers to something inside the play, perhaps even a "soul," or "indwelling form" (5–7).

11. Quoted in States, *Great Reckonings in Little Rooms*, 2. Martin Heidegger. *Poetry, Language, Thought*, trans. Albert Hofstadter (New York: Harper & Row, 1975), pp. 46–47.

12. Quoted in States, *Great Reckonings in Little Rooms*, 3. *Hegel on Tragedy*, eds. Anne and Henry Paolucci (New York: Harper & Row, 1975), 312.

13. Beckerman, *TP*, 104–105.

References Cited

Beckerman, Bernard. *Dynamics of Drama: Theory and Method of Analysis*. New York: Drama Book Specialists, 1979.

_____. *Theatrical Presentation: Performer, Audience, and Act*. Ed. Gloria Brim Beckerman and William Coco. New York: Routledge, 1990.

Crenshaw, James. *Education in Ancient Israel* (New York: Doubleday, 1998).

_____. "Transmitting Prophecy Across Generations," *Writings and Speech in Israelite and Ancient Near Eastern Prophecy* edited Ehud Ben Zvi and Michael Floyd, 31–44. Atlanta: Society of Biblical Literature, 2000.

Davies, Philip. *Scribes and Schools: The Canonization of the Hebrew Scriptures*. Louisville: Westminster John Knox, 1998.

Harper, William R. *A Critical and Exegetical Commentary on Hosea and Amos*. Edinburgh: T. and T. Clark, 1905.

Jeremias, Jorg. *The Book of Amos*, translated by Douglas Scott. Louisville: Westminster John Knox, 1998.

Mays, James Luther. *Amos*. Philadelphia: Westminster Press, 1969.

States, Bert O. *Great Reckonings in Little Rooms: On the Phenomenology of Theatre*. Berkley: University of California Press, 1985.

Wellhausen, Julius. *Prolegomena to the History of Israel*. Edinburgh: A. & C. Black, 1885.

Wolff, Hans W. *Joel and Amos*. Philadelphia: Fortress, 1973.

Theatre and Politics
A Review Essay
David S. Escoffery

Michael Patterson. *Strategies of Political Theatre: Post-War British Playwrights.* Cambridge: Cambridge University Press, 2003. Pp. xviii + 232. Hardcover $70.00.

S.E. Wilmer. *Theatre, Society and the Nation: Staging American Identities.* Cambridge: Cambridge University Press, 2002. Pp. 281. Hardcover. $70.00.

William Peterson. *Theater and the Politics of Culture in Contemporary Singapore.* Middletown, CT: Wesleyan University Press. 2001. Pp. xi + 287. Hardcover $60.00, pbk. $24.95.

African Theatre: Playwrights and Politics. Edited by Martin Banham, James Gibbs and Femi Osofisan. Oxford: James Currey, Ltd. 2001. Pp. xxi + 291. Pbk. $24.95.

In the post–9/11 world, it has become difficult, if not impossible, to draw a line between the cultural and the political. Of course, theorists since Plato have discussed the various ways in which cultural products, and theatre in particular, can and do influence the political sphere. In the past three decades, however, theorists influenced by feminism, post-colonialism, and cultural studies have provided writers with new ways to analyze the political implications of theatre. The four books reviewed here highlight many of these new approaches and provide good examples of their benefits and potential weaknesses.

Michael Patterson begins his *Strategies of Political Theatre: Post-War British Playwrights* with the claim, "All theatre is political. Indeed it is the most political of all art forms" (1). Although he is often forced to question the direct political impact of the British playwrights whose work he examines, Patterson does provide a thoughtful analysis of how even seemingly apolitical works can make political statements. In this book, Patterson has chosen to look at nine post-war British playwrights whose work "not only depicts social interaction and political events but implies the possibility of radical change on socialist lines" (3–4). His goal is to place these radical writers within the cultural context of post-war England, focusing especially on the 1970s.

Of course, one of the potential problems with the book is Patterson's restricting of his definition of "political theatre" to only those plays that reflect left-wing, socialist values. Patterson does justify this position, however, claiming that the common usage of the term "political theatre" in England at the time refers specifically to left-wing plays. After dealing with this issue, Patterson lays out his primary methodology. Working within the parameters of the Lukács/Brecht debate, Patterson identifies each of his nine playwrights as using either a "reflectionist" or an "interventionist" strategy. He describes these two approaches, saying,

> The reflectionist tradition asserts that the main function of art and indeed theatre is to hold up a mirror to nature and to reflect reality as accurately as possible.... The interventionist mode asserts that, even if it were possible to reflect reality accurately, the undertaking is futile, since it is the task of the artist and playwright to interpret reality and to challenge our perception of it [15].

Although this formula is a bit reductive and does not exactly reflect the ways in which theatre is created or consumed, it does provide a convenient framework on which Patterson structures his book. To help his readers understand how he plans to use these two categories, Patterson begins the meat of the book with a section he calls "Two Model Strategies." He includes a chapter on Arnold Wesker to demonstrate the reflectionist strategy and one on John Arden depicting the interventionist strategy. The next section of the book includes chapters on his other "reflectionist" playwrights: Trevor Griffiths, Howard Barker, and Howard Brenton. Finally, he has a section with chapters devoted to the other "interventionist" playwrights: John McGrath, David Hare, Edward Bond, and Caryl Churchill. Each chapter, along with a general discussion of the playwright and his or her major works, then goes into specific detail on one particular play, using that to explore the playwright's strategies for advocating political change.

In general, Patterson's book is rich in detail and thoroughly researched, providing a good discussion of the British context in which these writers were working. He does admit the reductive nature of the dichotomy he uses to structure the book, saying, "It would be more appropriate to think of the two strains as the ends of a spectrum rather than as mutually exclusive categories" (24). The fact that his book does position them primarily as "mutually exclusive categories" is a weakness, but it does not undermine the value of his analysis of the plays and the strategies used by these political playwrights to bring about "an awareness of the need for social change" (5).

One interesting theory that has driven much of the scholarship on political theatre in recent years deals with national identity — what it is, how it is created and maintained, and how it is changed. An excellent example of such a study is S. E. Wilmer's *Theatre, Society and the Nation: Staging American Identities.* Wilmer's goal is to take the theory of "cultural nationalism" (1) as put forth by Edward Said, Homi Bhabha, and Benedict Anderson and use it to examine the role of theatre in the construction of national identities.

Noting the complexities inherent in the theories of cultural nationalism, Wilmer argues,

> [O]ne could propose that notions of national identity are constantly being reformulated, revised and reasserted in an ongoing battle to assert and maintain a hegemonic notion of the nation. Likewise, subaltern groups have confronted the homogenous image represented by the dominant group in asserting a more pluralistic or counter-hegemonic identity [3].

One problem Wilmer sees with the work of Said, Bhabha, and Anderson, however, is that they "have undervalued the role of theatre" (1) in the shaping of national identities. Thus, he plans to use the American case as a means of demonstrating the importance of theatre in this process.

The book is organized with each chapter detailing how theatre functioned at what Wilmer refers to as "times of national crisis" (3). Significantly, he does not choose to discuss only "hegemonic nationalism" (3), as the majority of his chapters deal with marginalized groups attempting to change the national identity in some way. For example, Chapter 3 deals with the Ghost Dance religion that spread through Native American tribes, especially the Lakota, in the late nineteenth century, showing how this movement "reconfigured the nation, but from a Lakota perspective and in a Lakota idiom" (81).

Focusing on marginalized groups like the Lakota or the silk workers who staged the Patterson Strike Pageant in 1913 allows Wilmer to give time to aspects of American theatre that rarely get covered in history texts. One of the greatest strengths of the book, then, is the amount of historical detail that Wilmer brings to his discussion. Each chapter begins with an in-depth discussion of the historical context, followed by an extraordinary amount of detail about the specific theatrical event(s) he is analyzing.

Perhaps the only major problem Wilmer has is that his primary focus on marginalized groups tends to exaggerate the importance of theatre in changing our notion of national identity. Like Patterson, he is often forced to admit that the productions he has just analyzed in such detail were actually not particularly effective when it came to creating actual, perceptible changes in the national identity.

William Peterson is also interested in the ways in which theatre can be used to shape national identity. His *Theater and the Politics of Culture in Contemporary Singapore* looks at post-independence Singapore and the government's careful construction of a national identity. Since Singapore was almost unpopulated before being colonized by the British, there was no indigenous culture to fall back on when the country gained its independence. A Singaporean national identity had to be created from scratch, and Lee Kuan Yew's People's Action Party (PAP) used a number of different means, including theatre, to put forward the ideas of "soft authoritarianism" (9) and "Asian values" (20) as the models for that identity.

Like Wilmer, Peterson makes extensive use of Said's *Culture and Imperialism*, especially the claim that "reading and writing texts are never neutral activities" (qtd. 7). Also like Wilmer, Peterson seeks to expand Said's observations to include theatre as an activity that is "never neutral." Thus, he looks at the work of a number of Singaporean theatre artists to analyze the role theatre has played in the construction and contestation of a Singaporean identity.

One minor problem with Peterson's book is its organization. Some chapters are based on thematic concerns like the body, gender, or interculturalism, whereas others deal with specific forms of performance like festivals or the Singaporean musical. In the first three chapters, Peterson gives important background information on Singaporean history. These chapters are particularly important for people who are unfamiliar with the Singaporean context, though they are colored by Peterson's obvious dislike of the PAP government. He claims, "Because I have seen others persecuted in the courts and driven from Singapore for expressing their opinions openly, I cannot pretend to be neutral when it comes to the intersection between politics and the process of artistic creation" (8).

The book is important, however, in that it introduces Western readers to artists and events they may not otherwise hear about, including the work of Ong Keng Sen at TheatreWorks and the musicals of Dick Lee, "the pan–Asian pop star and prolific composer and lyricist who has been largely responsible for the indigenization of the genre" (182). Many in Singapore expected some of Lee's musicals, like *Nagaraland* or *Sing to the Dawn*, to make the move to Broadway or the West End, but they never managed to do so, making their inclusion here one of the few ways for Western readers to learn about them.

Another book that introduces Western readers to artists and styles they may not otherwise have heard about is the volume *African Theatre: Playwrights and Politics*, edited by Martin Banham, James Gibbs, and Femi Osofisan. Part of a series from the journal *African Theatre*, this collection features articles by scholars from numerous African countries, Germany, England, and the United States, all of which reveal the "underlying perception of the general political nature of theatre" (xi) that is clear in much African work.

As the editors note in their foreword, they tried to select "articles, reviews, interviews, and autobiographical statements that provide insights into the work of particular writers, including Bole Butake (Cameroon), Ojo Rasaki Bakare, Femi Osofisan and Sam Ukala (Nigeria), Joe de Graft, Mohammed Ben-Abdallah (Ghana), Khalid Al Mubarak Mustafa (Sudan), and Dev Virahsawmy (Mauritius)" (xi). As with many anthologies, the articles tackle the issue of political theatre from a number of methodological points-of-view, though most, not surprisingly, rely to some extent on postcolonial theory, especially the work of Ngugi wa Thiong'o and Frantz Fanon.

One problem with a collection like this is its unwieldy nature, which makes any sort of organization practically impossible. The editors have divided the book into sections that cover particular playwrights (Femi Osofisan, Joe de Graft and Mohammed Ben-Abdallah) or thematic issues (language and Shakespearean adaptations, puppets, theatre in development). The articles in each section range in quality from good to excellent, though even those that are least theoretically nuanced are still interesting in that they offer discussions of plays and playwrights rarely mentioned in the West.

The highlight of the collection, surely, is Nisha and Michael Walling's translation of *Toufann*, an African adaptation of *The Tempest* originally written by Dev Virahsawmy. This play is quite powerful, and it makes for an interesting intercultural document because of the way Virahsawmy has taken Shakespeare's story, added characters from other Shakespearean plays, and transformed the whole into a specifically African context. It may not answer any questions about power and society, but it raises them beautifully.

These four contemporary books on theatre and politics, in the end, are both inspiring and slightly unsatisfying. The many theories brought to bear on the subject show that the relation of theatre to the workings of political power has perhaps never been more critically examined. Unfortunately, in spite of all the careful analysis given here, most of these authors are in the end forced to admit that these plays and productions have not really had much effect in terms of real political change. What remains exciting, however, are the possibilities opened up by the many different strategies of political theatre examined here. Artists interested in using the theatre to inspire audiences to rethink the way society functions can learn a lot — about what works and what does not work — from the techniques discussed in these four books.

SOUTHWEST MISSOURI STATE UNIVERSITY

Review of Literature: Selected Books

Hellmut Hal Rennert, ed. *Essays on Twentieth-Century German Drama and Theater: An American Reception, 1977–1999.* New York: Peter Lang, 2004. Pp. xii+321. Hardcover $74.95.

Karelisa Hartigan founded the Comparative Drama Conference in 1977. While many areas of theater were represented at the Conference, German drama received particularly strong representation. Led by William Elwood, Jan-Lüder Hagens, Glen Gadberry, William Grange, Hellmut Hal Rennert and others — scholars with genuine bona fides in German theatre — German studies flourished during the Conference's initial two decades. Rennert has now gathered together the presentations on German drama, and has organized the collection into six sections: Performance and Theory, Expressionism, Third Reich, Bertolt Brecht, Post–World War II, and Contemporary. Each section, as well as Rennert's own concise introductory essay, sheds light on significant moments in German theatrical history. This anthology offers readers a way of observing the thinking of German theatre and drama from an American perspective. The essays, however, are of mixed quality. Many make noteworthy points, but some are of dubious merit. In addition, the proofreading is woefully lax.

In the opening section, William Elwood grapples with sweeping social and political developments. He argues for faith in the theatre over the past two hundred years and into the next two hundred. The piece (as well as many others) suffers from horrendous copy-editing: typos abound, sentences are grammatically askew, and poor proof-reading leads to phrases such as "To paragraph Schwanitz" (35) rather than "To paraphrase Schwanitz." The essay is also rife with generalizations and trivially true assertions: "As we progressed through the last half of our century, theater forms remained essentially realistic" (29); "The injustices to the American Indian must be redressed finally" (34); "Wife and child abuse are bad and we have to stop it by knowing how it starts" (35); and, "Homosexuality per se is neither here nor there" (35). The reader must wonder what these bromides have to do with German theatre.

The remaining essays in this section examine the differences between written drama and stage performance. Dean Wilcox presents a lucid description of Robert Wilson's anti-naturalist directing style. Jan-Lüder Hagens categorizes plays in which the staged or choreographed action is built into the play (what characters say, how they direct other actors, etc.). Sarah Bryant-Bertail argues that theatre has the ability "to spatialize time and temporalize space — that is, to concretize aesthetically the historical consciousness of a particular society" (54). Although interesting, Harris Gruman's essay on audience participation is marred by inexcusable typos ("eexperiments [63]," "acknoeledge [64]," "Everymam [65]," "fir example [66]," "sprectators [67]," "clainm [68]," etc.). William Gruber concludes this section with a convincing comparison of acting theories by Gordon Craig and Bertolt Brecht.

The "German Expressionism" section contains six essays by Elwood and one by Gadberry, providing expert testimony on this genre's significance. Elwood begins by spotlighting Georg Kaiser's *Von Morgans bis Mitternachts* (*From Morn to Midnight*), the story of a Cashier who, as part of an effort to alter his drab existence, absconds with funds. Elwood emphasizes the protagonist's existential dilemma by examining this paradigmatic expressionist play in view of certain of Sartre's ideas. In the next essay Elwood turns his attention to Ernst Toller's *Masse-Mensch*, arguing that the play represents the story of "salvation of the common soul" (89). His two following essays focus, respectively, on Walter Hasenclever's 1932 play, *Sinnengluck und Seelenfrieden* (*Peace and Pleasure*), from the perspective of Eastern philosophy, and Reinhard Goering's *Seeschlacht*, an often overlooked German Expressionist play. Along the way Elwood describes German Expressionism in the theatre as an attempt to create "the reality of the unconscious or the soul in an actual physical space with the limitations of gravity, the technology available to the theatre in the early quarter of the twentieth century, and on man's own inability to perceive with a rational faculty a non-rational phenomenon" (104). If, according to Elwood,

Freud and Jung were the "cartographers of the subconscious," then German expressionist artists were the subconscious's "expeditionary force" (105). In addition, he examines American Expressionism, comparing Hasenclever's 1918 play, *Die Menschen*, to Adrienne Kennedy's 1968 play, *Sun*, while his final piece compares expressionism and deconstruction. The section concludes with Gadberry's informative study of the Austrian left-wing expressionist playwright, Arnolt Bronnen (1895–1959).

The third section marches the reader intrepidly into a particularly nettlesome terrain. In its opening essay, "The Theater in and of the Third Reich," Gadberry contends that during the *Nazizeit* "German theatre excellence was to be demonstrated by production" (134). According to Gadberry, "most German theater during those years remained remarkably independent of national politics — despite intrusion, subsidy and the need of artists to exercise their art" (135). As a result, he notes, "the tradition of excellence" largely prevailed (136). For Gadberry, theatre artists — apparently without missing a beat from one regime to the next — exercised their art apart from (aloof from?) the surrounding brutality. Furthermore, he argues, the actors, playwrights, and directors at the time were "excellent" despite the purging of Jews who accounted for many theatre artists during the 1920s and early 1930s. Gadberry, however, fails to provide criteria determining "excellence" other than statistics confirming an active theatre scene, implicitly suggesting that quantity equals quality. Moreover, he pays scant attention to what "excellent" directors, playwrights, and particularly actors actually do: absorb and express current events and art. Another profession might flourish during a period of crimes against humanity, but actors, conditioned to *react* and *respond*, are unlikely to perpetuate a "tradition of excellence" while performing in a void. Insensitivity is antithetical to performance, which demands an emotional connection to the world, or at least the immediate social scene. Actors and directors of the period were either emptied out emotionally resulting from fear of reprisal or "excellent" *because* they enthusiastically endorsed the Nazi regime. The former is understandable, but if the latter, then what does this say about German theatre at the time?

The remaining chapters in this section describe a theatrical era replete with Nazi sympathizers. William Sonnega writes persuasively of Sigmund Graff's play *Die endlose Strasse* (*The Endless Road*), a drama which portrays the horrors of war *and* the German soldier as national hero. Gadberry attends to the Nazi history plays, which were "the most privileged serious dramatic form of Third Reich playwriting" (155). Certain historical plays in particular allowed Nazi ideologists to emphasize the *Widukind*, the "8th century Saxon chieftan [sic], who seemed to focus patterns of German racial destiny" (157). Nazi playwrights capitalized on the alleged heroics of their Aryan ancestors. In his next essay, Gadberry examines the influx of "Caroline Neuber plays," dramas based on the life of the famous Prussian actress/manager who is credited with helping develop the eighteenth-century German stage. While Neuber's well-known back-stage sexual peccadilloes offended the Nazis' prudish sensibilities, plays portraying her life were permitted by the authorities because she was deemed a "national treasure." Leigh Clemons follows with an essay on the dramatist Erwin Guido Kolbenheyer (1878–1962), a pro-Nazi writer of his-

torical novels and plays whose work echoed the Party's cultural critic, Alfred Rosenberg. Gadberry's final offering in this section examines Gerhart Hauptmann's five-act play *Die Ratten*. This play was originally written and performed in 1911. According to Gadberry, the 1936 revival was an unusual choice during the Nazi period given the play's depiction of decadence, rat-infested barracks, and dregs of society, hardly prototypes of Nazi uplift propaganda. The play "challenged" Nazi authority, but only up to a point; it also suggested the decay of the previous administration, the Second Reich, thereby pleasing Nazi officials. Gadberry again extols the "inherent humanity" of theatre, yet he also emphasizes that Gobbels, Schlösser, and Rosenberg — Nazi cultural watchdogs and Hitler's propaganda henchmen — "were quite successful impressing their vision upon the arts" (190). William Grange closes this section with an examination of Germany's popular "comedies" during the period.

The next section, "Brecht," opens the scholarship to wider possibilities. Graley Herren puts forth a counter-intuitive theory of Brecht's *Life of Galileo*. Rather than Marxist dogma, the play suggests "no doctrine or course of action as unquestionably true"; only the "act of questioning" itself is supported (208). Julie Klassen and Ruth Weiner examine Brecht's *Mann ist Mann* through the sociological lens of Victor Turner. Although absorbing, the article is undermined by missing numerical notations for endnotes (readers have to guess where the quotes are in the text). Inadequate copyediting plagues the next essay as well. In his article, "Saving the Fallen City of Mahagonny," John C. Nichols attempts to shed light on Brecht's opera by suggesting its importance in the Brechtian canon. While the argument is convincing, block quotes occasionally appear as text and the author's text as block quotes, creating confusion. Rebecca Hilliker also emphasizes Brecht's *Rise and Fall of the City of Mahagonny* as an important but overlooked work. According to Hilliker, Brecht's *Threepenny Opera*, despite being less demonstrative of Brecht's theory of *Verfremdungseffekt* than *Mahagonny*, has been popularized in the United States because its music achieves "its ultimate romantic outlook in such vocal interpretations as Bobby Barren's [*sic* Darren's] Mack the Knife and textual interpretations as the G. W. Pabst film version" (228). Leslie Ellis goes against conventional wisdom with an Aristotelian analysis of *Life of Galileo*. Brecht would likely reject the interpretation, but Ellis is persuasive in underscoring the play's Aristotelian influences such as actions of a noble character, *hamartia*, *peripeteia*, recognition, and even facets of modern existentialism. However, absent from the discussion is catharsis, which Brecht deliberately nullifies by placing Galileo's recantation offstage, thereby undermining the play's suspense. This lapse notwithstanding, Ellis presents a strong case for reinterpreting the play.

Hellmut Hal Rennert begins the next section, a study of post–World War II plays, by analyzing Max Frisch's *Die Chinesische Mauer* (*The Great Wall of China*, written in 1947, and revised in 1955 and 1972). According to Rennert, this is a language play attempting to come to terms with the war and its aftermath. Rennert's generally fine translation is marred at one point where he translates the German critic Christian Ferber's 1966 comment, "von dem [ein Aderlaß] sich unsere Bühne in diesem Jahrhundert nicht mehr erholen wird," as: "German stages will never not recover

from this bloodletting in this century" (248). The double negative in English is not only grammatically incorrect, it misconstrues Ferber's intent. Jürgen Schlunk looks at Martin Walser's obscure play, *The Rabbit Race*, as a work "which reflects all of Germany's historical reality" (257), while Patricia Stanley sheds light on Wolfgang Hildesheimer's *Das Opfer Helena*.

The final section covers the contemporary German theatre scene, and is, with one exception, superb. Christa Carvajal's study of avant-gardist Peter Handke's drama *Beyond the Hamlets* stresses the play's language as an expression of poetic testimony. If, according to Carvajal, Handke exemplifies verbal brilliance, then the next essay by Julie Klassen calls attention to Heiner Müller's visual strengths. According to Klassen, Müller's plays and directing challenge accepted notions of linear drama and Enlightenment reason. Instead of emphasizing narrative, Müller "inundates the viewers with an overwhelming amount of sense perceptions — demanding, sometimes surrealistic dialog, collage, mime, masks, music — simultaneously or in rapid succession" (282). This sensual cacophony yields spectatorial selectivity and places the responsibility of interpretation on the audience.

William Elwood's essay, "Darkness Visible: Peter Turrini and the Scripted Life," is a copyediting nightmare: 8 out of 18 numerical notations for the endnotes are missing in the text, making it nearly impossible to match quotes with sources. Elwood's argument that Turrini's plays align with psychologist Alfred Adler's theories of "scripted language" is hard to follow because, in several instances, quotes and the author's words are indistinguishable. The point of the essay seems to be that

Turrini's plays use language to obfuscate motivation. While accurate, this generalization can also be applied to just about any drama, movie, and novel.

The next two essays provide something missing from the book's previous contributions: examinations of women playwrights and female characters. Andreas Ryschka's "Woman Takes Center Stage" focuses on three plays: Kroetz's *Wunschkonzert* (*Taking Request*), Roth's *Ritt auf die Wartburg* (*On Horseback to Wartburg Castle*), and Reinshagen's *Die Clownin, Ein Spiel* (*The Female Clown, a Play*). Ryschka examines these dramas within the concept of *écriture feminine* (feminine discourse), but also compares these works to those of American dramatist Wendy Wasserstein and filmmaker Mike Nichols, both of whom question early feminism's hard line. Britta Kallin focuses on several dramatists of the 1980s and 1990s in light of their efforts to critique race and nationality in German theatre. Kallin explores a particularly ticklish situation: white authors who enjoy positions of privilege in Germany portraying women of color albeit condescendingly. Kallin boldly criticizes where criticism is due. Finally, Ralf Remshardt pinpoints the pros and cons of the dramatist Manfred Karge, who, according to Remshardt, "is one of the few genuine and unapologetic Brechtians remaining in the German theatre scene" (313).

This anthology deserves a place alongside *Playing for Stakes: German Language Drama in Social Context* and *Studies in German Drama: A Festschrift in Honor of Walter Silz*. It also deserves far better copyediting by the publisher. Another problem is that incomplete endnote citations and phrases such as "Today I will analyze..." (219) give the appearance of "Proceedings" from a conference collected without adjudica-

tion. The weakness of some essays suggests a collection rather poorly vetted and hardly selective. Still, readers will gain much from this anthology, provided they bypass the superficial and tolerate the lack of proofreading.

DAVID KRASNER
Yale University

Andrew Sofer. *The Stage Life of Props.* Ann Arbor: University of Michigan Press, 2003. Pp. 278. Hardcover $49.50, Paperback. $19.95.

Andrew Sofer's *The Stage Life of Props* is a witty, entertaining and–above all–thought-provoking study of a neglected subject. It is not a history of properties on the stage or a comprehensive overview of their deployment. It is, rather, a selective analysis of how meaning attaches to theatrical properties, a hermeneutics of their use. Since this is something that changes with the culture and with the nature of the staging, he chooses "to reconstruct the stage lives of five exemplary props from five pivotal periods of stage history: the Eucharistic wafer of the medieval stage; the bloody handkerchief of the Elizabethan stage; the skull on the Jacobean stage; the fan on the Restoration and early-eighteenth-century stage; and the gun on the modern stage," arguing that "taken together these case studies illustrate a common mechanism of appropriation whereby props are enlisted to address a wider semiotic crisis in the theater (and often the culture) of the day" (viii, xii).

In his Introduction, Sofer reviews Prague School linguistics for models of semiotics, but insists that "the language of props eschews a unitary syntax and grammar. There is no underlying logic of props, merely a variety of 'object-games' in circulation at a given time from which dramatists pick, choose and combine" (29). This conviction informs each successive phase of his argument, in a way that circumvents both predictability and over-certainty. The choice of his first "prop," the oble or eucharistic wafer used in medieval/early modern drama, therefore, seems at first sight perversely predetermined in its connotations: surely audiences then (and now) all knew what it "means"? But Sofer's point is precisely to demonstrate that there was no such certainty. Just as theologians argued over the status of "the Host" and its relationship to the body and blood of Christ — transubstantiation, consubstantiation, symbol, metaphor — so the status of a *representation* of the phenomenon (or conceivably a use of the thing itself within fictive dramatic space) was equally vexed. As he patiently shows, the hermeneutics all parallel doctrinal positions, with Roman Catholics, Lutherans, Zwinglians and Anglicans (after Hooker) all potentially seeing something different in the "same" stage property: "Once the unique property of the church, by the turn of the sixteenth century the oble (or something very much like it) was on tour as a *stage* property, where people may have paid for the privilege and enjoyment of deciding exactly what it was they were looking at" (49).

In the following two chapters Sofer concentrates on props which still resonate with religious significance, though in very different registers. Looking at a key item in the immensely influential *The Spanish Tragedy*, he argues that "[b]y introducing a bloody handkerchief into his revenge drama, Kyd deliberately exploited the medieval association between holy cloth and sacred blood–not in order to foment a Protestant aesthetics, but to appropriate the object's power on behalf of a newly invigorated professional theater forced from the or-derly bureaucratic surveillance of a clerical hierarchy" (75)–a suggestion which chimes closely with much recent work by Stephen Greenblatt on the early modern theatre's appropriation of the power of Catholic ritual. Moving on to skulls on the Jacobean stage, Sofer is anxious to stress that their significance is not circumscribed (as many critical accounts have suggested) by the memento mori tradition to which they clearly allude. He suggests that those who read the gravediggers' scene in *Hamlet* this way "miss the irony of the performance, whereby Yorick butts his way in to the foreground" (99). "The paradox the skull embodies in *Hamlet*, *The Honest Whore*, and *The Revenger's Tragedy* is precisely the paradox of 'property', its oscillation between live attribute and dead thing ... If we wish to understand the appeal of skulls on the Renaissance stage, we must see them not merely as symbols, but as characters in their own right who may be less self-effacing than they seem" (115).

The fan has good claim to be the archetypal prop of the Restoration stage, and one with no religious resonance at all. Yet its very familiarity has led critics to treat it as a known quantity, a predictable weapon in the war of the sexes, a device which speaks (as Addison once claimed) a very limited language. Sofer will have none of this, claiming that — even when we do not have eye-witness accounts of performances — "the fan's impact cannot be detached from the personality of the actress who wielded it in a given production" (140). This is a claim he makes good in some finely nuanced readings of key plays, which were written with particular actors and their styles in mind: "If *The Man of Mode* brandishes the fan as an emblem of female independence in the face of male tutelage, George Farquhar's *The Incon-*

Review of Literature (Krajewski)   221

stant ... presents the fan lesson as a displaced rape" (145). By the end of the chapter he has advanced a strong case that "the fan's theatrical energy derived from not only its male-scripted lexicon — a lexicon, moreover, that was considerably less codified than has sometimes been imagined — but from its incessant and continually improvised play in the hands of flesh-and-blood actresses" (163).

Sofer ends, appropriately enough, with the gun, a property deployed by dramatists in various genres for the last two centuries, as often as not as a way of ending their plays. But here again his emphasis is on the potential for difference and novelty within the familiar: "If Ibsen uses Hedda's pistols to kill time by transcending as well as fulfilling the telos of the female suicide play, and Beckett deploys Brownie [in *Happy Days*] to prolong time and frustrate the spectators' desire for closure, Fornes uses Fefu's final shot [in *Fefu and Her Friends*] to *buy* time–both for her protagonist and for her audience" (172). Witty and insightful to the end ("In its ironic nonresponse to Winnie's plight, Brownie exposes the bankruptcy of the revolver as a device to kill time" [191]), Sofer demonstrates time and again the inadequacy of complacent or formulaic responses to stage properties. Even the most familiar of them are indeed "characters in their own right" and this book will have succeeded in its purpose if from now on we treat them with the careful attention such a status deserves and requires.

RICHARD DUTTON
Ohio State University

Harold B. Segel, *The Columbia Guide to the Literatures of Eastern Europe since 1945*. New York: Columbia University Press, 2003. Pp. 776. Hardcover $95.00.

The number of unwritten dissertations and unexplored avenues of study becomes apparent while reading Harold B. Segel's most recently published book, *The Columbia Guide to the Literatures of Eastern Europe Since 1945*. The wealth of Eastern European literature and the talent of its various writers — from playwrights, short story writers, and novelists to essayists, critics, and journalists — are given the exposure that has often been denied due to an emphasis many university literature courses in the English-speaking world place on the Western European and American canons. This emphasis on Western Europe and America has in turn produced many notable scholars whose work pertains to the literary traditions of these parts of the globe, but not as great a number specializing in other world literatures such as those of Eastern Europe. Segel is one of the handful of Western scholars who goes off the well-worn path to focus on and give attention to Eastern European literary traditions not well known outside of their native areas.

Creating awareness of many Eastern European writers that are largely unknown in the West, Segel provides in his book a taste of the literature and literary artists of "those countries that were absorbed into or became otherwise aligned with the Soviet orbit of power, the Soviet 'bloc' as it has often been referred to, after 1945 and in direct consequence of the outcome of World War II, and were dominated by communist regimes until the late 1980s and early 1990s" (Segel 1). Segel does not allow his readers, however, to feast on an excess of information about the literatures and their various writers — hailing from Albania, Bosnia, Bulgaria, Croatia, the Czech Republic, Slovakia, the German

Democratic Republic (formerly East Germany), Hungary, Macedonia, Poland, Romania, Serbia, and Slovenia — nor is it his intention.

As stated in the title, the book is merely a guide. It is a reference work that is encyclopedic in its form, listing notable Eastern European writers since 1945 in alphabetical order. For each writer, Segel includes the basics: dates, country, genres, personal background information, works published, and a brief summary of major works. Depending on the importance of the writer and his or her contribution to a particular nation's literature, the entries are sometimes extended and go into further depth, supplying greater details on the impact of certain literary works on society.

In the case of certain playwrights, it is not surprising that some are given entries that are up to three pages long. Well known and highly regarded in the East and West alike, Czech dramatist Václav Havel is given considerable space in which his political activities, including his career as the first elected president of Czechoslovakia and later the Czech Republic, are addressed along with the subject matter and importance of his plays. Similar to Havel, Árpád Göncz, a Hungarian playwright who is a short story writer, essayist, and translator as well, has a longer entry that discusses at some length his *Hungarian Medea*, an update of Euripides' play, in addition to his political life that includes becoming the first democratically elected president of Hungary in four decades.

Besides providing information on the playwrights and their significant political activity, Segel also brings attention to major productions of key dramatic works as he does with those of Polish dramatist Janusz Glowacki, whose

Antigone in New York was produced at the Arena Stage in Washington, D.C. Segel does not fail to mention noteworthy awards won by playwrights such as Marin Sorescu of Romania, who received honors in his native country as well as in Italy and Austria.

Although the book focuses on Eastern European literature, including dramatic literature, Segel, as a literary and theatre scholar who previously translated and edited Polish anthologies (*Polish Romantic Drama: Three Plays in English Translation, The Major Comedies of Alexander Fredro*) and Russian trilogies (*The Death of Tarelkin and Other Plays, The Trilogy of Alexander Sukhovo-Kobylin*), does not neglect to list prominent theatre critics and educators such as Bosnian Dževad Karahasan and Serbian Vida Ognjenović, who in addition to being a playwright was also the dramatic adviser and director of the National Theatre in Belgrade.

Of particular interest to scholars and those seeking additional information on the playwrights are the sections, included at the end of each entry, on "Literature" and "Translations." In the former Segel includes a brief list of available works (with commentaries on their quality) pertaining to a particular playwright, while in the latter he lists English translations of a dramatist's plays and publishers. Besides being helpful in giving interested readers a starting point for further reading and study, Segel seems to be prompting scholars to take up the challenge of conducting further research on some of the lesser studied dramatists, possibly even setting forth an invitation to fashion more in-depth books focusing on certain writers or the writers of a specific nation.

Undoubtedly, Segel's *The Columbia Guide to the Literatures of Eastern Europe Since 1945* is an invaluable reference and resource for anyone interested in the literatures of Eastern European nations. Segel's well-written and finely organized Introduction, as is the case with the scholar's introductions to other previously published works, should not be overlooked if the reader wishes to understand the background — historical and political — in which the writers crafted their pieces and against which many of the works are set. Other features that are helpful are a nation-by-nation "Chronology of Major Political Events, 1944–2002," a list of "Journals, Newspapers, and Other Periodical Literature," a "Selected Bibliography," and an "Author Index." One element that is sorely missing is an index that categorizes authors by genre. Unless a specific dramatist is known and sought, anyone who wishes to look up Eastern European playwrights must resort to flipping through the pages to find the playwrights, especially those who are lesser known. Perhaps this is a call to theatre scholars to develop a reference work that focuses not only on Eastern European playwrights, but also on other theatre artists.

EILEEN KRAJEWSKI
University of Dayton

Elinor Fuchs and Una Chaudhuri, eds. *Land/Scape/Theater*. Ann Arbor: The University of Michigan Press, 2002. Pp. 390. Hardcover $65:00, Paperback. $29.95.

Bringing together an impressive list of contributors, the collection *Land/Scape/Theater*, edited by Elinor Fuchs and Una Chaudhuri, argues for a conceptual shift in theatre and performance studies away from "contested representations of the human subject" (4) and towards an analytic paradigm that organizes itself around the idea of land-scape. Building from their work in conceptualizations of space in drama and dramaturgical practice, the editors suggest that landscape provides a model positioned between the specificity of place and the abstraction of space, arguing that landscape "is more grounded and available to visual experience than space, but more environmental and constitutive of the imaginative order than place" (3).

The general trajectory of the book leads from theoretical "Overviews" to specific environments ("Groundings"), explicit attention to landscape as an aesthetic paradigm ("Steinscapes"), expanding into a range of performative situations ("Redirected Geographies"), and into dematerialized landscapes ("Out of Space"). The 16 essays deliberately explore the landscape of texts as well as physical and conceptual landscapes in order to avoid a mere focus on space.

"Overviews" consists of two essays by the editors that attempt to embody the paradigm of study they have invoked. Chaudhuri's essay charts the conflicts within the field of landscape studies, providing interdisciplinary theoretical contexts for the contributions that follow; Fuchs's survey of several canonical American plays from Miller through Shepard and Parks suggests that temporality has been replaced by spatiality as an organizing theatrical principle, extending beyond the construction of conflict to the very construction of character itself.

"Groundings" begins with Natalie Crohn Schmidt's exploration of the literal landscapes W.B. Yeats physically experienced as a key to understanding his work. Rather than assuming their metaphoric significance, Schmidt instead demonstrates that the literal place is a far more accurate source of the land-scape than any literary or mythological source, thus confirming the centrality of physical landscape in Yeats's work. Provocatively though less successfully, Joseph Roach creates a connection between the landscape of *Waiting for Godot* and the Irish potato famine. Stanton B. Garner, Jr., explores examples of contemporary performance that employ the activity of walking in the city as a creative activity that transforms the perspective of the audience participants, blurring the boundary between everyday life and performance in the urban space.

"Steinscapes," the most focused section, explores Gertrude Stein's explicit evocation of landscape as a theatrical aesthetic and her influence on later American dramatists, paralleling some of the generative work Fuchs accomplished in "Another Version of the Pastoral" in her book *The Death of Character*. Jane Palatini Bowers builds on her concept of Stein's "lang-scapes" to further explore Stein's attempts to escape the contradiction of theatrical construction that combines the immediacy of the visual with the linearity of the language. Bowers argues that Stein's project, most clearly exemplified in *Four Saints in Three Acts*, is to create a suspended experience of relative simultaneity. Acknowledging Bowers's work, Marvin Carlson extends her concept of the langscape to American nonrealistic theatre artists including Mac Wellman and Suzan-Lori Parks. Along with the contribution by Marc Robinson on the work of Robert Wilson, this section seems more invested in exploring an already existing landscape aesthetic.

"Redirected Geographies" expands the scope of analysis, invoking the Victorian geographic conception of the East, the political function of the Chautauqua tent, and Latino performances of the border. The most compelling essays in this section are Julie Stone Peters's account of the influence of the landscape of Mexico on the theatrical and philosophical conceptions of Antonin Artaud and Matthew Wilson Smith's exploration of Disneyland, which he theorizes as a contemporary example of *Gesamtkunstwerk* that shapes and controls the landscape of performance.

The final section, "Out of Space," is intended to explore "the point at which spatialization becomes an abstract principle" (6) through attention to the mindscapes of symbolist drama and the soundscapes of Robert Ashley. Using examples of both webcam and live performance, Alice Rayner's essay "E-scapes" argues that "cyberspace and performance manifest a shift from spatial to temporal modes of thinking" (360). In this she is offering a critique of landscape itself as a theoretical paradigm precisely because although it is a perspective, it is also referencing a "geometric space" elided in cyberspace itself.

Overall, the collection's attempt to shift critical practice away from old habits of psychology and subjectivity is crucially important; however, the very potential power of this reconceptualization is also the source of a potential critique of this collection. Because of the complex space articulated by the landscape paradigm, some of the essays that are excellent critical contributions in their own right fail to deploy landscape as a perspectival activity that is not merely reduced into place or space.

The essays most effective in maintaining the landscape paradigm elucidate the work of 20th- and 21st-century practitioners whose aesthetic practice is already invested in a notion of a spatialized, perspectival practice, such as Arthur J. Sabatini's analysis of the soundscapes of Robert Ashley's musical theatre.

But, when Marvin Carlson reads Stein's legacy in American drama, he uses languages of cartography and travel to discuss the work of Mac Wellman, much as Stanton B. Garner, Jr.'s piece on urban performance relies more on de Certeau and Benjamin as theoretical models than on landscape as an alternate conception of the city itself. Or, in another example, W.B. Worthen's excellent essay on Guillermo Gómez-Peña articulates a relationship between geography and identity that need not invoke landscape per se. In part the problem is that the very concept of landscape, space mediated through human perspective, emerging from a visual art construction but exemplified in a perspectival approach to space tends to fix or limit the temporal experience of the work. The critical difficulty here is maintaining a sense of landscape as opposed to two separate discourses of space and time. This critique of their project is not unanticipated by the editors, who visually suggest these potential fractures in the very title *Land/Scape/Theater*. And, in the very moment of presenting this critique, I recognize the very power of this collection, its ability to generate such a critique, and the ways it has haunted my thinking as I have visited and revisited these essays.

JON D. ROSSINI
University of California, Davis

Japan Playwrights Association. *Half a Century of Japanese Theater: 1970s.* Tokyo: Kinokuniya Company Ltd., 2003. Pp. 392. Papereback $40.

The latest installment of this important series of Japanese plays in translation features six playwrights who came to prominence in the 1970s. If the previous decade was marked by explosive changes in the institutions of Japanese theatre, the 1970s can be characterized as a period of transition, particularly in the area of dramatic form. Most of these writers were college students when the underground theatre movement took off, and some apprenticed with these troupes, or trained in filmmaking. Despite the diversity in training and artistic leanings, however, all became committed to the development of a literary theatre that could be responsive to changes in society and culture. The 1960s also witnessed new (and hybrid) ritual-based forms developed by such innovators as Suzuki Tadashi and Hijikata Tsutomu. With such predecessors, it is no wonder these writers felt compelled to undertake bold experiments with language to match the physical dynamism that was coming to dominate the theatrical landscape. In fact, language itself becomes the main source of conflict, when it is not a central theme in several of these plays.

In an informative prefatory essay, Ei Kisei credits the playwright-director Tsuka Kōhei with paving the way for a generation of theatre practitioners to establish a greater symbiosis between language and physicality. Tsuka is represented in this anthology by *The Atami Murder Case* (for which he received the Kishida Kunio prize). His depiction of an increasingly theatricalized police interrogation illuminates how even the most banal crime can be transformed into entertainment through the rituals of due process. While the play's meta-theatricality is evident in the dialogue, Tsuka's approach to physicality can only be gleaned from a few production photos accompanying the text. Nevertheless, *The Atami Murder Case* stands out as the one work still highly relevant to both contemporary and non–Japanese audiences alike, particularly in its scathing indictment of media sensationalism, and its privileging of surface over depth in criminal reportage.

Other plays explore the possibilities and limitations of language so thoroughly as to eclipse plot and characterization altogether. The sparse dialogue of Komatsu Mikio's *Mystery Tour* melds the ellipses and non sequiturs of Absurdism with the *renga,* a medieval verse form structured upon metrical precision. Spoken by nameless (but numbered) passengers on a bus that appears to have forever veered off course, Komatsu's language demonstrates how social cohesiveness can be disrupted in times of crisis, and implicates language in the irresolution of social problems. Through the repetition of aphorisms and character catch-phrases, Yamazaki Tetsu's *The Family Adrift: The Jesus Ark Incident* explicates the interpersonal dynamics of a notorious cult of the era, at the same time that the dramatist constructs a parable about fractured interrelationships in the nuclear family. In another vein, Takeūichi Juichirō's fragmentary and a-logical dreamscape in *Clair de Lune* relies upon the reader's recognition of the many allusions to the works of Franz Kafka.

The incorporation of dialect is another noteworthy feature of many plays from this period, which, as Ei Kisei points out, was another means of creating a "theatrical grammar" equivalent to the new emphasis on physicality. In *Ayako: Mom's Cherry Blossoms Never Fall,* Okabe Kodai employs the Matsuura dialect to distinguish his characters, and by extension, an entire sub-population and their experiences during the war era. Similarly, the villagers in Fujita Den's *The Amida Black Chant Murder Mystery* speak with northern accents, and chant prayers specific to the True Pure Land sect of Buddhism. In both plays, dialect serves to highlight the tensions between tradition and progress, and communalism and urbanization, themes which also appear in the works by Tsuka, Yamazaki, and Komatsu. The goals of re-imagining dramatic structure through linguistic ingenuity and the eschewal of the conventions of *shingeki* are fully evident throughout the collection. Read within this context, the plays by Fujita and Okabe seem anachronistic, even though they are meticulously constructed, and become, not coincidentally, the most accessible. Of the two, Okabe's is the more conventional, and could justifiably be labeled Chekhovian, while Fujita (the *eminence grise* of this collection) employs slides, flashbacks, masks, and ritualized speech and gesture, which are all evidence of his long involvement with leftist theatre companies and his early work with Murayama Tomoyoshi.

Overall, this anthology is testament to the wide-ranging dramaturgical interests of Japanese dramatists of the 1970s. It should be noted, however, that Okabe's play was composed in 1988, while Takeuichi's play, which was awarded the Yomimuri Literature Prize, was written in 1995. Accompanying each play are production photos and a prefatory essay contributed by a scholar or critic containing background information on the authors, and clues by which historical and culturally-specific references may be decoded. Without such information it would be impossible to construe the core conflict in *Mystery Tour* as a metaphor for the "floating vote" that occasionally upsets national and regional elections. Or that Atami is an archetype of popular tourism, where one can even find statues of the prototypes for the doomed lovers in Tsuka's play. Though helpful, some of these essays seem truncated, especially when providing just enough information to condition a particular reading, but not enough detail to enable readers to appreciate the wider implications of the material offered. Happily, no such ambiguities mark the play translations, and one can only imagine the challenges the six translators encountered given the idiosyncratic use of language and dialect. While all are to be commended for creating lucid and eminently readable translations, Mari Boyd's work on Yamazaki's imagistic *The Family Adrift* stands out as a poetic achievement in its own right, while Don Kenny's vivid renderings of Okabe's characters quite literally jump off the page.

Though it is unlikely that any of these plays will find an audience outside of Japan, when considered as a whole, they offer an overview of the dramaturgical variety of the period, as well as the social and cultural preoccupations of the era. Taken individually, any of them could serve as a rich case study in cross-cultural or comparative critical projects.

DAVID PELLEGRINI
*Eastern Connecticut
State University*

Index